# Best Pub Walks around EDINBURGH

## David Hunter

SIGMA
Leisure

**Published by** Sigma Leisure – an imprint of
Sigma Press, 1 South Oak Lane, Wilmslow, Cheshire SK9 6AR, England.

**British Library Cataloguing in Publication Data**
A CIP record for this book is available from the British Library.

**ISBN:** 1-85058-717-5


**Typesetting and Design by:** Sigma Press, Wilmslow, Cheshire.

**Cover photograph:** the city of Edinburgh and the castle, from Arthur's Seat *(Graham Beech)*

**Maps:** Jeremy Semmens

**Printed by:** MFP Design & Print

**Disclaimer:** the information in this book is given in good faith and is believed to be correct at the time of publication. No responsibility is accepted by either the author or publisher for errors or omissions, or for any loss or injury howsoever caused. Only you can judge your own fitness, competence and experience.

# Acknowledgements

The writer of a book is like the visible tip of an iceberg, with the other ninety per cent invisible under the water. This is to say thanks to all those unseen people who contributed so much to make this book possible. Firstly, my brother John and his family who put me up and put up with me while I was doing the research on this book.

Thanks also to Neil Clark for information on the John Muir Country Park and to Ally Knox for the history of the West Barns Inn. Clare White and Brian Vere-Stevens of the National Trust for Scotland, Culross were also helpful. Marlene and Michael Egan aided me with information about Girsey Nicols and put me on to a valuable book. John Adamson and Duncan Gillespie were forthcoming about the Mansfield Arms, as was Ian Murray of Alloa Library, local history section. Martin Dean supplied data about Gartmorn Dam Country Park. Thanks also to Mr Barker, Rose Cottage, Pencaitland for help with the history of the Winton Arms. Bill Bruce of Penicuik Local History Society helped me with the history of the Flotterstone Inn. Gordon Jardine, Isabelle Paterson and Mrs Dixon were invaluable in researching the history of the Gordon Arms. Thanks to Dr Munro for setting me straight about the Balgeddie Toll Tavern. Many libraries and librarians assisted me, including Sybil Kavanagh of West Lothian Libraries local history department and Marion Richardson of Midlothian Libraries local history section. Ian Nelson of local history, Edinburgh Libraries, and the staff at Bo'ness Library are also owed my gratitude for their help.

Rangers at Country Parks also deserve special mention and my grateful appreciation goes to Mary Konik, senior ranger at Almondell Country Park, Liz Flaherty of the Pentland Hills Regional Park and the staff at Beecraigs Country Park. Tourist offices etc. were also an invaluable source of assistance. The Kingdom of Fife Tourist Board were always willing, as was Dunbar Tourist Office. Scottish Borders Tourist Board and the West Linton Tourist Group are also worthy of my thanks, which is freely given, like their help. Sundry others helped as well – the Royal Commission on Ancient Monuments. the Dunfermline Press, the *Bo'ness Advertiser*, Julia Stephenson sales and marketing manager of the *Britannia* and the staff at Aberdour Castle. To anyone I have omitted, I apologise and offer my thanks, the fault is mine. There were many librarians, countryside rangers, local historians and publicans who gave freely and unstintingly of their time and knowledge, to you all many thanks – it is you who make this possible. Special mention must be made of the staff in Burnage Library whose patience and tolerance passeth all understanding and of Apex, Kingsway for putting up with my odd photocopying requirements.
*David Hunter*

*This book is dedicated to my brother John and his family –
Sarah, Rachel, Kate and Jack. Without their support, succour and
sustenance none of it would have been possible. It is also dedicated
to Che, beloved companion – many paths, many miles.*

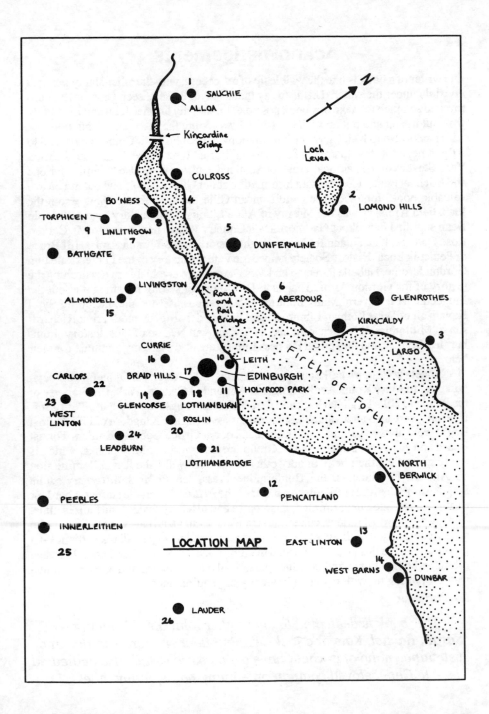

LOCATION MAP

# *Contents*

# Introduction

## The East of Scotland

This is royal Scotland. Nowadays it is Balmoral, but anciently Edinburgh was the court and capital of Scotland. It became this around the middle of the 1400s when Dunfermline was no longer considered secure enough to protect the monarch from his turbulent and rebellious nobles. Edinburgh Castle is a very secure defensive site. It is what is known as a 'crag and tail'. This is where glaciation has left a strip of spoil leading up to a crag. This provides access, but easily defended access, a natural fortress. Previously Dunfermline was Scotland's capital from its being united under Malcolm Canmore in the middle of the 11th century. Linlithgow was also a royal residence, in fact Mary Queen of Scots was born there. Even before this Fife was a kingdom and King Lot ruled Lothian from Traprain Law in modern East Lothian.

After Malcolm Canmore united Scotland around 1065, David I stiffened Scotland with Normans whose castles and churches brought a modicum of stability. The monks in places like Holyrood and Newbattle brought continental skills to Scotland such as weaving, spinning, brewing etc. The Normans and Scots fought together in the Wars of Independence. William Wallace kicked off at Lanark in the 1290s and Robert the Bruce scored the golden goal at Bannockburn in 1314. One of the major battles of these wars took place at Roslin, where 8000 Scots defeated 30,000 English in three battles in the course of one day.

During the Reformation most of the population of the area changed religion from Roman Catholic to Protestant. Subsequently, king and Kirk clashed over who should appoint clergy. Troops and Covenanters fought pitched battles in which many died, including the Battle of Rullion Green in the Pentlands near Edinburgh. The Jacobite Rebellion was warmly welcomed in Edinburgh when Bonnie Prince Charlie held court there for many months in 1745. His Highlanders camped on the slopes of Arthur's Seat.

Fishing and salt panning on the coasts and farming and mining inland were the original occupations. Fife later moved into weaving and other industries powered by coal and the water running off the steep southern face of the Ochil Hills. Clackmannanshire was a mining area and was also famous (and still is) for brewing. West Lothian was a mining area which later produced shale oil from mines, which accounts for its present day refining industry. Midlothian was a mining area and also prospered off salt produced by burning waste coal under pans of sea water. The monks started this here – hence the name Prestonpans, Priest's Town of the Salt Pans. East Lothian has always been mainly agricultural because of its rich farmland. The English taught the Scots about modern farming here, then a century later the English were coming to learn modern agriculture off the Scots. East Lothian is noted for its numerous 'agricultural improvers', people who invented new ways of farming or processing farm products. It is also Scotland's 'Big Sky Country'.

Lastly Auld Reekie, Edinburgh, prospered from being Scotland's capital. It also developed a very healthy finance industry, which is still very healthy as the recent take-over of one of Britain's major High Street banks by a major Scottish bank illustrates. In fact, I once saw a competition in the UK-wide magazine *Investors Chronicle* in which the first prize and six of the seven second prize-winners had Edinburgh addresses.

Today the area prospers on trades ancient (farming, brewing, distilling etc.) and modern (computers, finance, tourism etc.). Edinburgh's newest tourist attraction, the former royal yacht *Britannia* had nearly half a million visitors in its first year.

## Beers and Brewers

In pre-medieval times the Picts brewed heather- and spruce-flavoured ales. From the 12th century onwards these were replaced by practices which are the basis of brewing today and which were brought over by monks from Germany. Hops do not grow well in Scotland because of the climate, so there has been a historical preference for flavouring beer with roasted barley. This is akin to how whisky is flavoured: stopping the malting process by heating it over a peat fire.

In the past Scotland produced two main ales. One was Scotch Ale – powerful, blackish, sugary and heavy. The other was Tuppenny Ale, named after its price in 1707. This was produced by a second wash of the barley after it had been used for making Scotch Ale. This was a weak or 'small' beer. Around that time the introduction of 'common barley', as it is now known, greatly improved the quality of Scottish beers.

Brewing was traditionally a small-scale process until the markets were opened up by good commercial transport such as railways and canals. It then became concentrated in three main centres; Alloa, Edinburgh and Glasgow. Edinburgh and Alloa had good supplies of hard water and produced mainly pale ales. Glasgow has soft water and concentrated on stouts and porters. Towards the end of the 19th century brewing in Scotland tilted eastwards to Edinburgh and Alloa, and their highly hopped and decreased original gravity beers. These tended to travel soundly and keep well. These were exported to the Raj and became India Pale Ales, IPA. Scottish beer at this time made up a quarter of all beer exported from Britain. This first convenience beer could have been the start of the trend that has most people still drinking keg beers.

In Scotland the real ale tide came in and receded, but as with an incoming tide, the second wave is stronger and longer. New breweries are currently opening up faster than I can keep track of them. The major producers of real ale in Scotland are Belhaven, Caledonian Brewing, Maclays and Broughton. Belhaven is based in Dunbar and was opened in 1719. The company produces a regular range of real ales plus seasonal specialities. However, not all Belhaven products are real ale. In Edinburgh, the Caledonian Brewing Company, established in 1869, makes only its award-winning real ales. Maclays of Alloa, founded in 1830, makes both real and keg ales. Their Kanes Amber Ale is a tribute to Dan Kane, weel-kent man in Scottish cask-conditioned circles, now sadly deceased. In the Borders village of Broughton, the eponymous company creates real ale including its famed Greenmantle.

Of the smaller breweries, Harviestoun by Dollar produces only real ale and

Traquair is also noteworthy. In 1965 the Laird of Traquair, Mr Maxwell-Stewart, commenced real ale brewing after finding a complete old brewery and equipment on his estate. This apparatus is believed to have been made in 1720. The Inveralmond Brewery is based in Perth. Among other small brewers are Orkney, whose award-winning Dark Island is found throughout Scotland, and West Highland Brewers, based in an old railway station in Argyllshire. Independence brews in Invergordon and Stirling Bitter is a pleasant pint from the Bridge of Allan Brewing Company. Burntisland Brewery makes Alexander's Downfall, this brewery is closed as I write this but I am told that it will re-open. Sulwath Brewers (formerly Southerness) was established in 1996 and is now sited in Castle Douglas, Dumfries and Galloway. Its three main beers are Knockendoch, Criffel and Cuil Hill. These are made with Maris Otter barley, both dark and crystal malt. They use fresh whole hops, not extract, including Nugget, Fuggles, Golding, Bramley and Challenger. They brew without priming sugars, concentrates or colouring. Finally, the Mansfield Arms in Sauchie has its own in-pub brewery producing delectable ales not available anywhere else.

Real ale is a quality product and should be sipped and savoured like fine wine or malt whisky. Take a little into your mouth and let it trickle down the length of your tongue so you can appreciate the complex melange of flavours.

Finally, if you are a stranger to Scotland you will find a confusing plethora of shilling ales ranging from 60/- to 90/-. Historically this relates to the duty payable on a barrel of beer, so the higher the shilling number, the stronger the beer, as a rough rule of thumb. Very crudely, 60/- is alcohol by volume (ABV) 2.6 per cent to 3.7 per cent, 70/- is ABV 3.2 per cent to 4.2 per cent and 80/- is ABV 3.9 per cent to 4.5 per cent.

# Walking in Scotland

## Equipment

It is always wise to carry a backpack and a few basic necessities. Food and drink are essential – it is a good idea to include some instant energy food such as Mars bars or Kendal Mint Cake, and these can safely be left in your pack between walks. Fruit is another good source of easily ingestible sugar and is also good for thirst if you run out of drink. You only appreciate how much juice there is in an apple or an orange when you have run out of drink on a really hot day and one of these fruits is nectar for a desiccated gullet.

As to the nature of the drink that you carry, this is a question of personal taste. Soft drinks, non-diet versions, can be a useful boost if blood sugar levels fall. Some people carry beer, some squash and some tea or coffee but I carry just plain water. I got into this habit while walking with a dog that would not touch lemonade or squash even if his tongue was hanging out. You can also use water to rinse your hands or wash your face, or on a genuine scorcher you can even pour it over your head. If you want to be trendy use mineral water. But drinking from streams in the countryside is not be recommended although I confess that I have done it in the past.

## Clothing

Always have a hat with you: in winter it warms your head while in summer, in these days of ozone depletion, it protects you from the sun. You will also need a warm waterproof jacket. Remember that it can be much colder in the country than the city and for every 100 metres that you climb the temperature drops by one degree Fahrenheit. Walking can quickly make you warm and you can cool quickly when you stop so it is important to be able to regulate your temperature swiftly and easily. Consequently take two thin jerseys rather than one thick one and avoid jackets that do not open at the front. Strong trousers are a good idea; you may find yourself making an unplanned excursion through brambles or barbed wire. Shorts are fine on a hot day but be sure that you have something to cover your legs as the weather may change or your path may lead through a nettle patch. Lightweight waterproof trousers can be good for this. There are few things worse than sodden jeans so I do not recommend them for walking in the country. Straight-leg jeans are particularly unsuitable for walking in the country, although I wear them myself when not walking in the country. The trouble with these is that you go over one stile too many and they rip at the crotch. I love trainers and they are brilliant for walking city streets when you seem to float along on a cloud of air, but they are not for walking in the country. You will need proper hiking boots with ankle support in case you slip. And, with hiking boots, the cleats in the soles will make you much less likely to slip. Finally, to protect your feet, buy your hiking boots a size too large and wear two pairs of thick boot socks as well as ordinary socks. If this is good enough for the SAS yomping over the Brecon Beacons, it will be good enough for us.

### Finding your way

You will need to carry, and know how to use, a map and compass. I would advise getting laminated maps. They cost more but are worth it as they seem to last forever, while an ordinary map can be ruined on one wet day.

In navigation there is one simple rule: God is in the details. If you glance at a map impatiently and quickly rush off, I can guarantee that you will soon be lost. I have done it myself many times. Peer and squint at the map, take your time, work out where you are and where you are going, and if you do not know what a symbol means look it up on the edge of the map. If you do this you will seldom, if ever, get lost.

## Access to the Countryside in Scotland

These walks encompass country parks, recognised footpaths with stiles and/or kissing gates, canal towpaths and waterworks roads, cycle routes, farm tracks, parts of long-distance routes such as the Southern Uplands Way, minor roads, major roads (short distances only), forest roads, open moorland (occasionally) and rarely, rights of way. The Ordnance Survey maps seem deceptive to me. They say 'Public rights of way, not applicable in Scotland', but there are a small number of rights of way in Scotland. There is a Scottish Rights of Way Society. Its address is John Cotton Business Centre, 10 Sunnyside, Edinburgh EH7 5RA. The point is that I could not put together a book of walks around Edinburgh using only rights of way. Such a volume would not be slim, it would be anorexic.

Historically the status quo in Scotland has been that you can walk where you like as long as you do not cause any damage. But this is common law and is ambiguous. It is like the empty space of old maps that said 'here be dragons'. Insofar as I understand it you have unfettered access to unfenced land. Otherwise there is no law of criminal trespass in Scotland, in fact it is illegal to threaten trespassers with prosecution, but you can be sued in a civil court if you cause damage.

In practice you are unlikely to have any problems. Walkers are well tolerated in Scotland and the walks I have given you are all on recognised paths when crossing farmland. When I was researching this book, if I was balked or checked in any way, even by as little as a dirty look, then I abandoned the idea of that walk. I have walked all the walks in this book unhindered and frequently found friendly people along the way. The proposed 'Right to Roam' will no doubt be very good but this is for the longer term (as I write this in March 2000). One point worth remembering is that when a sign says 'Private Road' this normally applies to vehicular traffic not hikers.

Finally, please remember the country code. Take nothing but pictures and leave nothing behind you but closed gates (unless they are clearly intended to be left open). Keep your dogs under close control at all times and especially when near livestock. And remember people make a living in the countryside—it is not a theme park. So if a farmer closes a path in the lambing season, respect it so long as a suitable and temporary diversion is provided. And if a path is closed in the shooting season, it is your life that is being protected as well as the landowner's living.

# 1. The Wee County: Sauchie

**Route:** Sauchie – Gartmorn Dam Country Park – Blackfaulds – Devon Way

**Distance:** 6 miles

**Map:** OS Landranger 58, Perth and Alloa

**Start:** Mansfield Arms, Sauchie

**Access:** This journey is not advisable by bus as it would be a three-bus journey each way.

By car, take the A8 westwards out of Edinburgh towards the airport. At the Newbridge junction roundabout go right on to the M9 for Stirling. At junction 7 go right on the M876 for Kincardine Bridge. This becomes the A876(T) at the Bowtrees roundabout, keep along this and over the non-toll Kincardine Bridge. Once over the bridge bear left on the A977(T). At the Gartarry roundabout go left on the A907 marked for Alloa and Clackmannan. Once past Clackmannan and on the outskirts of Alloa turn right on the B909 for Sauchie and Tullibody. At the next roundabout go straight ahead. As you arrive in Sauchie there is a sign on the right for Gartmorn Country park. Turn left immediately after this, doubling back on yourself. The Mansfield Arms is about 50 metres up here on the right. The car park entrance is on the right just before the pub. If the car park is full you can park in the lay-by across the road from the pub, so mine host assures me. Note: If you see a second sign for Gartmorn Dam you have gone too far and will have to turn back.

---

## Mansfield Arms. Tel: 01259 722020; Fax 01259 781 324

The original building on this site in 1750 was a weaver's cottage. All the plots of land along this side of the road were occupied by weavers' cottages. This was before industrialisation and when weaving was done at home on a handloom.

Before 1820 there were no meeting places in Sauchie except pubs. These put on displays of bare knuckle boxing and cock-fights. There were many bets on the outcomes of such contests. Around

1850 the Railway Arms opened on this site when the railway arrived in Sauchie. It served the men who were building a two-arched bridge outside the pub. One arch covered Coalgate, the wagon road for the coal, the other covered Coal Faulds, the route to where the coal was stored. The landlord at this point was George Walls. He sold the pub in 1879 to Isabella Snaddon. In the early part of this century it was in the hands of the Sirkett family. It was now called the Mansfield Arms after the Earl of Mansfield whose family had owned the Sauchie estate. The burn just beside the pub marked the boundary between the Sauchie estate and the Alloa estate of the Earl of Mar. This is why the road it now stands in is called Mar Place. So the Mansfield Arms functions like a boundary marker, when you see the Mansfield Arms you are entering the Mansfield estate.

By the end of the Second World War it was owned by Youngers of Alloa, the brewers. But it was bought by the Gibson family in 1985, which is good for us as they installed a micro-brewery on the premises and now we have the choice of some unique real ales. These are Devon Original, a hoppy, light-coloured beer of 3.8% ABV; Devon Thick Black, whose name aptly describes it (ABV 4.2%); and Devon Pride, a traditional Scottish Export of 4.8% ABV. These beers have won the Scottish CAMRA award for 1993 and local Forth Valley CAMRA awards in 1991 and 1996. On keg are their own Devon Cream, Calders 70/-, Skol Lager, Carlsberg Lager, Guinness and Dry Blackthorn. Opening hours are Monday to Thursday 1100-2300, Friday and Saturday 1100-0030 and Sunday 1230-2300. Inside it is an attractive high-ceilinged kind of old-fashioned pub, and I mean old-fashioned in the nicest possible way. It has a kind of 50s/60s retro ambience about it. If you want to step back in time and taste real ale the way it was before mass production (mass murder of good beer more like) and sample the atmosphere of a pub 30 to 40 years ago, then this is your time machine.

And talking of time, food is served 1200-2100 Monday to Saturday and 1230-2100 on Sundays. The food is not all old-fashioned, although some classics like steak and kidney pie could be thus labelled. It also includes more modern foods such as pasta dishes and vegetarian choices. It is all home cooked and delicious. The choice ranges from hot rolls and baked potatoes all the way up to steaks. The present landlord, Martin Gibson, is happy to see walkers enter his door. There is a children's licence, kiddies' meals and high chairs.

## Gartmorn Dam Country Park

The country park's history is intimately connected with that of nearby Sauchie. In the early 1700s Sauchie was a mining village. As the miners delved deeper in search of more coal the colliers began to encounter serious flooding problems. The well-known engineer George Sorocauld was consulted. He decided on a very elegant solution: to use water to remove water. An enormous waterwheel was built to power the pumps that took the water out of the mines. As there was not enough water-power in the local burns to turn this wheel more water had to be found. So a two-mile long lade (mill leat) was built from the Black Devon River to the east of the country park to fill the swampy depression that existed on this site then. A dam of earth was thrown up at the west end of this depression to create a body of water which would always supply enough water-power to pump the water out of the mines. This was the largest non-natural loch in Scotland at this time.

The tail race, which is the water flowing away after powering the waterwheel, was used to power local industry. At one time this loch powered three mines and nine mills. By early last century the growing industry with its concomitant increase in population had outstripped the capacity of Alloa's wells. So the landowner gave permission for water to be abstracted from the tail race. As steam power increasingly took over from water power so this water source was freed to become drinking water. The Alloa Water Act of 1891 caused this reservoir to be increased in size and filter beds built. This water supply is the oldest artificial one currently working and is run by East of Scotland Water.

It became a country park in 1982 to protect wildlife as it was anticipated the recreational demand would increase. The council leased the land to East of Scotland Water. The reservoir is nowhere very deep, never being more than 7.5 metres in depth. The water is rich in food, supporting a large population of photosynthetic algae which can sometimes explode into life creating what is called an algal bloom. The rich diversity of water plants has led to this area being created an SSSI, a site of special scientific interest. These plants support the next step up the food chain, invertebrates such as shrimps, snails and fly larvae. These invertebrates feed the next link in the chain, the fish. The loch has pike, perch and trout. The abundant water wildlife also attracts birds. Resident wildfowl include little grebe, great crested grebe, herons, mute swans and mallards. Migrants include large numbers of cormorants, whooper swan, greylag geese, wigeon (a grey duck with a red head and orange forehead), teal, pochard, tufted duck, goldeneye and ruddy duck. It is a good spot for birdwatching, especially in the winter.

## The Walk

Turn left out of the Mansfield Arms and walk up to the main road and the panda crossing. Cross the main road, then bear diagonally right on the footpath and left at the end of it along Gartmorn Road. Walk along here for about a quarter of a mile until the houses end on your right. Go past the shop and bus shelter on your right and then squeeze through a narrow gate on your right and walk along with the line of trees on your right. About 200 metres along here a field gate appears in front of you. At this point turn left onto the well-defined cart track. At the end of this negotiate two field gates to arrive at a bend in a farm road. Ignore the road to the right and go straight ahead, bypassing another field gate by a gap beside it. Proceed directly ahead on this farm road, crossing over a tarmac road.

This terminates in a T-junction with the tarmac road to the visitor centre at the country park. Here go right towards the now visible reservoir. The visitor centre has diagrams, maps, displays and general information about the park. This is a park of 150 hectares. The dam was built in 1713 by the Earl of Mar to provide water-power to pump water out of the mines. It also provided a fresh water source for the area. It is an important stop over on wild fowl migration routes. It became a SSSI in 1971.

Go past the visitor centre and along the edge of the water following signs to the sunken garden and barbecue site. Here look out for the old pump-house of the waterworks. Once across the dam turn left following the public footpath signs. The sunken

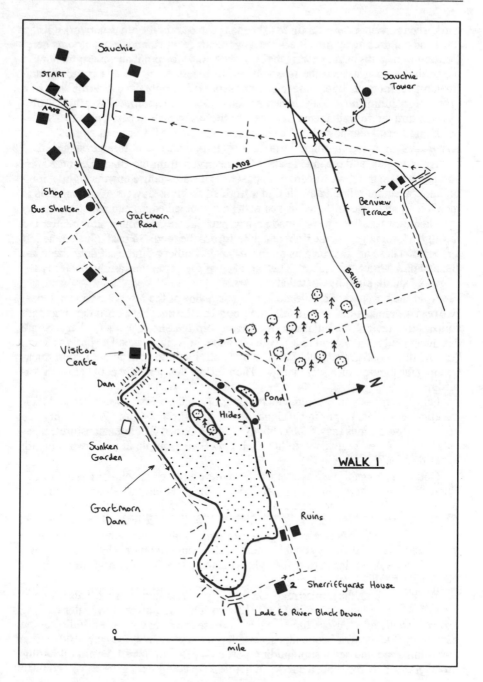

garden can be visited here, this used to be the filter-beds of the old waterworks. Keep dogs and children away from the water as you can get poisonous algal blooms here. Continue along this path, ignoring the bridleway and viewpoint on your right. For the next mile or so just keep the reservoir on your left. Keep on this broad, beaten earth/gravel footpath, bypassing minor paths to left and right. It crosses the neck of a promontory jutting out into the loch but soon rejoins the shoreline. Just after the picnic area turn left to walk up the short axis of the reservoir. Go past a path to a viewpoint and a path signposted to Clackmannan via Linn Mill on your right. As you arrive at a sign saying Gartmorn Dam Country Park there is a footbridge on the left.

Traverse this, and the lade feeding this reservoir from the Black Devon River, and proceed up the boardwalk to walk past Sheriffyards house on your right. Along here in the summertime you will find a froth of fragrant flowers of cream. This is meadowsweet. It has tri-lobed leaves with saw-toothed edges and red stems.

Then turn left along a well-made broad path labelled for the visitor centre. Go through a kissing gate to the right of a pole across the road. Go past ruins on the left and right. These are the remains of Sheriffyards Colliery. In the summer these are flushed pink with Herb Robert. This member of the geranium family has ferny foliage and small, pink, five-petalled flowers.

After the best part of a mile along this north side of the reservoir you walk past two bird watching hides on your left with a pond on the right between them. This path follows the track of the old mineral railway from the Sheriffyards Colliery. Some 300 metres after the second hide a path on the right is signposted Devon Way 3km. Ascend this broad gravel path. Keep on this path into trees and across a farm track, keeping the picnic tables on your right. Then follow this beautiful path across a footbridge.

I am enormously impressed with the quantity and quality of footpaths and their excellent directional signs in Clackmannanshire. Take a bow, the Wee County. To other local authorities I say "Look aboot ye" (the motto of Clackmannanshire), especially at the Wee County, and follow their excellent example in your own footpath networks.

Continue along this path as it veers right where a cart track comes in from the left. There is an arrow here with drawings of horses, bicycles and pedestrians which is labelled 'CCPN', I presume this means Clackmannan County Footpath Network. Follow the arrow. This comes to a T-junction with a forest track. Here go left as indicated by the CCPN arrow. Keep up here past a public footpath sign pointing in your direction of travel. Stay on this forest track for approximately half a mile, going past a farm track coming in from the right. This leads to a T-junction with a minor tarmac road, the B9140.

Walk left along the tarmac road. On your right front here is Alva. This is one of the mill towns at the base of the Ochil Hills which were powered by water rushing down from the hills. At one time the line of these towns in the Devon Valley at the base of the Ochils was Scotland's second largest textile area. Roughly 100 metres along this road you see a sign guiding you right, Devon Way 1.5km. Follow this broad gravel path for about a quarter of a mile, bypassing field gates as you come to them by walking over cattle grids. As you crest a small rise the flat, fertile farmland of the Devon Valley appears ahead, backed by the brooding bulk of the Ochils. Note the steep faces of the hills, they would provide plenty of power for the mills.

This path terminates in a T-junction with a narrow tarmac road. Bear left here as the signpost, Devon Way 1km, indicates. On your right front here is Tillicoultry, another mill and textile town. Stay on the right side of this road so as to face the oncoming traffic. About half a mile on follow this road right between a few houses, Benview Terrace, to the main road, A908. The road layout here is virtually the same as on the 1817 map, which indicates a lack of imagination or more likely a pragmatic appreciation of the geographical realities. Once over the main road cross the minor bridge. As the road ahead bends right a sign on your left points left to Devon Way, Alloa 3.5km. Go along this broad, well-laid path. On your right here there used to be pits and the Devon Ironworks. Approximately half a mile along here, where the pylons pass overhead and two bridges cross the Devon Way in front of you, there is a sign pointing back and right for Fishcross. Go up here. At the top of the slope, where there is a T-junction of paths, go right downhill into the trees. After about 200 metres you reach a bend on a tarmac road. Go left here and keep with this road as it goes right and left to reach the remains of Sauchie Tower.

Sauchie Tower was built by the Schaws around the start of the 1400s. It is made of ashlar (square-hewn stone) and is roughly 12 metres by 10 metres. This four-storey building has a spire on a corner of the roof. This is a cape-house and covers the internal spiral staircase. The roof has an overhanging parapet with machicolations. These are holes through which stones, boiling oil etc. could be dropped on attackers.

The Schaws were an important family in Scotland. They were granted the barony of Sauchie in 1529. Around 1631 they built an adjoining manor house as times grew less perilous. This house was burnt down in 1775, severely damaging the tower. Then the Schaws lost the land and absentee owners had no reason to do anything with this tower. For that reason, this tower is a particularly fine example of how a tower house was in the Middle Ages, as it is relatively little altered by time.

Retrace your steps to the Devon Way and walk under the two bridges. Keep on this path for roughly the next mile. This path marks the route of the Tillicoultry branch of the Stirling and Dunfermline Railway. It was opened in 1851. Trains travelled about 20mph and there were four classes. The fourth was a discount fare of a penny a mile on one train a day as provided for by an Act of Parliament. It was called a parly. Cross over a footpath cutting across your front at bollards and pass under a bridge. The footpath ends at a tarmac road. Here turn right and the Mansfield Arms is some 50 metres on your right.

# 2. The Kingdom of Fife: Lomond Hills

**Route:** Wester Balgeddie – Glenlomond – Glen Vale – Harperleas Reservoir – West Feal – Balnethill

**Distance:** 8 miles

**Map:** OS Landranger 58, Perth and Alloa

**Start:** Balgeddie Toll Tavern, Wester Balgeddie

**Access:** By bus, this walk is just about feasible. If you get a bus to Kinross or Milnathort from Edinburgh (reasonable service) you can then get a local bus to the Balgeddie Toll Tavern. However, this bus does not run on Sundays and the last bus leaves the Balgeddie Toll Tavern about 1730. Perhaps if there is a group of you your best bet would be to get a bus to Kinross and then taxis to and from the Balgeddie Toll Tavern. Bus details are available from Kinross Passenger Transport Information on 0845 (local call rate) 301 1130. Or phone 'Traveline' on 0800 232323 if in the Edinburgh area or 0131 255 3858 if outwith Edinburgh for details of buses from Edinburgh.

By car, take the A90 (Queensferry Road) out of Edinburgh and follow signs for the Forth Road Bridge. Cross this toll bridge. Keep straight ahead on the M90. At junction 5 run off to the left and then go right along the B9097, signposted for Glenrothes. Once over the motorway turn left along the B996, signposted for Glenrothes and Scotlandwell. Then turn right along the B9097, signposted for Scotlandwell. Drive along past the RSPB centre of Vane Farm on your right and Loch Leven (a National Nature Reserve) on your left.
At the T-junction with the B920 go left and after about 100 metres go left again, still on the B920 signposted for Scotlandwell. At Scotlandwell you run directly on to the A911 without stopping. A mile after Scotlandwell you pass through Kinneswood. A mile beyond this the road forks. The Balgeddie Toll Tavern is on the apex of the fork with its car park behind it. You can go right and then left or left and then right into the car park.

## Balgeddie Toll Tavern. Tel: 01592 840212

The date 1534 displayed outside is far too early. This building was built in the 1720s. In the 1770s the Turnpike Act caused a number of these toll roads to be laid out. The toll charge here was 1d. The Statute Labour Trustees, the heritors or landowners of the parish, organised this and held their meeting in the Balgeddie Toll Tavern. At one time this was a major road running to Scotland's capital at St John's Town of Perth. It also connected royal residences and hunting palaces such as Falkland, Dunfermline and Edinburgh. It was known as Bodgers (beggars) Road. Mr Sharpe, who lived here as it became a toll road, brewed his own ale (as many did in those days) and saw his chance to ease the pain of paying the toll and of travel generally by turning his house into a public house. Nowadays the drink-drive laws have turned it into a country restaurant and a pub for the locals.

In the last century, James Beath from local Glenvale Farm was a noted poet and songwriter. He used to recite his poetry and sing his songs in the Balgeddie Toll Tavern. These songs were bothy ballads, songs workmen used to sing to entertain themselves when working away from home and staying in huts in the countryside.

You will not be serenaded today but the food is pure poetry. There is an excellent selection of local home-cooked food (including vegetarian) at reasonable prices. The most telling points about the food are the awards it has won. These include the 1991 Guinness Award for excellent standards in pub food, a commendation in Eating Out in Fife 1999, Les Routiers 1997 and 1998 Customer Awards and a 1999 Les Routiers Hospitality and Customer Awards. The service is friendly and attentive. Food is served Monday to Saturday 1200-1400. In the evenings Monday to Thursday it is 1815-2100 and Friday and Saturday it is 1730-2100. On Sundays, food is on offer all day between 1230 and 2100. Children are welcome until 2000 in the elevated portion of the bar.

The awards continue when we look at the beer. The pub is a member of the Guild of Master Cellarers. It is in *The Good Beer Guide 1999*. It was awarded a cup by Burtons for the Best Burton Ale in the UK in independent houses. The real ale, unsurprisingly, is Burtons. The kegs supply Strongbow, Guinness, Tetleys, Kilkenny, Calders Premium Cream Ale and Carlsberg Lager. Opening hours are Monday to Thursday 1100-1500 and 1700 -2245, Friday 1100-1500 and 1730-2345, Saturday 1100-2345 and Sunday 1230-2245. They stock a good selection of wines.

Jocelyn Glebocki and Mrs C (Christie) welcome walkers and many currently use this pub. It is a lovely old atmospheric country pub with a piano, so I suppose that you might be serenaded after all. There is some old period/antique furniture. Dark wood beams, light plaster and stone walls paint a pretty picture for you. The dining room, which can hold up to 40, is warm and comfortable with stone cladding for ambience. Back in the bar, flowers, dried flowers and pictures by local artists (for sale) create a good impression. There is a beer garden outside.

## Loch Leven

Finds of Roman coins, swords and helmets around the loch seem to indicate that the Romans were here for quite some time early in the first millennium. However, recorded history starts here around AD490 when several old texts state that there was a fortalice on Castle Island built by Congal, son of Dongard, King of the Scots.

By AD600 a hermit's dwelling existed on what is now called St Serf's Island. In AD838 this became a religious house of St Moak by the good offices of Brudeus, King of the Scots. By AD843 this was dedicated to St Servanus (Serf). Around AD980 this became a priory. In the 1040s history records MacBeth, King of Scotland, giving various lands to this priory. The island then became St Serf's. These monks are of the Celtic Church and are variously called Keledei or Culdees.

In 1146 David I gave St Serf's Island and Priory to the Priory of St Andrew. David I and his queen, Margaret, were energetic reformers of the faith in Scotland. This time marks the start of the decline and fall of the Celtic Church in Scotland and the rise of Roman Catholicism. In 1257 Alexander III and his queen were seized at Loch

Leven and forcibly carried off to Stirling. This does not seem to have put him off as it was a royal residence of his later in his reign in 1275.

In 1563 Mary Queen of Scots and John Knox had a two-hour religious debate at Loch Leven Castle. In 1567 she was imprisoned in the castle. Her jailers were the Douglas family, who had been granted these lands by Robert III, their kinsman, in 1390. They held these lands until 1676 when support for the Stuart kings had beggared them. Mary Queen of Scots flirted with a teenage Douglas boy who obtained the keys, released her, locked up the castle again and rowed her to shore while casting the keys into the loch. These keys were recovered some three centuries later. In 1570 St Serf's Priory was given St Leonard's College, St Andrew's, thus ending nearly a millennium of religious history here.

The castle remained habitable until at least 1650. In 1793 an old person locally remembered that in his lifetime there had been 52 beds in it. But by then it was a ruin.

The other interesting thing about Loch Leven was the fish. In 1722 Daniel Defoe, author of *Robinson Crusoe*, said that Loch Leven had the finest fish in the world. In 1803 the Reverend Jones, while touring Scotland, highly rates the fish of Loch Leven. Every year, he says, the fishing is let for a goodly sum and the fish caught are eels, carp and trout of up to 6lbs in weight with excellent reddish flesh. In medieval times, commoners, who did not like eels, are recorded as paying part of their rents to the nobility in barrels of eels. The nobility obviously didn't share their aversion.

In 1844 a successful experiment was carried out locally in tinning trout from Loch Leven. The fish was still fresh when the tins were opened three months later. How come I never see tinned trout on the supermarket shelves? The local fish must have had a shock in 1846 when a great storm blew in a flock of wild white geese from the Bass Rock. These must have been gannets, also known as solan geese, which nest on the Bass Rock. They are prolific eaters of fish.

## The Walk

Turn left out of the Balgeddie Toll Tavern and walk along the main road, A911. After around 150 metres you will come to a sign on the right pointing left to Glenlomond and Wester Balgeddie. Just prior to this cut left up the bank by the seat and then bear left along the minor road. This cuts off the corner. Go along this road and follow it as it goes sharply left as a farm road comes in from the right. About 100 metres beyond this you will notice a farm gate on your right with a rough road behind it. Pass through the gate and proceed up the track.

Climb over a padlocked gate and continue along the rough track towards the Lomond Hills looming in front of you. This rough track peters out, at which point you should go left, keeping the line of fence and dyke on your left. There is a faint path here. Keep with the fence and dyke and break right as it cuts across in front of you. Then go left through the fence/dyke between you and the Lomond Hills at a field gate. Next double back to your left on a sunken track. Continue with this track to another field gate. After this gate keep ahead on the cart track over a small rise with the fence and dyke on your left. Contour along the hillside with the fence/dyke on your left and passing the radio transmitter on this little-used track. Once past another field gate a footpath ahead starts to become visible on the contour line. This leads you through a gap in a fence across your path and to the right of a field gate. The fence/dyke on your left starts to bend to the right ahead of you. Follow this up to two field gates close together.

Go through the left-hand gate and immediately turn right with the right-hand path. Follow this path up the right-hand side of the Glen Burn. This is now a well used path. Close the gate behind you please. As you walk up this valley you will notice caves in the crags on the opposite side of the valley. These caves are in the softer layer of old red sandstone (compressed sand) that underlies the Lomond Hills. This Glen Vale has cut a cross section through the hills, exposing various rock strata. On top is volcanic rock, below this is hurlet limestone, deeper again is another layer of volcanic rock (a sill) which has another layer of hurlet limestone beneath it. A sill is an extrusion of molten lava that moves horizontally between or within strata of rock. In this case it has split the hurlet limestone layer in two. Underneath these four layers is a layer of calciferous sandstone which is based on the old red sandstone. Glen Vale is quite a good place to look for fossils.

Near the top of the valley the path swings left and right across the valley to lead you onto a plateau. Continue along this path, heading for the trees in the distance. The large hill on your left is West Lomond. Up here in summer it can still be a mass of white. But this is not snow, but cotton grass. This gets its name from its white, fluffy seed heads. It is seldom found on lower ground. In fact, a nature reserve near

West Lomond, above the moorland plateau

Kilmacolm in Renfrewshire notes on its display board that this is one of the very few places in the country that it grows at anywhere approaching sea level. Cotton grass is a biological indicator of bog. However the path here is dry and firm, although there are some boggy bits nearer the trees.

As you walk over this moor Harperleas Reservoir comes into sight before you. Just after you cross a stream, go right down a path towards a gate 50 metres away. Pass through the gate and walk along with the dyke on your right, heading for Harperleas Reservoir and the trees around it. Ford another burn and go through the kissing gate at the junction of dykes. Walk along a narrow, boggy path, keeping the dyke and then a fence on your right. Just before Harperleas Reservoir go right through a kissing gate and across a concrete footbridge. Then go along the cart track to the right of the trees. A couple of hundred metres along here, past a sign on the right that says Harperleas Woodland, you arrive at a wooden sign on your right with a yellow arrow and path printed on it. Go up this rough road.

At the top of the rise bear right with the track. On your left are two new reservoirs, left to right these are Ballo and Holl Reservoirs. On a clear day there are grand views over the Firth of Forth from here, sometimes you can even see the Bass Rock and Berwick Law. This path now curves left downhill in a U-shape to bring you to a very minor cart track. Cross this and the stile in front of you and follow a faint path straight ahead through the heather towards the Firth of Forth. This leads you down into a small declivity and up the other side. This then upgrades to a cart track. Continue along it as it goes left and right and then left and right again. Then it opens out just before a fence. A sign facing the opposite way tells people that this is Harperleas Woodland. Go over a stile behind this sign, but negotiate it with care as it was a bit shoogly when I was there. Then follow the cart track, with the fence on your right, towards the hut on the skyline. Pass through a farm gate and about 20 metres beyond this turn right onto a gravel track. Go over a cattle grid, heading for the farmstead of West Feal, visible ahead among trees.

This track takes you around West Feal with the farm on your left. On the other side of the farm there is a stile to the left of a farm gate. Once past this stile, walk uphill on a rudimentary cart track with the dyke and pine plantation on your left. Bear right at the top of the hill as the dyke cuts across your path. Just after a farm gate on your left is a stile on the same side of you. Cross this stile and go right, uphill, on the grassy path between the trees. If you look back from here a new reservoir on the right is the Arnot Reservoir. Go over another stile to the left of a farm gate. From here you may here the whistling diminuendo of a curlew. On this path in summer you may see a four-petalled blue flower, this is field gentian.

At the end of the forest, clamber over a ladder stile on the right of a gate. Then proceed dead ahead on the rough track. This is lovely walking, bouncing along on the springy turf. Some 300 metres along here the Ochil Hills become visible before you. Then this track takes you to the pièce de résistance of this walk, a stunning view over Loch Leven and the valley floor from the crest of the Lomond Hills. Below you may see gliders, both constructed (from the Levenmouth Gliding Club) and natural, as buzzards frequently wheel and mew in the skies around here.

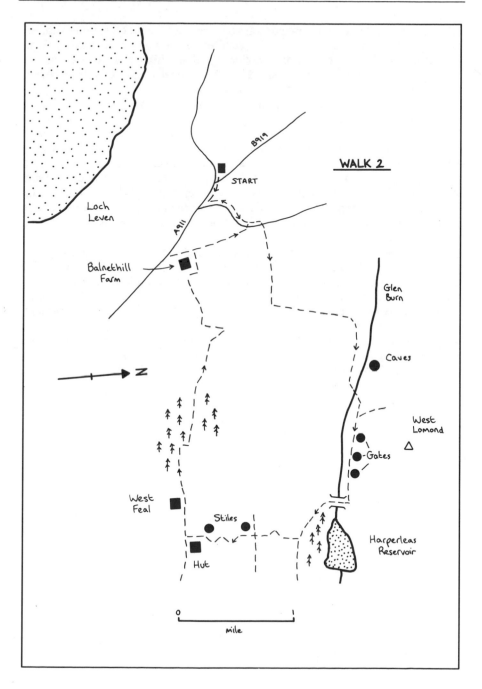

Loch Leven

B919

START

WALK 2

A911

Balnethill Farm

Glen Burn

Caves

West Lomond

-Gates

△

West Feal

Stiles

Harperleas Reservoir

Hut

N

0                                1

mile

After some 300 metres along the crest you arrive at a fence across your path. Ignore a gate in it and descend 50 metres to your left to find a broad hill track, snaking steeply downhill, chewed out of the hill face. Go down this, despite its steepness. I was amazed when two farmers on a quad-bike had enough torque to stop and chat to me and then get started to ascend the hill again.

This hill track terminates at the bottom of the hill at a field gate. Go right along the obvious footpath on the nearside of the gate. When this path breaks right into the hills, stay along the line of the fence on your left until you reach another field gate on your left. Negotiate this gate and walk down beside the fence on your right until it becomes a dyke. On the other side of the dyke, parallel to your direction of travel, is a cart track with a field gate across it. Just past the field gate, cross right over the dyke. It is an easy step over some low barbed wire to the top of the dyke and a simple jump down onto the cart track. Go left down this cart track and through another gate. This terminates in a T-junction with another farm track, here go right away from the farm buildings.

At the end of this track go straight ahead on the clear footpath flanked by fences. On your left here the long, low-lying island is St Serf's, where the priory was. The higher wooded island on the right of this is Castle Island where Mary Queen of Scots was imprisoned in Loch Leven Castle. Cross a not-too-visible stile on the extreme left of a field gate. Keep along the line of fence and ditch on your left. Pass through another field gate onto an enclosed farm track. About 50 metres along here you arrive at a bend in a tarmac road. Walk to the left down here, keeping to the right-hand side of the road so as to face the oncoming traffic. Once past the houses take the slight path on the right by the seat to cut the corner to the main road, A911. Go right along this and the Balgeddie Toll Tavern is at the apex of the fork in the road about 100 metres along.

# 3. The Kingdom of Fife: Largo

**Route:** Lower Largo—Scotland's Larder—Chesterstone—Upper Largo—Kiels Den

**Distance:** 4.5 miles

**Map:** OS Landranger 59, St Andrew's

**Start:** Crusoe Hotel, Largo

**Access:** By bus, there is an hourly direct service from Edinburgh to Lundin Links. Ask to be put off at Durham Wynd. From here it is a few minutes walk downhill into Lower Largo, where buses do not go because of a weak bridge. This service runs from Monday to Saturday. Watch your time as the last bus leaves Lundin Links around 1815. These buses depart from St Andrew's Square bus station in Edinburgh. Sunday is not advisable for this journey as it would involve a three-bus journey. For details phone the Fife Passenger Transport Information Service on 01592 416060. Or ring 'Traveline' on 0800 232323 if inside the Edinburgh area or otherwise 1031 225 3858.

By car, take the A90 (Queensferry Road) out of Edinburgh and follow signs to the Forth Road Bridge. Cross the bridge (toll) and go straight ahead onto the M90 at junction 1. At junction 2a turn right onto the A92 for Glenrothes and Kirkcaldy. After about eight miles on this fast dual carriageway go right at a roundabout onto the A921 for Kirkcaldy East and Central. After around three-quarters of a mile on this, take the A915 signposted for Leven and St Andrew's. At the first roundabout go generally left and straight ahead on the A915, still signposted for Leven and St Andrews. After some seven or eight miles along here, at Lundin Links, you will see a sign pointing right for Lower Largo, Robinson Crusoe's birthplace. Turn right and follow this road down to the seafront where it makes a T-junction with Drummochy Road. Here go left. This road takes you down by the harbour. The Crusoe Hotel is on your right immediately after the bridge. The car park entrance is just before it, also on the right. If the car park is full then go left just over the bridge and uphill under the railway viaduct to double back right following the signs for free parking. From here you can follow the stairs downhill and to the right to reach the Crusoe Hotel.

---

## The Crusoe Hotel. Tel: 01333 320 759

This building is over 300 years old. The seaward side was always a pub for the sailors of Largo. The landward portion was a granary and the outside shows the outlines of the entrances where the carts used to reverse in to be loaded. In the centre of these, now much smaller, are the windows. There are rumours of a ghost upstairs.

The theme of this hotel is the story of Robinson Crusoe. A signpost in the car park points 7500 miles to Juan Fernandez. This is the island that Alexander Selkirk, the real Robinson Crusoe, was marooned on. A notice on the wall of the bistro says that Robinson Crusoe was the only person to get his work done by Friday. There is also a picture of the Hotel Robinson Crusoe, Tobago, West Indies on the bistro's wall.

There is an Alexander Selkirk Museum in the hotel which you can visit for free. There is a plan of Juan Fernandez, a photograph of Juan Fernandez and a picture of the commodore's tent on Juan Fernandez. There is a framed newspaper clipping about Alexander Selkirk's experiences which includes a feature on the Crusoe Hotel. Details about privateering are given and a copy of Alexander Selkirk's will is shown. The story of Alexander Selkirk is on the wall of the bistro.

The bistro is one of three places to eat in the hotel. It has a no smoking rule. There is a formal dining room upstairs. On the other side of the bistro in formality (informality?) is the bar, where only snacks like soup and toasties are served. It was from this bar that I saw Concorde fly past accompanied by the Red Arrows. It was the day of the opening of the Scottish Parliament.

The food is wonderful. Your host Bob Jorgensen is one of Scotland's top chefs. This hotel was highly commended by the BBC's Radio 4 programme 'Breakaway' as a place to visit on vacation. Famous guests have included Sean Connery, football stars and some of the cast of 'High Road'. When the Open is at Carnoustie or St Andrew's this hotel can be fully booked. Not surprisingly, the house speciality is seafood. In summer lobster and crab are supplied by local harbour fishermen. Fresh fish comes from nearby Fife fishing villages and Fife also supplies local vegetables. Food is served in the bistro 1200-1430 (Sunday 1230) and 1800-2100. The restaurant is open from 1900-2145. Soup and toasties are available in the bar at any time.

Opening hours are 1100-2400 Monday to Thursday and Saturday, Fridays 1100-0100, Sundays 1230-2400. There are two real ales which are both guests. They were Deuchars IPA and Boddingtons when I was there. Keg beers etc. included McEwans 80/-, McEwans 70/-, Guinness, Dry Blackthorn, Miller Pilsner, Kronenberg 1664 and McEwans Lager.

The bar has a pool room off it with a real fire. Dark wood, light plaster and stonework set the scene for you. The television has its own little alcove in the stonework. Some of the stonework is nicely carved. Look out for a corbel, an angled support bracket between the top of the wall and ceiling. Usual amenities include cigarette machine, telephone and jukebox. The bar overlooks the harbour and there are tables outside as well. This is a family bar. Generally, high chairs are available in the hotel. Walkers can be sure of a warm reception here.

## Largo

Largo comes from the Celtic 'largaugh', meaning sunny, seaward slope and the sea has been very important in the history of Largo. From the sea came the Vikings who held this coast for about a century in the 800s. Later Largo was part of the Earldom of Fife but it was forfeited to the Crown by the disgrace of Murdoch, Duke of Albany in 1425. James III gave these lands to Sir Andrew Wood, the famous naval warrior, in 1482 for services against pirates, particularly the English. He gained much practice at repelling French and Portuguese pirates while trading as a merchant. In 1487 he became leader of Scotland's embryonic navy, giving up trading and commanding a princely fleet of two vessels, the *Yellow Carvel* and the *Flower*. In 1488 his ships carried James III to Fife to rally support from the people after his nobles rose in rebellion against him. James III was killed. Then the rebels asked the sailors of Leith to attack Sir Andrew but they refused to do so. In fact, they said that even with ten ships to Sir Andrew's two, this son of a Leith shipmaster, whom they knew well, would win.

Sir Andrew made peace with the rebels and the new king, James IV. In 1489 Sir Andrew's two old luggers defeated and captured an English pirate fleet operating off Dunbar. In 1490 the English king, Henry VII, anxious to have revenge for this insult, sponsored an English fleet of three large, powerful vessels to defeat Sir Andrew. This fleet hid behind the Isle of May at the mouth of the Firth of Forth waiting for Sir Andrew to return from Holland, to where he had escorted a Scottish convoy. The ships pounced on Sir Andrew and he gave battle. The fight raged all day but eventually, at the mouth of the Tay, the English surrendered. In 1491 Sir Andrew Wood was granted a charter to build a castle at Largo. In 1495 he safely carried James IV on a visit to the Hebrides. In 1496 he was appointed Governor of Dunbar Castle.

Another famous Largo mariner was Alexander Selkirk, the real life Robinson Crusoe, who first saw the light of day here in 1676. Selkirk appears to have been a turbulent man and after one too many conflicts with the Kirk he went to sea. Later he became sailing master in the *Cinque Ports* under Captain John Dampier. This vessel carried letters of marque, making it a semi-pirate ship only capturing ships of the country's enemies. Quarrelsome Selkirk contrived to fall out with the captain. Rashly he said that he would rather be put off at the nearest land than sail any further with the captain. He was then marooned on the Isle of Juan Fernandez, some 800 miles from Chile's capital Santiago, the closest landfall. He had only his sea chest, gun, kettle, axes and a few other sundries. He spent four lonely years there before being picked up by another ship. He returned home in 1712.

Daniel Defoe, supposed to be an English spy and editor of Scotland's first newspaper, the *Edinburgh Courant*, used Selkirk's story as the basis for his novel *Robinson Crusoe*. The first edition of this book was published in 1719.

Largo and the Crusoe Hotel

# The Walk

Leave the car park of the Crusoe Hotel and turn right away from the weak bridge. Then follow the road as it kinks right and left – this is not the road to the right of the Railway Inn. Walk along here for about a quarter of a mile until a wider road to the left bends away uphill and a narrow road goes straight ahead. The road left uphill is signposted to the main coast road. Your route is up here to the left. However, if you go 50 metres ahead on the narrow road ahead, on your left is the site of the house where Alexander Selkirk was born. It has a carving of him on the front. The house was built by Stuart Barret of Edinburgh as the original house was demolished. It is marked by a tourist board sign.

Halfway up the hill you will find a set of steps on your right. Ascend these to the Fife Coastal Path on the old railway line in front of you. The Fife Coastal Path is not too well signposted here. Leave Largo on the Fife Coastal Path. Here, in winter, you may see scaup. The females of these ducks are brownish and nondescript but distinguished by a whitish patch around the base of the bill The males are characterised by ash-grey backs. These ducks feed on, among other things, mussels. 'Scaup' is an old Scottish word for 'a mussel'. The Firth of Forth has lots of scaup in the winter. Walk along the Fife Coastal Path for the next half to three-quarters of a mile. Bypass footpaths and cart tracks left and right. The signing of the Fife Coastal Path improves here. Bypass a field gate by a kissing gate on its left. At this point your path has upgraded to a rough track.

Eventually you will reach ruins on the left and right of the track. Go to the left here via a kissing gate to the right of a farm gate. Proceed up the small slope with the fence on your close left. You have now left the Fife Coastal Path. At the top of the field go through a kissing gate to the right of a farm gate. Then follow the cart track as it veers right and then left. The hill straight ahead of you here is Largo Law. This is an extinct volcano which has summits topped with basic basalt. It used to be used as a beacon hill to warn people of impending danger. 'Law' is an old Scottish word for 'a rounded hill', most often utilised when the hill is detached from other hills, making it more obvious.

Just before the farm in front of you follow the footpath sign left through a kissing gate. Go right and left on the footpath to arrive in a car park. At this point follow the green arrows straight ahead and right past Hansel and Gretel's workshop (I kid you not) on your left. Walk past Scotland's Larder on your left on the same road. You can visit the exhibition here, taste food, buy a snack or food to take home with you. It is Scotland's only Commended Food Visitor Attraction (sic). They also do mail order. Walk up the tarmac drive to the main road, A917, and walk to the right along this.

About 100 metres along here, bear left up an overgrown path between a hedge on the left and a fence on the right. Keep the telephone wires on your right. This path starts just before the farm road to Monturpie bed and breakfast. The walking is better on the left-hand side of this path. This brings you out on the main A915. Walk left along here for about 50 metres and then go right up the farm road to Chesterstone Farm. Proceed up to and around the outside of the farm, keeping it on your left. Having done a U-shape around the farm you will come to a cart track on your right at the

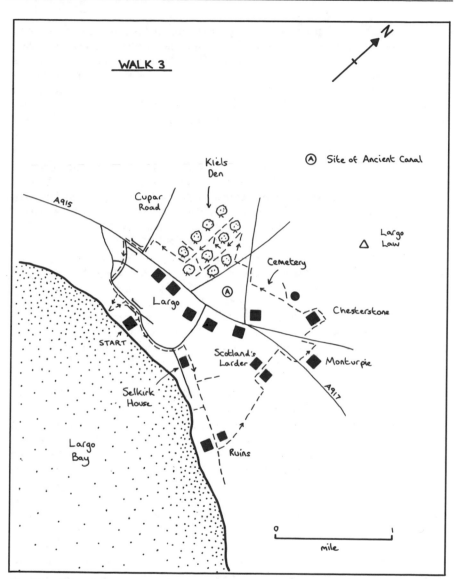

WALK 3

(A) Site of Ancient Canal

far side of the farm. Go down this cart track. There is a dog at the farm but it only barked at me. Wander down past Chesterstone Farm Cottage on your right to a fork in the track. Here choose the left fork downhill.

As this cart track ends in a field, walk along a footpath ahead of you that is rather obscured by plants, keeping the fence on your right. After passing the cemetery on your right you arrive at a tarmac car park for the cemetery. Walk through this to the tarmac road at the end of it and turn right up the tarmac road. At this point, if you look over the dyke on the opposite side of the road from the cemetery you will see what appears to be a deep ditch diagonally to your left. This was Scotland's first canal. As the great Largo seafarer Sir Andrew Wood retired and became infirm he had this canal dug by captured English pirates to connect his house (ahead of you but out of sight) to Largo Church (visible below and to the left of you). Every Sunday these pirates would row Sir Andrew to church and back again in his admiral's barge This was in the late 15th century.

Just past the main gates of Largo Cemetery on your right, you will find a kissing gate on the left of a field gate on the left-hand side of the road. Pass through here and contour along the hillside, keeping close company with the dyke on your left. Walk along two field margins, still accompanying the fence/ dyke on your left, and through a kissing gate to the left of a field gate. Keep ahead on the beautiful grass path to the tarmac road and go straight across where a footpath sign points to Kiels Den. Here a seat enables you to enjoy beautiful views over the Firth of Forth.

Contour along the hillside on this well-traversed path. Pass through a gap in a fence to arrive at a T-junction with a much used path running along the top edge of the river valley of Kiels Den. Descend to the left at this T-junction. Approximately 200 metres downhill a footpath goes right and then right again, doubling back down into the valley of the Boghall Burn. This is your way. At the bottom cross the burn by a footbridge. Pause to enjoy the peaceful glen. This Kiels Den was a favourite haunt of Alexander Selkirk subsequent to his return to Largo following his four year lonely sojourn on Juan Fernandez. Bear left uphill having traversed the bridge. At the top of the opposite bank this path makes a T-junction with another path which follows the course of the burn. Here drop left with the path, keeping the burn on your left. Walk past minor paths to the left and right.

At the end of the wood exit via a kissing gate. Then follow the path ahead of you by the barbed wire fence on your left. At the end of this well-walked path negotiate a kissing gate to the left of a field gate and turn left along the surfaced road. At the end of Cupar Road go right along the main road, A915. Cross the bridge and take the first road on the left after the bridge. There is a house called Wellford here. Keep with this road to the right and up and over the hill. Then go straight ahead at the crossroads to go down Emsdorf Road. At the T-junction descend to the left down Drummochy Road.

Just after the Fife Coastal Path signs on the right, turn right down Drumpark. This is signposted facing the other way so you have to look behind you. As you near the sea go left up the little alleyway. This takes you around to the left and brings you out into an open grassy area with seats. On the other side of the harbour you can see the Crusoe Hotel. Drop down to the main road and go right over the bridge. Then bear right into the Crusoe Hotel car park.

If the tide is extremely low you may see the remains of a submerged forest of oak, birch and hazel in Largo Bay. This has been caused by the sea rising or the land falling — opinions differ.

# 4. The Kingdom of Fife: Culross

**Route:** Culross – Culross Abbey – West Kirk – Blair Moss – Fife Coastal Path – Culross Palace

**Distance:** 3.5 miles

**Map:** OS Landranger 65, Falkirk, Linlithgow and Dunfermline

**Start:** Red Lion, Culross

**Access:** By bus, this needs to be a two-stage journey. First you go to Dunfermline and then from there to Culross. There is a good train service to Dunfermline, ring 0345 484950 for details. There are numerous buses to Dunfermline. From Dunfermline an hourly service runs to Culross, even on Sundays. For bus details call Passenger Transport Information on 01592 416060, or 'Traveline' on 0800 232323 in the Edinburgh area or 0131 225 3858 if calling from outside Edinburgh.

By car, take the A90, Queensferry Road, out of Edinburgh and follow signs to the Forth Road Bridge. Once across this (toll) bridge take the junction left just before the start of the M90, signposted A985, Kincardine Bridge. Go through three roundabouts in quick succession and then, about five miles after the third roundabout, you arrive at a fourth. Here go left on the B9037 signed for Culross. Drive through Torryburn and Valleyfield villages for about two and a half miles. At the far side of Valleyfield take the road going diagonally left ahead for Culross. After another half a mile or so you arrive at a free car park on your left. This is a good place to park. You then leave the car park and walk left up the road into Culross, the road you have just been travelling on. The Red Lion is about 150 metres up on your left. Alternatively you can drive directly into Culross and take a chance on getting into the Red Lion's car park. The entrance to this is on your left immediately before the pub. There is another free car park on the far side of Culross.

## The Red Lion. Tel: 01385 880 225

This is a listed building. In the 1976 listings it is recorded as 'an eighteenth-century inn, two storied, rendered. slated, altered. Later addition at the east end'. However, like the east end of the pub, its history has also lately been extended. Originally the pub was believed to have been a private house erected in 1746. Then in 1983, during renovation, workmen discovered intricately decorated beams, very much like those found at Culross Town House. These beams had been assessed by experts as four centuries old.

Because this is a listed building the proprietors sent for specialists from the Royal Commission on Ancient and Historical Monuments. They dated these beams as between 1570 and 1640. Specimens and photographs of these beams are currently being studied in an effort to age them more precisely. Meanwhile the beams have been covered up again to protect them from pollution such as smoke. When the car park was relaid evidence such as coal and iron rubble indicates that this was a forge at one time. So the cloudy history of the Red Lion is being clarified by time. The pub is believed to have been a coaching inn on the coast road in the last century.

This century it still serves travellers with excellent food. The local farmers supply the pub with potatoes and meat. While I was there I had a beautiful meal of haggis, whisky and cream in a ramekin served with a delightfully dressed, high in herb flavour salad and oatcakes. There is an extensive range of home-cooked food. This is available from 1200-2100 seven days a week.

Opening hours in winter, between October and Easter, are 1200-2400 seven days a week. In summer the opening hours are 1100-2400, 1130 on Sundays. There is a guest real ale in summer and sometimes in winter. On keg are Tennents 60/-, Tennents Special 70/-, Maclays Cooper Ale, Grolsch Premium, Guinness, Caffreys and Dry Blackthorn.

Landlord David Alexander welcomes walkers. There is a children's certificate until 2000. There are also high chairs. Inside it is a lovely old country pub. It has dark wood exposed, beams framing painted walls and ceilings of various colours. There are old wooden tables and lots of pictures of old Culross. The dining room has stone walls and pictures by local artists adorning the walls, these are for sale. Other amenities include a pool table, fruit machine, darts, cigarette machine and television. A patio/beer garden overlooks the Firth of Forth. They also take credit cards and serve coffee.

## Culross

If you could put whole villages into time capsules and leave them for 200 years then you would get Culross. The village is like a history theme park, a fact not lost on film makers and TV producers who often use it as a setting for their work. For some unknown reason the Industrial Revolution did not disturb the sleep of this Rip Van Winkle village. Then in the 1930s the National Trust for Scotland started occupying properties in the village. This, with the Trust's 'Little Houses' scheme to encourage private owners to keep their dwelling harmonising with the rest of the village, resulted in Culross awakening in the latter half of this century as a tourist attraction.

The market cross and Oldest House

That was how Culross ended up as it is today, but how it started up was quite another story. Culross was first recorded as a religious centre with monks of the Celtic Church here in the 6th century. Princess Thenew (St Enoch of Glasgow), daughter of King Lot of Lothian, was disgraced and cast away in a tiny boat to die in the deep. This boat grounded at Culross and her son was born here. This Kentigern grew up under the auspices of St Serf at Culross. Later, as St Mungo, he founded Glasgow Cathedral. St Serf's day is the first of July.

In 1217 Malcolm, the seventh Earl of Fife founded a monastery here. This was part of the (Roman) Cistercian order and had to say masses for his soul in perpetuity. The Cistercians are members of the Benedictine order which came from a father house in Citeaux, France and was founded in 1098 by Bernard of Clairvaux. He softened the hard edges of poverty, prayer and austerity that was killing the Monastery of Citeaux. The Cistercians said less prayers than other members of the Benedictine order. They went in for plain, unadorned churches, normally in towns. They did physical labour, studied and did not eat flesh.

These hard working monks provided the prosperity of Culross. As so often in Scotland, it was they who started mining coal. This primitive industry was kick-started into a much bigger one by George Bruce, a descendant of Robert the Bruce. He rented one of the Cistercians' mines. Then, using modern methods to improve production, drainage and ventilation, he made enormous increases in tonnage possible. He also treated his employees as human beings at a time when most miners in Scotland were effectively serfs.

This increase in coal production led to an increase in salt production. Sea water was heated in large pans by burning coal to evaporate the water and leave the salt behind. In those days salt was a very valuable commodity as there was no refrigeration. This abundant energy source also helped the production of a unique Culross speciality, the baking girdle. Rumour has it that the blacksmiths of Culross created this cooking implement first. Certainly their monopoly right to produce cooking girdles was recognised by James VI in 1599.

After the death of the then Sir George Bruce in 1625, Culross slipped into decline. Bad weather damaged the undersea mining. Then in 1760 foundries at Carron started producing cheaper girdles of cast iron. Culross tried shoemaking for a while, exporting these to the colonies in the New World. However, after the American Revolution this dwindled away. Then Culross slept until the National Trust's handsome prince kissed awake the sleeping beauty of Culross in the 1930s.

## The Walk

Turn left out of the Red Lion and along the main road. After about 20 metres you arrive at the electricity substation on your right. If you wish you can go 20 metres on to the townhouse on your right and buy an all inclusive ticket for the Study, Palace and Townhouse, which are all on the route of this walk. Keep the electricity substation on your left and walk uphill towards the Dundonald Arms. About 30 metres up here on your right a plaque reveals which was Bishop Leighton's house. Walk past the

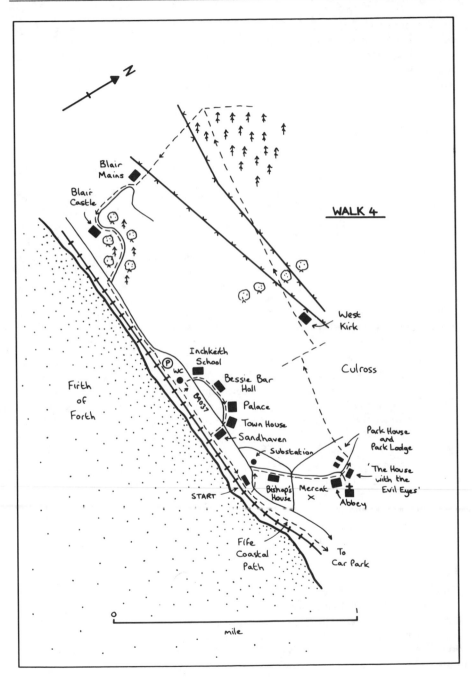

Z

Blair
Mains

Blair
Castle

WALK 4

West
Kirk

Culross

Inchkeith
School

P
WC

Bessie Bar
Hall

B9037

Palace

Town House

Firth
of
Forth

Sandhaven

Substation

Park House
and
Park Lodge

'The House
with the
Evil Eyes'

Bishop's
House

Mercat
×

Abbey

START

Fife
Coastal
Path

To
Car Park

0                                              1

mile

Dundonald Arms on your left to the market cross. On your left here is the Study. This was used by Bishop Leighton and has a painted ceiling and original panelling from 1633. On its left is the oldest house in Culross, with the date 1577 on its gable. Keep going straight ahead uphill after the market cross. For National Trust for Scotland opening times of the Study etc., phone 0131 226 5922.

As you start to climb Tanhouse Brae, a Greek inscription over on the windowsill on your left means God provides and will provide. This was the home of a God-fearing sea captain with an interest in Hellenic culture. Number 4, on the left, was the butcher's and has the date 1664 and a cleaver and stele (knife sharpener) on a plaque on the wall. The yellow house on the corner where a road goes off to the left is the Tan House. Subsequent to the flooding and collapse of coal mining here in 1625, many merchants turned to shoe and boot making. Their products were exported to America via Glasgow.

Opposite the Tan House is Snuff Cottage, where an engraving from 1763 reads, "Who would ha' thocht it". This next line of this old poem reads, "Noses would ha' bought it." The complete inscription was on a different snuff manufacturer's house in Edinburgh. The white house on the right just past the junction on the left is the Coachman's Cottage, with foundations dating back to the beginning of the 1600s. The coachman worked for the owner of Park House, further up on the left. Walk up past Culross Abbey and Church on your right. This became the local church in 1633. The Bruce Vault off the north transept has a lovely alabaster memorial to Sir George Bruce. In this church is one of the very first examples of the printing of the Authorised Version of the Bible from 1612. At the triangle of stone in the middle of the road you go left. About 20 metres up here on your right look through the gates of Parklayhill House to see the gable end with the high windows in Dutch style. These give the house its nickname – the house with the evil eyes. If you want to protect yourself against the evil eye make a fist and extend the fore and little fingers and point it at the house.

Go past Park House and Park Lodge on the left and about 10 metres past these is a gap in the wall, also on your left. There is a gate here and a signpost guiding you 'Footpath to West Kirk', take this path. This right of way is known as Coachman's Road. Walk along the field edge with the trees on your left until you reach a road via a gate. Go straight ahead on the cart track here. Follow this cart track as it decays into a footpath. At the T-junction with another footpath turn right, as suggested for West Kirk. Here you may find red campion, a pinkish/red five-petalled flower with a bulbous bit just behind the flower head. The hills you can see ahead are the Ochils. Keep on this path as it bends left towards pylons, go left with it and you arrive at the West Kirk. This church dates back to the 12th century and was the original parish church for Culross.

Continue along this well-maintained and mown path, a right of way called the Moor Road. You arrive at a junction where a cart tracks go right and ahead and a path goes to the left. Go straight ahead on the cart track. The large chimney ahead on the left is Longannet Power Station. This cart track degrades into a narrow but followable footpath after you go under another set of pylons. Contour along the hillside on this footpath and through a kissing gate to the right of a field gate. Ignore a stile on the right leading into a pine wood and walk along the obvious path ahead on the field margin between the wood and the telephone wires. Bypass another stile on the right, marked grave. This marks the grave of girdlesmith James Bald's three bairns, Jean, Agnes and Robert, who all perished of the plague on a single day – 24th September 1645.

Go through a kissing gate at the end of the field and straight ahead through the wood. At the end of the path is a T-junction with a dirt track, go left down this. Walk under two sets of power lines and past Blair Mains Farm on the right. Just after the farm the road forks, follow the fork to the right. Approximately 200 metres along here, as the house appears in the trees ahead, go left on a track. Go along this, cutting across the fork of the Y-junction, and after some 20 metres go left onto the other fork of the Y onto the tarmac. It would be best not to pick any flowers or shrubs here as the landowners are quite strict about this. Descend through woods on this tarmac road to arrive at the coast road at the entrance to Blair Castle, now a home for convalescent miners. Just to your left around the bend is Dunimarle Castle, where in 1999 scenes from the film *The Little Vampire* with Richard E. Grant were shot.

Cross the road, bearing slightly right. Just to the right of an upright metal post with fluorescent strips on it is a faint path ahead. This leads you onto the Fife Coastal Path via a stile or kissing gate. Turn left towards Culross. The railway on your right between you and the Firth of Forth is a mineral railway.

About 50 metres past the west car park at Culross, turn left through the children's play park and then bear left again towards the public toilets. Swing right by the war memorial to reach the main road. Cross the road and walk up the cobbled path, with Inchkeith private school on your left. Follow this little ox-bow shaped street around to the right. On your left you will see Bessie Bar Hall. Bessie Bar was a niece of Sir George Bruce and this was her malt-house. It also had a well.

Wander past the sundial at Sandhaven on your left and the Tron Shop, Town House and the Palace. The tron was on the right of the Tron Shop. Its stone base supported a beam for weighing goods for export so as to assess the tax liabilities on them. The sundial at Sandhaven is a restored one. The Palace was never a royal palace although James VI stayed here, but the residence of Sir George Bruce. Its title deeds specify it as "The Palace of Great Lodgings in the Sand Haven of Culross". The gardens are laid out in medieval fashion. They are planted with crops of the period such as onions, peas, beans, kale, skirret (a kind of bitter parsnip) and salsify. It is also planted with herbs typical of the era like mugwort, madder, French lavender and dwarf broom.

At the Town House turn right and cross the main road and go ahead up the concrete path with the wall of Sandhaven House on your left. Then go directly ahead and turn left onto the Fife Coastal Path. About 100 metres along here the car park of the Red Lion is on your left. Another 200 metres along, at the end of the concrete footpath, go left through the gate into the car park. A display board here gives details of Preston Island ahead.

# 5. Kingdom of Fife: Dunfermline

**Route:** St Margaret's Cave — North Urquhart — Dean Plantation — Crossford — Urquhart — Pittencrieff Park

**Distance:** 5.5 miles

**Map:** OS Landranger 65, Falkirk and Linlithgow

**Start:** Old Inn, Dunfermline

**Access:** By bus, the service between Edinburgh and Dunfermline is sometimes good but always adequate. For information call 'Traveline' on 0800 232323 if calling from the Edinburgh area, otherwise ring 0131 225 3858. You can also ring Fife First on 0131 663 9233 or Scottish Citylink on 0990 505050.

From the bus station, go into the shopping mall behind and attached to it. Follow it around past the escalators then be guided by the signs to High St. When you emerge into High Street, turn right along it. About 100 metres on, turn left down Guildhall Street. Then around 100 metres down here go right along Abbott St. Walk past the pink medieval Abbots House, which can be visited. You may see peacocks wandering the streets here. At the T-junction at the end of Abbots Street the Old Inn is just ahead and to the left of you.

It is possible to go to Dunfermline **by train** but the station is quite a long walk from the Old Inn. Train details can be accessed on 0345 484950

By car, take the A90 (Queensferry Rd) out of Edinburgh and follow signs to the Forth Road Bridge. Cross this (toll) bridge. Go straight ahead onto the M90 at junction 1. Get off the M90 at junction 2 onto the A823 (M), signposted for Dunfermline. From here, depending on the day, take one of the following options:

On **Sundays and public holidays** follow the A832 (M) to the roundabout at the top of the hill where the A907 is shown as the second left. However, you take the first left off the roundabout, marked Central Area Car Parks, Town Centre, Museum and Carnegie Hall. Shortly after this turn left down New Row at Marks and Spencer's. Then turn right along Canmore St. Follow this along past the pink medieval Abbots House on your left. Past here there is a parking bay free on Sundays. If this is full the road ends in a T-junction at the Old Inn. There are parking spaces left and right but left is probably a better bet. Watch out for peacocks around the Abbots House.

**Mondays to Saturdays** — take the second left at the roundabout at the top of the hill, the A907 for Alloa. Go along this dual carriageway for about 300 metres. Just before the bridge turn right up Bruce Street, signposted for car parks. Use either of the car parks on either side of Bruce Street, both are long stay. Walk back down Bruce Street to the A907 and cross the main road at the traffic lights to keep on down a narrow, cobbled continuation of Bruce Street towards the steeple. Cross over High Street and stay ahead on what is now Kirkgate. You will see Dunfermline Abbey and Palace ahead on your left. The Old Inn is directly opposite the Abbey on your right.

## The Old Inn. Tel 01383 736652

As the name implies, this is a very old pub. It was an old coaching inn and a plaque outside on the wall by the door gives details of its history. As you are probably going there and will be able to read it for yourself I won't spoil it for you by repeating it all, but I will give you a taster of this tavern's history.

In 1806 Laurence Miller, then the landlord of this pub, started to run a coach called The Fly. This ran to Aberdour, from where passengers could get a ferry to Leith. As there was then no coach service to the world outside Dunfermline, this attracted much business. Sadly the service stopped the next year when his horses died under a fall of masonry from a dilapidated turret of Dunfermline Abbey. In 1885 Dunfermline Athletic Football Club was founded in this pub. This is marked by football memorabilia on the walls of this hostelry.

And hospitable it is, too. A walkers' club meets here every second Wednesday so ramblers can be sure of a friendly reception from landlord Mr Hegarty and his staff. This tavern also has a children's licence. Brewing cartoons in the hallway may amuse the children. The hallway is brightly coloured in yellow and orange. This leads up to the large bar at the back which can also be accessed via the long, narrow public bar on the right of the hallway. The lounge is spacious and graciously decorated with jazz memorabilia and a ceiling fan and soothingly furbished in blue. There are framed articles about The Old Inn on the walls of the bar, some from the *Dunfermline Journal* as far back as 1838 and one from a book called *Scottish Taverns* by Rankine Taylor. There are photographs of the pub from days gone by, in-

The Old Inn

cluding one of a horse and cart delivery of barrels of ale. The brewery theme is continued with decor detailing old processes such as filling machines, bar engines and imperial measures. There is a picture in cross-section of an old brewery. Stained glass pictures about brewing adorn the wall behind the bar.

And talking of brewing, this establishment normally stocks four real ales. McEwans 80/- and Courage Directors are usually the residents. The two guest ales when I was there were Deuchars IPA and Harviestouns Bitter and Twisted, the champion beer of Scotland for 1999. Issuing from keg pumps were Becks, McEwans 70/-, Miller Pilsner, Guinness, Strongbow and McEwans Lager. Opening hours are 1100-2400 Monday to Saturday and 1200-2400 on Sundays. There is a jukebox and fruit machine

There is no food. However this pub is in central Dunfermline overlooking the Abbey, the Abbots House and the Palace. There are plenty of places to get something to eat, including The Creepy Wee Pub next door to The Old Inn. The history of The Old Inn and its choice of real ales tilted the balance in its favour when I chose the pub for this walk.

# Dunfermline

Dunfermline means 'fort at the river bend with a waterfall'. This fort was built by the first king to live at Dunfermline, Malcolm Canmore, in 1065. Dunfermline had been a centre of the Celtic church so when Malcolm married an intensely pious English-woman, Margaret, it was natural to her to supplant these establishments with a church of her native Catholic faith. This church had a holy relic, a black rood (cross), and so became a place of pilgrimage. Thus Dunfermline was established on the twin foundations of medieval life: church and state.

Queen Margaret's sons helped Dunfermline. Alexander I made it into a royal burgh. David I transformed Margaret's church into a Benedictine abbey rich in lands and possessions. The first part of the abbey was dedicated in 1150. In 1243 it became a mitred abbey with some 50 monks. In 1250 Queen Margaret was canonised. The town prospered as the royal court and abbey brought people and business to the town. Tax was recorded as being paid on luxury items such as pepper, ginger, raisins, rice, almonds and figs.

In 1303 Edward I of England, having stayed at the abbey for the winter, gave orders for it to be torched as he left. Although much was destroyed, much was saved. In 1322 Robert the Bruce, who spent a fair bit of time here, granted the abbey the right to collect taxes for the town. After the assassination of James I in 1436 Dunfermline was considered insufficiently secure to protect the king from his nobles so the royal residence was moved to Edinburgh and Dunfermline lost one of the twin bastions supporting it. At the Reformation in 1560 many of the contents of the abbey were taken out and burnt (paintings, relics etc.) and the building was used as a public quarry for stone. Only the nave escaped as it was the parish church. The abbey lands etc. went to the crown, who visited a bit more in less perilous times. In fact James VI gave these lands to his wife, Anne of Denmark, as a wedding gift. However, after the union of the crowns in 1603 Dunfermline only ever saw kings when they were in trouble and needed something from the town.

By the early 1700s Dunfermline was in a poor state after the loss of its earnings from church and royalty. Daniel Defoe, author of *Robinson Crusoe*, was less than impressed with it in 1723. Coal continued to help and with the advent of the Industrial Revolution was a positive advantage. Foundries were founded on local coal and iron. However Dunfermline's main industry, which continued into the 20th century, was textiles. The advent of looms, and particularly power looms, brought prosperity to the town. Linen, especially damask linen, was Dunfermline's pride and joy. Andrew Carnegie, local lad made millionaire in America, gave much money to the town. Today the 'Auld Grey Toon' is trying to encourage tourism, one of the current growth industries.

## The Walk

From The Old Inn turn left and walk uphill along Kirkgate. At High Street there is an old church on your left which is now the town hall. A little way left on High Street is a cannon. This is a Carron Ironworks cannon which has been here since 1772. The streets here are all cobbled. Cross High Street and continue uphill. About 100 metres up here, just past Queen Anne Street on the right, is an old church on your left which was a carpet warehouse when I was there. Turn left down the alleyway immediately before this church, following the sign to St Margaret's Cave. At the end of the steps in the alleyway go right to reach St Margaret's Cave. This is free. You can walk down to reach the cave where the holy Queen (later Saint) Margaret retreated to meditate. Information boards give a chance to rest on the way up. Turn right once out of the cave.

Walk under the bridge and hairpin right onto a flagged path and then bear left with the path onto Bruce Street, Go right along Bruce Street and then turn right across the bridge you have just passed under. This is the Glen Bridge, a plaque on the parapet on your right gives details about it. Once over the bridge, immediately turn right off the A907 up Chalmers St. After about 50 metres along here go left along Dewar St. In the old Scottish pre-Catholic Celtic Church a dewar was a guardian of holy relics. About 100 metres along Dewar Street break right at the first junction. Around 50 metres along here bend left into Cameron St. Cameron Street ends in a T-junction with the main road, A907. Slightly to your right, across the road, is a footpath sign to the Dean plantation, proceed along there.

After some half a mile on this beaten earth footpath between lines of trees you will arrive at a four-way junction of paths roughly 50 metres before a field gate. Bear right towards North Urquhart Farm on the hill above you. Follow the path/cart track left and right past this farm on your right. When this cart track bends sharply right, go left through a gap in the bushes. There veer right on to a grassy track that aims for a farm just to the left of the three signal towers ahead. On this path you may put up coveys of partridge. These are grey partridge, although I always find them more brown than grey. They can be identified by a rusty red tail which is prominent as they take to the air. They are about the size of a town-square pigeon.

Proceed on this path through rough ground between fields and then along the left-hand side of a field with a high hedge on the left. This terminates in a T-junction with the tarmac road to Mylesmont Croft. Turn left and walk through the farmyard. At the far end of the farmyard a path is evident between low trees on either side. About 50 metres up this path turn left through a gap at the left of the path and them right over a fence. Then walk parallel with but to the left of the path. The path ahead was impassable when I was here. I wished that I had been carrying a machete.

At the end of the field a barbed wire fence ahead and to the right presents an obstacle. However it is quite easy to cross at the junction of fences. Once over the fence break left onto the path between bushes which is now passable. Hopefully you will not to have to take this little diversion off the path as it will be passable all the way along when you get there. I have been in touch with the local authorities about this. Some 50 metres after climbing over the fence this path terminates in a T-junction with a farm road. Turn left along this and bear right with it, keeping the narrow strip of woodland on your right.

At the bottom of the hill veer right, keeping the farm buildings of Berrylaw Farm on your left. Cross a tarmac road and go directly ahead along a gravel track. Keep with this through a narrow belt of woodland then bear right and left with what is now a cart track and walk along with the hedge on your right. Continue on across the field to the footpath sign at the road ahead. A Scottish Rights of Way Society Sign informs you that you have been walking along a cycle path.

Turn right up the metalled road, following the sign to the Dean Plantation. Walk past Furness House and another house on your left. After approximately 100 metres, turn left on to a drive. About 10 metres along this turn left on to a footpath through the wood. Follow the path and each time it forks take the left option. There is a maze of paths in here and you have to keep to the southern (Firth of Forth) side of the Dean Plantation. After paralleling the edge of the plantation on your left at about 10 metres distance, the path then breaks left and right to run between the plantation and its fence.

At the bottom of the valley here, at the burn, step left over a beaten down piece of fencing and go straight ahead to follow the line of trees on your left that marks the course of the burn. Keep with the burn as it bears left. When it breaks sharply left around 30 to 40 metres beyond this, go to your right up a farm track. This comes to a T-junction with a very minor paved road at a farm. Here walk left along this road. After just under half a mile on this road, now degraded into a cart track, you arrive at a four-way junction. Cross the tarmac road to a tarmac road on its far side called Kirkwood Crescent.

When a sign ahead says Knockhouse Gardens, turn left just before it to walk up a metalled road. Walk up here for roughly half a mile until you reach the farm. Turn right along the farm road with the farm on your right and houses on your left. Bypass a cart track on your left and jink left and right past the farm buildings. A grassy track ahead takes you away from the farm between a field on your right and a hedge on

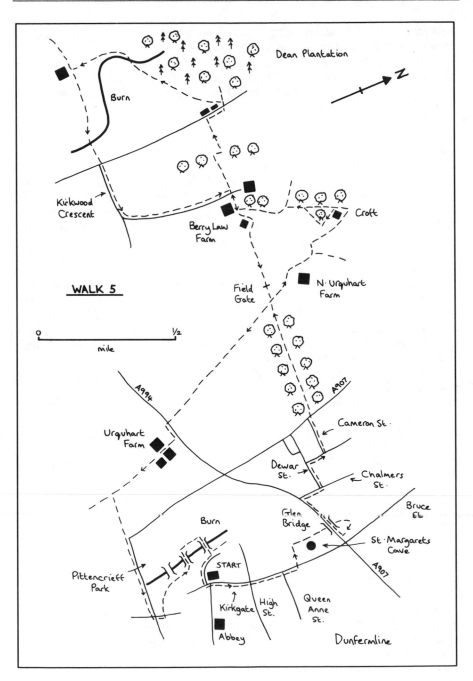

Dean Plantation

Burn

Z

Kirkwood
Crescent

Berry Law
Farm

Croft

**WALK 5**

N·Urquhart
Farm

Field
Gate

0       ½
      mile

A994

A907

Urquhart
Farm

Cameron St.

Dewar
St.

Chalmers
St.

Bruce
St.

Burn

Glen
Bridge

St·Margarets
Cave

Pittencrieff
Park

START

A907

Kirkgate

High
St.

Queen
Anne
St.

Abbey

Dunfermline

your left towards Dunfermline on the skyline ahead. Look to your right for good views over the Pentlands and Forth rail and road bridges. About a half a mile along this track negotiate a field gate to arrive at a four-way junction some 50 metres beyond it.

Turn right downhill and follow this track flanked by hedges to the main road, A994, at some half a mile's distance. At the T-junction with the main road, walk left along the busy road for around 50 metres. Then at the Dunfermline Tourist Attractions sign turn right and proceed along a minor tarmac road. There are houses on your left and Urquhart Farm on your right. About 100 metres after the houses and farm buildings end, a rough road goes off to the left. Take this and after approximately a quarter of a mile walk past the boom at the end of this road that blocks vehicular access to it.

Your route lies straight ahead. On your left front is Pittencrieff Park with a tall wall around it. What is the point of having a public park when the public cannot get into it! Walk ahead, keeping to the right-hand side of the road so as to face the oncoming traffic. For the first 100 metres there is no trace of a pavement so some care is needed. After this there is a semblance of a footpath. After some 200 to 300 metres along this road you arrive at a T-junction with a tarmac road. Here go left and then quickly left again into the park. Then immediately go right past the children's play area. Follow this path up with the burn on your left. Cross the burn at the second footbridge and continue on with the burn now on your right. You will often here jays screeching harshly here. These shy woodland members of the crow family are more often heard than seen. In flight, a crow-sized bird with a prominent white rump identifies a jay.

This path then takes you across the burn by a third footbridge. As soon as you are over this bridge turn right uphill. This glen has been amazingly quiet so close to a town. You have no aural indication that you are surrounded on all four sides by busy roads and town. This new path takes you to a T-junction with a tarmac park road. At this point turn right uphill. This takes you to a tarmac traffic road opposite Dunfermline Abbey. An information board here gives you details about Pittencrieff Park. Turn left up St Catherine's Wynd and The Old Inn is soon to be found on your left.

# 6. The Kingdom of Fife: Aberdour

**Route:** Aberdour – Silver Sands – Bendomeer – Dalachy Farm – Humbie Wood – Aberdour

**Distance:** 5 miles

**Map:** OS Landranger 66, Edinburgh

**Start:** Woodside Hotel, Aberdour

**Access:** By bus, you need to take two buses, one to Inverkeithing and one from there to Aberdour. A Stagecoach service runs from St Andrew's Square bus station to Inverkeithing. This is a good service Monday to Saturday, on Sundays it reduces to an hourly service. From Inverkeithing a half-hourly service runs to Aberdour Monday to Saturday, on Sundays this bus runs hourly. For times of buses ring 'Traveline' on 0800 232323 if in the Edinburgh area, if outside the Edinburgh area ring 0131 225 3858. The number for Stagecoach (Fife) is 01592 261 461.

Probably a better bet for accessing Aberdour by public transport is the train. Aberdour Railway Station is a Victorian gem and the rail journey takes you across that icon, the Forth Rail Bridge. In addition, this is a direct service with no need for changing. Weekdays and Saturdays trains leave Edinburgh's Waverley Station for Aberdour at half-hourly intervals. On Sundays it is an hourly service. For train details ring 0345 484950. From Aberdour Station take the exit to the main road, A921. Turn left and follow the road as it kinks left and right over the railway, and some 150 metres past the railway bridge the Woodside Hotel is on your right.

By car, take the A90 (Queensferry road out of Edinburgh) and follow signs along this to the Forth Road Bridge. Cross this toll bridge. Once over the bridge, just before the motorway (M90), turn right onto the A921. Pass by Inverkeithing by two roundabouts. Then bypass Dalgety Bay on two roundabouts. Two miles further on, go straight ahead at a roundabout as the B9157 goes off on the left. As the A921 enters Aberdour the Woodside Hotel is on your left. Some 30 to 40 metres past it a nameless, unsignposted little road on your left leads to the hotel car park.

---

## Woodside Hotel. Tel: 01383 860 328

The Woodside Hotel was built as a coaching inn to service the traffic on the main road just outside in the early 18th century. It was then called the Bell Inn. In 1873 it was taken over by the Greig brothers of nearby Inverkeithing whose great grandfather founded the Russian navy. It was then called Greigs Hotel. After the Greigs died it was known as the Late Greigs Hotel. On the lintel above the door at the main entrance is a carving in stone of the face of one of these Greig brothers. In 1894 it became the Woodside Hotel.

In 1926 the blue riband transatlantic liner the *Orontes*, built in 1901, was being scrapped at the ship breaker's yard of T.W. Ward in nearby Inverkeithing. The roof of the first-class smoking salon was then incorporated into the fabric of the Woodside Hotel. Today it is the roof to the ante-room of the bar. You will know it when you see it as it has a sign up that says 'First Class, Please Mind the Step'. The ceiling portion of this is of stained glass, magnificently patterned. The ceiling surround is ornately and superbly carved, highly polished wood. It is altogether a work of art. The bar has a floor of lightly polished wood. The decor is, not unexpectedly, of a naval theme. It is comfortable and well appointed.

In this bar you have a good selection of food. There are vegetarian starters and main courses as well as desserts, a sandwich menu, cappuccino, regular coffee, tea, biscuits and shortbread. In-season vegetables come from the hotel's kitchen garden. Local fish comes from Pittenweem and Anstruther close by. The beef is all Scottish, as is the venison. All the food is fresh and home cooked. The frequently changing menu is created by a two rosette chef, making this one of the best of Scottish pubs to eat in. Outside of normal food hours soup and sandwiches are available. Food is served 1200-1400 and 1800-2130 Monday to Saturday and on Sundays from 1200-1430 and from 1700-2130.

Opening hours, for the bar, are 1100-2345 Monday to Saturday and 1200-2345 on Sundays. The one real ale, not on when I was there, is Alexander's Downfall by the Burntisland Brewery. The kegs on offer were Guinness, Belhaven Best, Tennents Ember, Tennents Lager and Tennents Velvet.

Proprietors Lesley and Stuart Dyke are happy to see walkers entering their establishment. The hotel is not a child-free zone. A beer garden is planned to be completed by the summer of 2000. In the winter a real fire is a warming sight, or should it be site. Credit and debit cards are welcome apart from Diners.

## Aberdour

Two neighbouring medieval structures, originally built in the 1100s, make up the heart of this ancient village. These are St Fillan's Church and Aberdour Castle. The church is an excellent example of early Norman construction. It became disused when a new parish kirk was erected in 1790. However, it was renovated in 1926 and once again became the parish church. There are stained-glass, 20th-century windows by Alexander Strachan.

Aberdour Castle has been modified and expanded throughout its life. It was also left to decay subsequent to a major fire towards the end of the 1700s. Between 1342 and 1924 it was in the possession of the Douglas Earls of Morton. It was then taken over by the government as a national monument. Aberdour Castle, Historic Scotland, is a semi-destroyed 12th-century tower house with renovated rooms from the 1600s, 17th-century pleasance (walled garden) and a doocot from the 1500s.

In the 19th century, as trades such as handloom weaving and other hitherto customary types of work started to decline, locals saw possibilities in tourism created by mass transport such as steam trains and ferries. The Earl of Morton sold land for wealthy visitors who came for the beach and sea to erect houses on. Manse Road and Seaside Place were the centre of Aberdour's new town. Along with these semi-resident holiday visitors came the day trippers. Up to nine steamers a day came here from Leith. When the rail access opened up with the completion of the Forth Rail Bridge in 1890, even more tourists came from the West of Scotland. The line through

Aberdour was called the missing link as it connected the Fife railways to the Forth Rail Bridge of 1890. Pierrot shows on the seafront were an Aberdour speciality.

Aberdour Harbour started off in industrial use. In the 1870s coal carts were commonly seen in the streets by the pier. Then it was used by ferries, now it is only utilised by pleasure craft. The now ruined wooden pier built in 1866 could disembark passenger ferries at any level of the tide.

St Fillan's 12th century Kirk

## The Walk

Exit the Woodside Hotel and walk left along the main road, A921, for about 100 metres. Then turn right down Shore Road at the Foresters Arms. After a couple of hundred metres down here, go left at the seafront as indicated by the sign for the Fife Coastal Path. Walk around the inner perimeter of the harbour. Proceed to the left of the café and follow a concrete footpath to a footbridge over the Dour Burn. Once over the burn ignore paths to the left and right and stay with the signed Fife Coastal Path to walk towards the point sheltering the eastern end of Aberdour Harbour. On your right here you will see the island of Incholm. This was called Aenemia before it became the Isle of St Colm. It was also called Druids Isle in advance of it being known as the Isle of the Saints. It was sacked by Vikings and after one unsuccessful raid Shakespeare wrote that Sweno King of Norway paid MacBeth and Banquo $10,000 to have his slain buried there.

Alexander the Fierce, King of Scotland, was shipwrecked here and taken care of by a holy hermit. He fed the king on cockles, dulse (edible seaweed) and milk from the cow he kept. In recognition of God sparing his life and to thank the holy man, the king endowed a priory of Augustinian canons here. This was a rich establishment with many land rents and taxes to be paid to it.

The area between Incholm and the mainland is called Mortimer's Deep. This recalls a rapacious and overbearing landowner, William de Mortimer, Lord of Aberdour in the 12th century. He was dumped in the sea here by long-suffering monks.

Near the derelict pier a rough road comes in from the left. Dog-leg left up here for about 10 metres. Then go right up steps to a footpath, as signed by blue arrows. As the rough road comes in from the left you can go ahead through houses to a footpath bearing left to visit Ha'craig, where climbers frequently practice. However this is neither an alternative route or a short cut but a dead end. You have to return to the rough road. At the top of the steps follow the well worn, beaten earth/grassy footpath across the neck of the point. Keep with this path towards a building that looks suspiciously like a lighthouse. Then be guided left along the tarmac road by the blue arrows. Walk past Silversands beach on your right here. This was Scotland's only blue flag beach in 1999, although whether you will see the blue flag flying is debatable. As I write this in July 99 the blue flag has recently been stolen from the flagpole, again!

Just past the café, bypass a gate by a gap to your left. About 50 metres past this gate walk to your right at a T-junction then go left along a tarmac path after some 50 metres. Bear right into the trees as guided by the Fife Coastal Path sign, Aberdour to Burntisland section. Walk along this path at the edge of the sea on your right for about a mile. Across the water you can see Edinburgh with Arthur's Seat and Salisbury Crags. The Pentlands fade away to the right of the city. The path then cuts left under the railway on your left and then bears right. Continue with this path.

After a couple of hundred metres you arrive at a very attractive cascade with a waterfall behind it. It is a very pleasant spot. About 50 metres past the cascade you come to a rough road athwart the path. Your route is to the left here. Then hairpin left with this crude road up to the main road, the A921. Bear right on the A921, the pavement is on the opposite side of the road from you. About 100 metres along the A921, just past a house on your left, is a farm road also on the left. This is your road.

Approximately 150 metres up here there is a five-way junction with two parallel roads on the left. Your way lies along the first of these roads on your left. Proceed past where the parallel road joins this road and continue on it, contouring along the hillside. Beside this road you may see a blue dandelion-like flower in summer. This is chicory. Its leaves can be blanched for salads and its roots dried, roasted and ground to be used as a flavouring in coffees.

Roughly 100 metres past a farm road coming in from the right, this track terminates in a T-junction. Go left downhill for around 100 metres. Here a narrow footpath through a gap in the trees on your right goes for some 10 metres to join a parallel farm track. Pass through here to turn right up this other farm track towards Dalachy Farm. Keep on this road past a house on the left called Green Kip and three houses on the

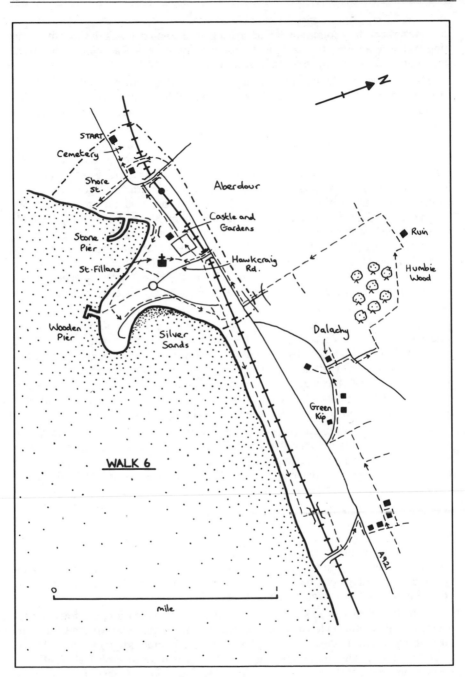

START

Cemetery

Shore St.

Aberdour

Castle and Gardens

Stone Pier

St. Fillans

Hawkcraig Rd.

Wooden Pier

Silver Sands

WALK 6

Ruin

Humbie Wood

Dalachy

Green Kip

A 921

0

mile

right, heading up in the direction of the farm. There is a fork in the road just before the farm and you should take the right fork.

At Dalachy Farm turn right just before the farmyard and walk through the farm outbuildings on a cart track between dykes uphill. Ignore a cart track to the left immediately after the farm. Follow this cart track uphill until it ends in a T-junction. At this point go right. After some 100 metres on the new track take a farm track on the left which has a dyke on its right and a fence on its left. Enjoy the views over the Firth of Forth up here. The islands between Incholm and Edinburgh are, believe it or not, part of the City of Edinburgh. Around 200 metres along this track, go with it as it bends sharply left through a field gate. Please close this gate behind you. There are two other field gates on the crown of this bend.

Ahead of you is Humbie Wood. The track takes you right at the edge of Humbie Wood. Keeping Humbie Wood on your left, proceed around two sides of it (going through field gates as you come to them). Eventually the wood fades away on your left. At this point a fence crosses your path. Go through the field gate in front of you into the crop field. After about 20 metres, follow the fading track to your right. At the end of the field ahead of you, at some 50 metres distance is a rocky ridge with gorse on it. Once atop this small ridge, turn left along it. There is no path on the ridge but if you follow its spine along you will not go wrong.

After some 200 metres along this ridge you will come to a ruined farmstead. There is a grassy cart track on its left. This is your way. Bypassing a field gate (and cart track behind it) on the right at the farmstead, go through a field gate ahead of you and keep on the track in front of you, firstly contouring along the hillside and then descending it. This ends at a fenced dyke blocking your route ahead. Here go left through the gate between two lime trees. Then stay on the overgrown cart track as it goes downhill with hedges on each side of it. After some 200 metres down here, walk past a well-marked cart track on the right. Continue downhill on what is now a footpath flanked by hedges. This is a bit overgrown with meadowsweet, willowherb and thistles, but it is quite passable.

Ignore a gate on your left. After around a quarter of a mile this footpath widens to an open cart track ahead of you. Bypass a farm track to the left. Shortly after this cart track your track narrows among hedges and then degrades to a footpath. It then opens out again to a wide, rough road. When this rough track ends, go directly ahead on the tarmac road in front of you, bypassing tarmac roads left and right of you. At the main road, A921, proceed right along this. Some 150 metres along here, past the sign to the police station, you reach Hawkcraig Road on your left. Go up here. Once over the railway bridge you will see a sign on your right to Aberdour, St Fillan's Ancient Church. You can go down here to visit the church, it is only a hundred metres or so diagonally to the right. At ninety degrees right here is a door in a wall that is dated 1632 on its lintel. When you return from St Fillan's, or if you choose not to go there, this is your route. This is a courtesy footpath for local people allowed by Historic Scotland, the custodians of Aberdour Castle. The opening hours for this path are 0900-1800 in summer and in winter 0900-1600 except on Thursdays. If the door is closed then return to the main road, A921, and walk left along it. At the railway bridge some 200 metres along here, turn right on the minor road signposted for Aberdour Cemetery and pick the walk up here again.

If you are able, go through the door into the walled garden and head for the right-hand door of the two in its far wall. In Sassanid, the language of the ancient Persians, paradise was their word for a walled garden. Once out of the walled garden, Aberdour Castle is on your left. You can visit it for a small charge. Having visited or bypassed the castle, go straight ahead past the castle on your left and out on its tarmac exit road past Aberdour Station. Then turn right across the railway via Station Place. Once over the railway go straight ahead on the minor road signposted for Aberdour Cemetery, where you will be joined by those who found the door locked.

About 50 metres down this minor road turn left where the sign points to Aberdour Cemetery. Cross the footbridge over the railway, and where the track veers right in the direction of the cemetery go diagonally left to pass through a gateway in a wall into the old cemetery. Follow the path ahead down between the church hall on your left and a house on your right. Swing left around the front of the church hall. A memorial in front of the church hall remembers a local hero who won the Victoria Cross. From this plaque go right on to the main road, A921. Then turn right along the A921 to find the Woodside Hotel roughly 100 metres further on.

# 7. West Lothian: Linlithgow

**Route:** Linlithgow – Union Canal – Parkley Place – Beecraigs Country Park – Kipps – Williamcraigs

**Distance:** 7 miles

**Map:** OS Landranger 65, Falkirk and Linlithgow

**Start:** Four Marys, Linlithgow

**Access:** There are frequent bus and train services to Linlithgow from Edinburgh. For train times call 0345 484950, local call! From the station descend into the busy main street guided by the traffic noise. Turn left along this busy road and the Four Marys is about 100 metres along on your left.

For bus information ring 'Traveline' on 0800 232323 in the Edinburgh area or 0131 225 3858 if outside Edinburgh. You can also phone First Midland Bluebird on 01324 613 777. Timetables can also be obtained from the bus shop at St Andrew's Square bus station. These buses stop in Linlithgow, outside the door of the Four Marys.

By car, take the M8 out of Edinburgh westwards. At junction 2 take the M8 then M9 for Stirling. At Junction 3 on the M9 take the A803 for Linlithgow. The Four Marys is on your left just before Linlithgow Cross. High St parking is limited. An alternative would be to turn right at Linlithgow Cross, immediately after the elaborate stone fountain cum well. After some 30 metres turn left, with the 17th-century, white-harled Cross House on your right. Ahead of you is the Euro car park. It cost £2.50 a day when I was there, free on Sundays. It is open 0900-1800. It is free outside these hours.

## The Four Marys, Linlithgow. Tel: 01506 842171

This pub was originally a house built around 1500. At that time many noble families lived in this area to be near the Royal Palace of Linlithgow. There is an archway in the pub large enough for a horseback rider to clear without dismounting. Local legend has it that this led to a tunnel to Linlithgow Cross across the road. It then split; one part going to the palace and the other to the West Gate of Linlithgow Town. Perhaps this was to enable discreet royal assignations.

Later, in 1813, David Waldie was born here. According to the locals, who are vehement about this, he was the real discoverer of chloroform as an anaesthetic. The Waldie family had a chemists shop. David Waldie mentioned his idea about chloroform to Dr James Young Simpson and then Simpson appropriated the idea and got the glory and recognition. There is a plaque on the outside wall of the pub commemorating David Waldie. Subsequently these premises were a newsagents, printers and a tea-room before becoming a pub in 1975.

The name The Four Marys refers to the four ladies in waiting to Mary Queen of Scots, who was frequently in Linlithgow. These Four Marys, according to the old song, were Mary Beaton, Mary Seton, Mary Carmichael and me. There are various theories as to what the fourth Mary's surname was, Fleming, Livingston or Hamilton. My local informant says that it was Fleming. The interior has numerous mementoes of Mary Queen of Scots including a piece of her bed curtains, a copy of the original warrant for her execution, a reproduction of the report of her execution and a facsimile of her death mask. Another royal connection is in an alcove where a board gives details of six kings of Scotland named James.

The bar is L-shaped and the furniture is mahogany chairs around stripped period and antique tables. The walls are mainly of ancient stone with some excellent stonework at the back. The bar counter is of wood from a disused church. Serving hours for lunch are from 1200-1430 Monday to Saturday and on Sundays from 1230-1430. Evening mealtimes are Sunday to Thursday from 1730-2030, and on Friday and Saturday from 1730-2100. That great old traditional Scottish meal, high tea, is served on Sundays from 1730-2030. The food is all good, home cooked and fresh apart from the chips and scampi. The food includes home-made pasta, salads, kids' meals, baked potatoes, snacks, toasties, burgers and vegetarian choices.

The choice is also excellent in the real ale department. There are four permanent real ales, Belhaven 70/-, Belhaven 80/-, Belhaven St Andrews and Deuchars IPA. There are also three or four guest real ales which change all the time. Twice a year this pub has real ale festivals with up to 10 beers on offer. Keg products include Belhaven Best, Belhaven Extra Cold, Guinness, Dry Blackthorn, Skol and Tennents Lager. Opening hours are 1200-2300 Monday to Wednesday, Thursday to Saturday 1100-2345 and on Sundays 1230-2300.

Ian and Evaleen Forrest are pleased to see walkers and are to be commended in running a pub that seems to have everything: decor, comfort, history, hospitality and excellent food and ale. Children are welcome until 2000, but if an order for food is taken before 2000 they can stay on to finish their meal.

## Linlithgow

Linlithgow means 'the place in the hollow by the loch'. Linlithgow is an ancient and historic burgh. This walk barely scratches the surface of it. For example, it does not visit Linlithgow Palace or St Michael's Church, both of which are fascinating to explore. An idea might be to get to Linlithgow quite early in the morning and visit these two sites before having lunch and doing your walk. The tourist information centre at Linlithgow Cross is a treasure trove of information about the town. Just outside it is an elaborately carved well/fountain, Cross Well. This was sculpted in 1806 by a mason called Robert Gary, he had only one hand so worked with a mallet tied to the stump of his maimed arm.

On the coat of arms of Linlithgow is a black dog. This commemorates a local man who was tied to a stake on an island in the loch to die of hunger. But his black bitch swam regularly across to him, bringing food. Today the people of Linlithgow of both genders are known as 'black bitches'. The Black Bitch is the oldest pub in town.

In the Wars of Independence local agriculturalist William Binnie helped take Linlithgow for Robert the Bruce. He hid men-at-arms in one of his regular deliveries of hay. He then stopped the wagon in the gateway to prevent the gates or portcullis from blocking the entrance. Meanwhile the men-at-arms held the garrison at bay while supporting troops rushed up to take Linlithgow for the Scots. Linlithgow was a walled town with three gates at that time.

In 1368 Linlithgow became a royal burgh, one of the four famed royal burghs of Scotland and supplanting Berwick which had then been taken by the English. The royal link was continued with the palace, which had existed since David I lived in the town in the 1100s. This was burnt down in the 1420s. James I (of Scotland) started the palace reconstruction quite soon afterwards. He also struck a coin with Linlithgow imprinted on it as Linlithgow had the royal mint in those days. Mary Queen of Scots was born in Linlithgow Palace. At the nuptials of her father, James V, and Mary of Guise, the octagonal fountain in the palace courtyard flowed with wine. Just after the English Civil War Cromwell's troops were quartered in the palace for about ten years. The Roundheads are supposed to have taught the local people the art of tanning. This later became the main industry of Linlithgow and led to the comment that you could smell Linlithgow before you saw it.

Bonnie Prince Charlie visited here in 1745, and shortly afterwards fire reduced the palace to an empty shell. Another famous visitor to Linlithgow was Daniel Defoe, the author of *Robinson Crusoe* and reportedly an English spy. He wrote that around the end of the 17th century the main industry was bleaching. However, later shoemaking was the main industry. In 1793 the Earl of Hopetoun ordered 700 pairs of shoes for his regiment from the cobblers of Linlithgow. Today Linlithgow is a county town and tourist destination.

## The Walk

Come out of the Four Marys and turn right along the main road, A803. About 100 metres along on the pavement you will find St Michael's Well. This dates from 1720 and the words on it 'St Michael is kind to strangers' are the town motto of Linlithgow. Turn right up St Michael's Wynd just before the well. Follow this road around to the left and then go right with it under the railway station. Bear right again with this road once past the railway and keep with it left uphill. Then hairpin sharply left with it and after about 20 metres go right and across the road to find the Union Canal. Just to your right along the canal is the canal basin where Hugh Baird, the canal engineer, stayed while he was building it. Also here is the Linlithgow Union Canal Society's Museum and a doocot for some 370 pairs of birds. Walk left along the towpath with the canal on your right. Around 200 metres along here the building on your left with the ornate towers is St Magdalene's Distillery. Originally a lazar or leper house stood here. It was outside the town walls where it would not contaminate the inhabitants. Continue along the towpath as the B9080 passes **under** the canal. You may see white-faced, black-bodied coots here, these can be egg thieves of unguarded nests of other waterfowl.

About half a mile further on, at the first bridge **over** the canal, take the footpath just before the bridge going left up the bank. Go right along the farm road across the bridge. Continue on this track up a slight hill. After some 200 metres turn right by the house called Eastwood at a T-junction with the B9080. Walk along the B9080 on its

Linlithgow: The Four Marys

right-hand (pavement) side for another 100 metres. Then turn right up a minor road signposted for Parkley Place and Porterside. The signpost faces away from you. Keep on this road as it goes right and left to Parkley Place Farm. You get a good view behind you of the Forth road and rail bridges. At Parkley Place Farm go right, left, right and left in quick succession to find the dirt track going round the right-hand side of the farm. Follow this dirt road right and left until it terminates in a T-junction with a tarmac road. Then turn right up this road, keeping to the right-hand side so as to face the oncoming traffic.

About 300 metres up here you will find a footpath sign on your left to Beecraigs Country Park. Go over the stile and head right towards the wooden marker post. About 20 metres past it turn left up the side of the wee burn, keeping the burn on your right. Go across the field, aiming just to the left of the farm of Hilty which is slightly to your right. When you are about level with Hilty Farm cross the plank footbridge in front of you. On its other side go diagonally left up the field, heading for the left-hand edge of the belt of trees above and to the right of you. About 10 metres from the fence at the field top go right up to the steps that you will find there and over the stile. Go straight ahead after the stile for around 20 metres and then break left along the farm track cutting across your line of travel. After some five metres on the farm track go right where a signpost guides you to Beecraigs Country Park. Follow these path markers to Beecraigs for some 200 to 300 metres until you reach a T-junction of two tarmac roads. Cross the road and go down the long arm of the T.

Go down this road for roughly 200 metres and past the restaurant on your right. At a five-way junction go left as signposted for Beecraigs Park Visitor Centre and Deer Park. The visitor centre is on your left with the grass roof. It sells frozen trout and venison from the park's own farms and ice lollies, fizzy drinks etc. It has toilets and information about the park.

Go past the visitor centre on your left and over the high wooden bridge marked deer walkway and trout farm. Once over the bridge walk forwards between the fences of the deer enclosures. Follow this path right and downhill through the trees until you reach the loch. Here turn left, keeping the loch on your right. About 100 metres along this path on your left is an information board about the badger sett here.

At the fork that follows go right across the dam. This dam was built by German prisoners of war in 1914 to 1918. The dam was constructed of earth with a waterproof clay core. The stone used to line this reservoir was quarried on Riccarton Hill on your left front using a winch-powered endless railway. This, as I understand it, is a conveyer belt which brings stone down and then goes 180 degrees under itself and back to the top again where another wheel takes it 180 degrees over itself to be refilled with stone.

Go across the dam and descend on the steps to your left to the trout farm. **You cannot walk all the way across this dam,** a sluice channel prevents you from reaching the other side. If the trout have not had their daily rations by the time you get there, you can buy food and feed them. Go past the trout farm on your left after crossing the footbridge at the foot of the steps then walk up beside the sluice on your right. Keep with this road as it breaks right, staying with the reservoir on your near right. Beecraigs has resident greylag geese. These geese normally overwinter here and summer in Scandinavia. They can be distinguished from a number of similar brown geese by their orange bill and pale pink legs. In the loch here, in springtime, you will see the large spade-shaped leaves and the large buttercup-shaped and coloured flowers of marsh marigold growing in the water.

At the end of this road, having left the reservoir behind, you will arrive at a T-junction with a tarmac road with a car park on the far side of the road. Turn left up this road. About 50 metres up here on the right is a forest road signposted to Balvormie, this is your way. Go past a footpath cutting across the forest road at right angles and about 50 metres past that go right up a broad footpath, almost a forest road. Bear left with this path and around 100 metres past the bend bypass a rough track on the right and continue along this path. When you reach a T-junction with a semi-tarmac road, go left. As you do notice the large ash tree on your left, on the crown of the corner, with metal spikes driven into its trunk. The deer hunters would use these spikes to climb up the tree to see where the deer were feeding that day. Go along this semi-tarmac road, past paths to the left and right and a children's playground, until it makes a T-junction with a tarmac road.

Go right up this road for about 50 metres, then proceed left through gates into an open space. At the far end of this open space is a signpost saying 'Cockleroy'. Be guided by this sign to what is first a broad and grassy path ahead which then becomes beaten earth. When this reaches a tarmac road, go over the stile and walk left up the tarmac road. About 300 metres up here turn right, signposted for Kipps Farm. At the end of the trees on your right and just before the farmyard, go right on a farm road. Follow this track around to the left through a farm gate, closing it behind you.

The ruined building on your left is Kipps Castle which was built in 1625. It was the home of Sir Robert Sibbald. This interesting polymath was physician to Charles II, Geographer Royal for Scotland and West Lothian's first proper historian. In addi-

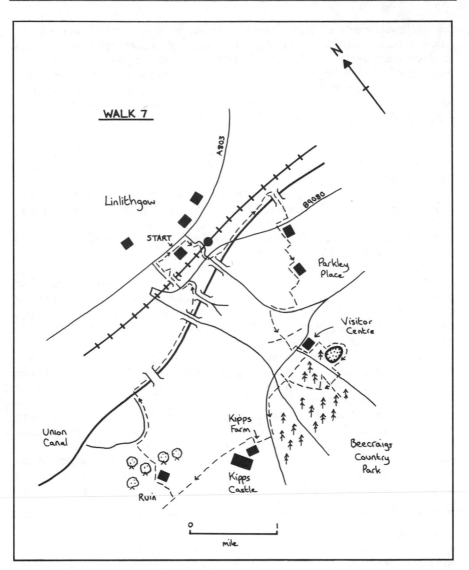

tion, along with another chap, he saved a rare plant collection in Livingston when the owner died. This plant collection became the foundation of what today is Edinburgh's Royal Botanic Gardens.

Go along this red earth track until you come to a gate on the right with a track behind it going uphill beside a line of trees. Quite what the metal contraption beside it is I do not know, possibly a ramp for quad bikes. Go uphill on this track. At the top pass through another gate and bear diagonally right downhill on a rapidly fading track aiming for the left-hand edge of the thin line of trees connecting two woods. When you reach the edge of the forest on your left, follow this as it breaks sharply away to the left. As the dyke at the edge of the trees turns 90 degrees to the right, at this point you will find a low piece of dyke that is easy to scramble over. Once over turn immediately right to ascend a low embankment and then walk to the left along this embankment. A fence then cuts across your path and veers away from you to parallel the edge of the forest on your left. Go left just inside the edge of the forest with the fence on your right. About 100 metres after this you will find gaps in the fence between the lower mesh part and the upper barbed wire. Turn right through the fence here and go straight ahead, uphill among the gorse.

Once atop this little knoll walk straight ahead to a gap between two dykes. Once through this cut half left through the field to a field gate. Once through the field gate follow the faint track diagonally left through this next field to find the field gate leading into the farm road below you. Go through this field gate and turn right down the farm road. Keep on this road past the golf course, it gradually becomes a metalled road. Pass under the bridge and beneath the canal.

At the far side of the bridge, steps on your right lead you up to the canal towpath. At the towpath turn left and walk along with the canal on your right. Go under two bridges then just before the third bridge go up the steps on your left to the road. Go left away from the canal and keep with this road as it bends right and left. When it terminates in a T-junction, go left along Royal Terrace. About 100 metres along here walk right over the footbridge crossing the railway. Once over the bridge turn right and double back left at the end of the railings. Then walk right downhill to the centre of Linlithgow. At the bottom of Lion Wynd turn right along Linlithgow High St.

Roughly 100 metres along here you will come to the Sheriff Court on your right. On the wall of the Sheriff Court is a plaque commemorating the assassination of Regent Moray on this spot. This was Scotland's first assassination by the newfangled firearms.

The Sheriff Court stands on the site of what in the 1500s was Riccartons Lodgings, the Linlithgow residence of the Archbishop of St Andrew's. From here Hamilton of Bothwellhaugh (a kinsman of the Archbishop) shot Regent Moray in 1570. Moray subsequently died of his wounds. Hamilton of Bothwellhaugh was the Jackal of his day. His preparations were very thorough, he put mattresses on the floor so that his footsteps would not be heard. He hung black curtains on the wall so that his shadow would not be seen. He removed the lintel of the back gate so that he could ride his getaway horse directly out of it. He went onto a career as a professional assassin on the Continent. It was pretty ungrateful of him to kill Moray as Moray had previously spared Bothwellhaugh when he was guilty of serious crimes. Bothwellhaugh was also thoughtless about the repercussions of this as his kinsman the Archbishop was later executed for complicity in this crime. This was all part of the bickering between the Protestant Lords of the Reformation and the mainly Catholic nobility who supported Mary Queen of Scots. A further 100 metres on past the plaque the Four Marys is on your right.

# 8. Calatria: Bo'ness

**Route:** Bo'ness and Kinneil Light Railway – Birkhill – Kinneil Estate – Bo'mains Farm – North Bank – Bridgeness – Grangepans

**Distance:** 6 miles

**Map:** OS Landranger 65, Falkirk and Linlithgow

**Start:** Girsey Nicols, Bo'ness

**Access:** By bus, there are direct bus services between Edinburgh and Bo'ness every day except Sundays. On Sundays an hourly service runs to Linlithgow Cross, from where another hourly service runs to Bo'ness. For details of times etc. ring First Midland Bluebird on 01324 613777 or 'Traveline' on 0800 232323 if inside the Edinburgh area, if outwith the Edinburgh area call 0131 225 3858. From the bus station go onto the dual carriageway beside it and walk to the left up this. About 150 metres up this road you will arrive at a roundabout, Girsey Nicols is on the opposite corner of the roundabout.

By car, take the M9 westbound out of Edinburgh towards Stirling. Come off at junction 3 and go left on the A803 signposted for Linlithgow. About half a mile past Linlithgow Cross go right on the A706 for Bo'ness. Cross the motorway and descend into Bo'ness. As you reach the old part of town near the sea you will see Girsey Nicols on your left just before a roundabout. Turn right at the roundabout and immediately left into the free parking by the Information Centre. Girsey Nicols is diagonally across the roundabout from you.

---

## Girsey Nicols. Tel: 01506 829204

This pub was a real find. None of the reference books about pubs or real ale that I read mentioned this place or anywhere in Bo'ness. Then I literally stumbled across this cracking pub with excellent food and six real ales.

Girsella Nicols was a notorious landlady in Bo'ness in the last century. The reason for infamy was her blatant flouting of the licensing laws. She sold drink where and when it was illegal to do so, and when it was legal to sell drink she sold larger amounts than the law allowed. About four years ago Steven Bundy bought two adjoining pubs, the Criterion, which was furthest away from the roundabout, and the Masonic. Then he merged them. He next held a competition for a new name for the pub and the winner was local historian Marlene Egan with the name Girsey Nicols. Needless to say, the licensing laws are observed by the modern day Girsey Nicols.

This is a lovely pub. There is a motor cycle in the roof of the bar. The lounge is lower ceilinged and has a dedicated dining section which is pleasantly furbished with check tablecloths and flowers. The bar has old beer barrels as tables, recessed windows and is decorated in wood and stone. There are pictures of old Bo'ness and snaps of the old pubs that make up the present pub. There are fruit machines, a jukebox and machines dispensing sweeties.

Food is served at lunchtimes only. Monday to Friday the hours are 1200-1500 and on Saturdays and Sundays they are 1000-1500. An all-day cooked breakfast is available in the above hours. There is a good selection of good home-cooked food including daily specials on the blackboard. At night toasties are served in the bar.

The real ales are Orkney Dark island and Raven, Inveralmonds Independence, Ossian and Lia Fial and Belhaven St Andrew's. Keg products include Cruz Campo, Belhaven Best, Strongbow and Tennents Lager. Opening hours for drink are 1100-2400 Sunday to Thursday and 1100-0100 Friday and Saturday. Both walkers and children are graciously greeted, but children only if they are having a meal during mealtimes. There is a small beer garden at the back.

## Bo'ness

Bo'ness is short for Borrowstouness, 'burgh town on the point'. Bo'ness was built on coal, which is why it is now subsiding. The final pit, the Kinneil Colliery, closed in 1984, thus ending a chapter of Bo'ness history of over eight centuries. As in so many other things, such as brewing and weaving, it was the monks who were the innovators here of coal mining in the 1100s. These holy men were from Holyrood (holy cross) Abbey in Edinburgh. This coal could be shipped as sea cargo from the port of Carriden. This was at the eastern end of Bo'ness and was reputedly the eastern end of the Antonine Wall. This was a great advantage in those days of appalling and atrocious roads.

Later this coal was shipped to Scandinavia and the return boats were filled with pit props from the Scandinavian forests. But before this era of pit props, which gained Bo'ness the nickname of Pitpropolis, simpler mining techniques were used.

Steam engine at Birkhill station on the Bo'ness & Kinneil Light Railway

Firstly horizontal shafts into the hillside were utilised called locally ingaun ees (in-going eyes) because the miners candles in the blackness of the mine appeared like demoniac eyes gazing out across the Firth of Forth. The bell pits were used, their name explained by their shape. Later mines were dug like today's mines but with deposits of coal mined around and left to provide supports. The only problem here was when greedy owners ordered the removal of these supports and collapses and fatalities did occur. In 1883 such a sit (local name for a collapse) did happen and destroyed Bo'ness church tower just as a sermon was being given in the town about the fall of the Tower of Siloam. The miners were serfs/slaves and were not allowed to leave their employment except with the consent of their bosses, which was very rarely given. This also applied to the whole family, so children were born into slavery.

A by-product of the coal industry was the salt industry. Waste coal was burned under pans of sea water to evaporate off the water and leave the salt behind. The figures are staggering, 100 tons of water took 50 tons of coal to produce three tons of salt. These salt pans burned day and night except Sunday. Sabbath salt, formed when the fires were out, had larger crystals and was considered a delicacy and thus was more expensive. Interestingly, sea salt is making a return as a gourmet seasoning these days.

Being in shipping and the wood business, Bo'ness soon developed a shipbuilding industry. Henry Bell, the designer of the *Comet*, the world's first ocean going steamship, served his apprenticeship here. After having a successful year with the *Comet* on the Clyde in 1812 he brought it to Bo'ness in 1813 for servicing.

Another Bo'ness industry was pottery. There was coal to fire the kilns and raw clay nearby to be mined. Other advantages were a ready supply of cheap labour in the miners' wives and children and sea transport for other raw materials to be brought here and safer transport by sea for the delicate pottery. These transport problems made the English Midlands potters build canals. Wedding jugs were a favourite Bo'ness product. They were inscribed with the names of the happy couple and their wedding date and site. Rather like wedding lintels over the doors of houses built for newly-weds in Scotland.

Coal and local iron led to foundries being established in Bo'ness. A speciality of these foundries were the harpoons used by the town's whaling fleet. This was another use for Bo'ness-built ships. Bo'ness ships went to the Arctic in the summer. Whales were killed from small boats with harpoons. This was difficult and dangerous to do. The men then donned spike-soled boots and flensed the whale i.e. they stripped the blubber off it for oil. Whalebone was also sold for corsets. Primitive oil refineries were established in Bo'ness to process the blubber into whale oil products. As the whales ran out, Dr James (Paraffin) Young arrived and coincidentally discovered shale oil deposits in West Lothian which kept the refineries going.

## The Walk

This is a walk which can be done two ways. Route 1 tells how this walk can be done in conjunction with a trip on the Bo'ness and Kinneil Light railway. Route 2 gives directions on how to join this walk at Kinneil Museum without using this railway should you not want to or should there not be a suitable train. At point **A** in bold type in the text both routes come together into the same walk. For train timetable information call 01506 822298, or visit the website www.srps.org.uk. Kinneil Museum is open Mondays to Saturdays 1230 – 1600 all year except public holidays.

## Route 1

Come out of Girsey Nicols and go directly across the roundabout to the A904, signposted for Edinburgh, South Queensferry, Bo'ness and Kinneil Light Railway and Clay Mine. About 300 metres down this dual carriageway, as you walk past the railway with its old-fashioned signals on your left, is the station. This is a genuine Victorian station brought from Fife. There is a railway museum here which can be visited. Buy a single ticket to Birkhill and settle back to enjoy what is normally a steam train journey.

Down this line in May 1910 came a train filled with hundreds of Glaswegian blacklegs to break a strike of pit prop workers. A pitched battle ensued with numbers and ready availability of pit props as weapons on the side of the Bo'ness men. The Glaswegians fled, leaving 50 seriously injured behind. Many of these strike-breakers avoided Kinneil Halt, between Bo'ness and Birkhill, where they had disembarked and fled over country to Manuel, where the Bo'ness spur left the main Edinburgh – Glasgow line, to return home from there.

At Birkhill walk up out of the station and across the bridge spanning the railway. Those who want to visit the fire-clay mine should accost one of the uniformed guides to be found loitering on the platform. It takes about an hour to visit the mines so walkers should consider this in their calculations. It is also cold down there so some warm clothes may be needed.

Having crossed the bridge, proceed ahead up the rough road for some 200 metres. At a T-junction with a minor metalled road go left along this. After about half a mile on this road you arrive at another T-junction with another tarmac road. Go left, which because of the bend appears to be straight ahead, on this second tarmac road, keeping Upper Kinneil Farm on your right. From up here you can sometimes see buzzards wheeling and mewing in the sky above you, within a mile of Grangemouth Chemical Works below and to the left of you.

Descend this road for around half a mile, enjoying views over the Firth of Forth in front of you. Bypass a road to the left near the bottom of the hill and bear right with the road. Some 200 metres after this bend you will find a well-defined footpath up steps to your right. Follow this path. Where it forks, go left and then walk past another footpath on the right.

When the path bends right at the end of the pond on your right, go left down a small set of steps. Then go straight ahead to the small knoll where there is an information board about Kinneil Roman Fortlet. You are now on the line of the Antonine Wall. A shallow depression running in a line to the north of you is the remains of the ditch in front of the Antonine Wall. From the fortlet go half left ahead, seeking the left-hand edge of the hedge and ditch running directly across your front. At the gap in the hedge turn right on to a well-marked footpath aiming for Kinneil House, which you will have seen among the trees ahead from the Roman fortlet. Stay with this path as it bears right and then left towards the gable end that is all that remains of Kinneil Kirk.

At this ruin an information board tells you about the church. From the church go slightly right ahead on to a beaten earth path which veers right with a fence along its left-hand side. Ignore steps down to the left and proceed along this path between hedges until you reach two stone gateposts on your right, here go left over the foot-bridge. At the far end of the footbridge is James Watt's cottage and an information board telling you about it. Go left after the footbridge and then right past Kinneil House on your right. Walk along beside a wall on your right, behind which is the kitchen garden and orchard of Kinneil House, to arrive at Kinneil Museum. This was the stable block of Kinneil House. Kinneil House was most likely started in the 1500s as a fortified tower house. Some of its gunholes can be seen at the back of the building. The Hamiltons, who became the owners of Kinneil House in 1323, subsequently added more comfortable quarters as times became less violent and defensive qualities in housing less necessary. A later tenant of this house was Dr John Roebuck who had a finger in most industrial pies hereabouts. There is a story that when James Watt's early steam engine would not hold pressure, Dr Roebuck sealed it by cutting off the top of his riding boot and using that to create the world's first cylinder head gasket. The house is not open to the public, which is a pity because it has magnificent murals including one illustrating the parable of the Good Samaritan. These wall paintings are about the best in Scotland. From Kinneil Museum retrace your steps to Watt's Cottage and recross the footbridge. Here both routes join so go to **A** in the text ahead.

## Route 2

Turn left out of Girsey Nicols and walk along Corbiehall, the street the Girsey Nicols fronts. About 200 to 300 metres along here you reach number 193 on your left. At this point cross the road and go up the rough track opposite you and carefully cross the railway. Around 40 metres over this level crossing the path splits, take the left-hand one and bypass another path on the right to walk between the railway on your left and the Firth of Forth on your right. Look out for sea buckthorn here, a silvery grey, scrubby bush with willow-like leaves. This grows to about two and a half metres high and has orange berries in summer. Because of its attractive fruits and foliage it is often cultivated in gardens.

As you cross the base of the point the meadowland is beautiful with flowers and butterflies in summer, ox-eye daisy, cornflowers, vetches and orchids. After around a quarter of a mile on this path take the right-hand fork towards a promontory as the path divides. Follow this path around the edge of the promontory and it breaks back left inland. This path then bears left again where there is large gap in the trees on your right. Keep with it for some 100 metres as it heads back to Bo'ness. Then you come to a level crossing on your right. Negotiate this level crossing and once over the railway bear right with the path. As you traverse the railway the remains of Kinneil Halt are on your left with two tracks and the remains of platforms. In 1910 this is where the Glasgow strike-breakers disembarked before the Battle of Bo'ness. Continue along the path beside the railway line on your right, bypassing a couple of paths to the left. This takes you through trees onto the A904.

Turn left along the A904 for roughly 20 metres and cross it to go directly up the footpath opposite. At the top, where the path meets a road, go right down this A993. At the bottom a sign points right to Bo'ness and the railway, just before this descend left down the bank and along the disused road at the bottom of it. After about 300 metres along here, dogleg left onto a minor road where a metal gate bars the way for traffic. Stay with this minor road as it goes left and right uphill.

At the top of the hill Kinneil Museum is straight ahead of you through the concrete bollards. The cottages on your left were originally built under the auspices of the Duchess of Hamilton as quality housing for estate employees. Turn right before the bollards and proceed along beside the wall of the walled garden and orchards on your left. This route here parallels the course of the Antonine Wall, which was about 20 metres to your right. Bear left past Kinneil House. The house is closed to the public which is a shame as its magnificent murals are about the best in Scotland. Then go right over the Gil Burn by a footbridge and past James Watt's Cottage and its interpretative board on your left.

## Routes 1 & 2

**A:** Once across the bridge turn left uphill. Go through a small car park and on to a path ahead with a hedge on its right and the Gil Burn on its left. A sign on your right informs you that you are entering Kinneil Woods. At a T-junction with a forest road turn left along the forest road. Fifty metres along, go right along another forest road at another T-junction. Bypass a forest road coming in from the right. At the four-way junction that you come to next, go left. At the fork just before the road, go right uphill and paralleling the road on your left. This brings you out on a drive, cut straight across this and break right up the minor road. Ascend this gentle incline for about a quarter of a mile, ignoring the drive to Woodland Farm on your right.

Then you will see a sign on your left just before the trees telling you that this is Scottish Wildlife Trust, Bo'mains Meadow Wildlife Reserve. About 20 metres beyond this sign a well-marked path/track goes left into the trees. After around a quarter of a mile along this, hugging the edge of the wood, it terminates in a T-junction with a farm track. A path goes off to the left here. Go right along the farm track. At its T-junction with a tarmac road go left along the road. After a quarter of a mile or so, carefully cross the A706 athwart your route and go directly forward where a sign points to West Lothian Golf Club. Walk along here for about three-quarters of a mile, past two minor roads and the golf club house on your right. At the end of the golf course on your left, as a line of trees descends the slope on the left, you will see a sign guiding you left on a public footpath to Bo'ness.

Go downhill on this path between a fence and trees on your right and telegraph poles on your left. Look out for yellowhammers here. When you first see one you might at first think that you have seen an escaped canary. Its greenish/yellowish

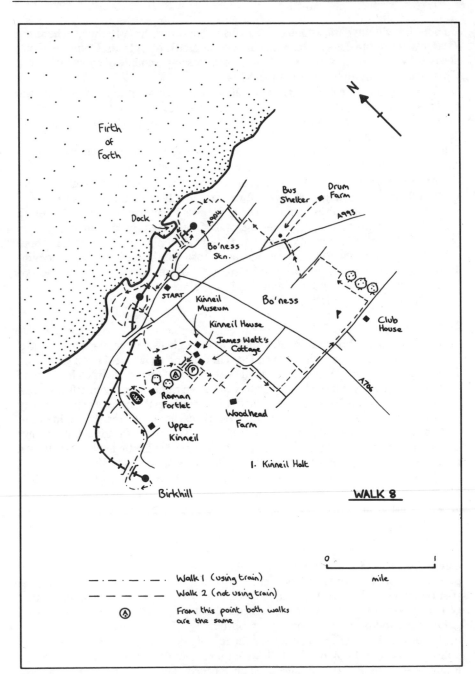

N

Firth
of
Forth

Dock

Bus
Shelter

Drum
Farm

A904

A993

Bo'ness
Stn.

START

Kinneil
Museum

Bo'ness

Kinneil House

James Watt's
Cottage

Club
House

A706

Ⓐ

Ⓟ

Roman
Fortlet

Woodhead
Farm

Upper
Kinneil

1. Kinneil Halt

**WALK 8**

Birkhill

0                                    1

mile

—  ·  —  ·  —  ·  —        Walk 1 (using train)

—  —  —  —  —              Walk 2 (not using train)

Ⓐ                          From this point both walks
                           are the same

feathers make it resemble this. This path takes you through a kissing gate. Past this turn left downhill, sticking with the fence on your left. Pass through another kissing gate and keep to the left-hand edge of the field. From up here people used to wait each year to watch for the safe return of the whaling fleet.

At the minor metalled road turn left for about 10 metres. And then go right down a farm road. Follow this track down to the right, keeping the Kinglass Community Woodland sign on your right. Cut across a crossing grass pathway as the track becomes grassy and head for the main road visible ahead. As this track degrades to a footpath bear left with it, keeping in close proximity with the hedge on your right.

At the end of the field walk straight ahead with the fence on your left. Cross Drumore Road and go up Drum Road to the main road. Cross this A993 to the bus shelter and turn left along Drumside Terrace. The main road now veers away to the left. The farm road to Drum Farm is not the correct road. At the end of Drumside Terrace pass over a road in front of you to find a tarmac footpath downhill to the right of Range Loan. At the end of this path go left along Philipingstone Road and right down Cowdenhill Road, in its day this was the garden city part of Bo'ness. Then traverse the main road, A904, and proceed directly ahead down Hainey's Way. Follow this around to the left, right, left and right again as it becomes a dirt road along the waterfront, with the Firth of Forth on your right.

As you see the track ahead bear left, take the path that develops to the right at this point. Follow this path around the headland with the river on your right. Go past the old dock on your right. Bo'ness is mentioned in contemporary accounts as being a port as far back as 1565. A proper harbour was ordered by an Act of Parliament in 1707. The present layout was completed in 1881. Coal and salt were the main exports, the main imports were timber, flax and grain.

This leads you to a footbridge over the railway. Once over the footbridge, turn to the right up the road and about 200 to 300 metres up here you will see Girsey Nicols on the opposite side of the roundabout.

# 9. West Lothian: Torphichen

**Route:** Torphichen – Cairnpapple Hill – Witches Craig – Beecraigs Country Park – Kipps – Craigend

**Map:** OS Landranger 65, Falkirk and Linlithgow

**Distance:** 6 miles

**Start:** Torphichen Inn, Torphichen

**Access:** By bus, there are no direct bus services between Edinburgh and Torphichen. A frequent service runs from Edinburgh to Linlithgow and from there a reasonable service runs to Torphichen. The bus goes past the pub door so ask to be put off there. For details phone Midland Bluebird on 01324 613777, or ring West Lothian Council Travel Helpline on 01506 775 288. It is also possible to get the train to Linlithgow – for information on this call 0345 484950.

By car, take the M9 westwards towards Stirling and leave at junction 3. There go left on the A803 through Linlithgow. In Linlithgow you take the A706 on the left for Bathgate. About four miles along here turn left on the B792 signed for Torphichen. The pub is on your right, opposite the memorial in the middle of the village. The car park behind the pub is accessed to the right of the pub.

## Torphichen Inn. Tel: 01506 652 826

The Torphichen Inn was a real find for me, and I am not the only one to have found it. It has won a string of awards. In the lounge/restaurant there proudly sits the Wallace Sword for best bar with a Scottish theme. It has also been commended for wines in bars, won the Free House of the Year Award at a ceremony in the Grosvenor Hotel in London and landlord Jim Boyd has been awarded the Licensee of the Year Award. He is the only Scottish publican ever to have been so honoured. In 1999 he was given Bells Community Pub of the Year Award.

The building is some three hundred years old and was originally a corn barn. Later it was a hospital and in 1999 it celebrated its centenary as a pub. The public bar used to be the whole pub and the restaurant used to be the cellars. In 1967 a function

suite was added. It is reputed to be haunted in the balcony area. According to psychics and clairvoyants this is a figure in a long coat wearing a broad-brimmed, flat hat of a style from about 200 years ago.

If you enter the Torphichen Inn by the front door to the left, the first thing that you will see is the 5500-piece mosaic of the cross of the Knights Templar on the floor. The eight points symbolise the Beatitudes and the four arms the Christian virtues of justice, fortitude, temperance and prudence. The Torphichen inn is one of only two pubs in Scotland with such a tiled mosaic entrance. There are details about the knights on the walls and also of Sir William Wallace (Braveheart) who held his last parliament in Torphichen in 1298. Additionally there are a number of rare licensed trade mirrors and windows featuring famous names from brewing and distilling in Scotland. The crests above the bar of MacGregor, Robertson etc. are from Dalhousie Castle. The Welsh dresser was Jim Boyd's great-grandmothers. The blackboards for daily specials are rimmed with local burr elm. Burr elm comes from the lumps and bumps on the trunks of these trees and is rare and expensive as well as very attractive. The beams in the restaurant are of cherry-wood. The bar has a wooden floor and a log-burning stove. It also has William, the African grey parrot, who is very talkative and a great favourite with children. As a country pub it has frequent entertainment including free food for children and a magic show on Sundays 1700-1900. There is a beer garden.

The food is exceptional. Try Chicken Cockleroy (named after a local hill) which is fresh, free-range chicken breasts stuffed with local haggis and rolled in oatmeal. A first-class meal beautifully presented and very reasonably priced. The other speciality is seafood. Jim Boyd reckons that his chef is one of the best in Scotland. They welcome walkers. Jim and his chef go Monroe bagging every week. Food is served 1200-1430 and 1730-2100 on weekdays and all day on Saturdays and Sundays.

There is one pump of real ale, which features Orkney Dark Island, Timothy Taylors Landlord, Deuchars IPA or Belhaven St. Andrews. The real ale here is very well priced, often less than the price of many a pint of keg. Belgian Hoegarden White Beer is also available here. On keg are extra-cold Guinness, Caffreys, Tennents Lager and Belhaven Best. There is also an excellent choice of malt whiskies including 18-year-old Glenfiddich matured in an oak cask. Opening hours are Monday to Thursday 1100-2300, Friday and Saturday 1100-2400 and Sunday 1230-2300.

## Torphichen

Torphichen means 'hill of the raven'. An early Christian here was St Vigeon. His nickname was Fechan, which is Gaelic for 'raven', because of his dark appearance. So came Torfechan, hill of the raven, later corrupted into Torphichen.

King David I, 1084 – 1153, granted the Knights of St John lands around Torphichen with the right of gyrth, which is sanctuary. This sanctuary extended around the village for one mile in diameter. These boundaries were marked with sanctuary stones, two of which still stand. These boundaries were enforced by the knights. Sanctuary protected alleged offenders against summary justice i.e. lynch law, but they still had to stand trial.

The Knights of St John were fighters, religious men and healers. One famous patient was Edward I of England who came here on the night of the Battle of Falkirk after his horse had kicked him and broken his ribs. They had a herb garden at their preceptory in Torphichen. The ruins of this preceptory remain. It was a fortified building as these were troubled times. It had a moat and is built on oak piles. It is called a preceptory as they lived by certain precepts i.e. moral commands. Their primary function was to help pilgrims on a caravan, or crusade as we call it nowadays.

At the Reformation the preceptory was sold to the then preceptor by Mary Queen of Scots in 1564. Sir James Sandilands then became Lord Torphichen and his descendants today are still Lords Torphichen and live nearby in Mid Calder. This caused a problem when the local laird built a new church in 1756 with a laird's loft accessed by outside stairs. Lord Torphichen claimed exclusive rights to use this as feudal superior, a decision which was upheld in court. So poor John Gillon never got to use the loft he had paid for.

As you walk up towards the church through the graveyard you will see, on the left, the central sanctuary stone. It is about three-quarters of a metre high and has a cup-shaped depression in the top of it. This could have been for collecting blood as the stone is thought to have come originally from Cairnpapple Hill nearby. It is carved with a cross and cup marks.

At the gate of the churchyard is a small building put up to shelter watchmen as they guarded bodies against being body-snatched. Opposite the main door is a table-top gravestone which was put on top of the lair to protect it from grave robbers. In the church is a memorial to Henry Bell, a native of Torphichen. Bell built the *Comet*, the world's first ocean going steamship. Also on a religious note, the local Covenanters were supposed to have been so elusive that Tam Dalziel o' the Binns got so frustrated that he imported grey cloth from the Netherlands to camouflage his troops. Thus giving rise to the Royal Scots Greys.

## Cairnpapple

This site has been occupied for some five and a half millennia. The original occupiers were Neolithic people of whom little trace remains apart from some pottery shards, remains of hearths and axe heads. One of these axe heads came from Cumbria and the other from a factory in North Wales. So even in those days there was manufacturing, travel, trade and commerce.

About 5000 years ago the people here constructed a henge. This consisted of a circular bank and ditch some 60 metres in diameter. Inside this a ring of timber posts enclosed or hid the central area. Perhaps it was here that local people carried out secret or sacred ceremonies. The central sanctuary stone at Torphichen is reputed to have come from here and has a cup-shaped hollow, perhaps for catching blood. Roman cartographers located a spot near here called Middle Nemeton, the Middle Sanctuary. So with nearby Torphichen's record of being a sanctuary, this could have been the place which Romans recorded as being a Druid sacred site and burial place.

This last is interesting as around 4000 years ago, at the dawn of the Bronze Age, the beaker people arrived and started burying their dead here. They buried their dead with beakers. Various graves were excavated in 1949, some were chiselled out of rock and others were cists i.e. lined with slabs of stone. Some cremation sites were also found. Today a concrete dome shelters the cairns that used to cover a Bronze Age chieftain's burial site.

Cairnpapple Hill burial cairn is open April to September from 0930-1830 seven days a week. October and November it is open 0930-1630 Monday to Saturday and 1400-1630 on Sundays. It is closed from December to March.

## The Walk

Come out of the Torphichen Inn and turn right up the main road, B792. Follow this up a slight rise until you come to a four-way junction. Turn left here where the sign-posts point to Beecraigs Country Park and Cairnpapple Hill. About a quarter of a mile along here, at the end of a tongue of trees on your right, is a break in the dyke and a path up to a field gate. Bear right and ascend this. Walk along beside the fence and trees on your right. Keep with the fence as the trees become bushes and it bends around to the left. After roughly a quarter of a mile you arrive at a field gate at a minor tarmac road.

Traverse the road directly ahead to where a footpath sign points in front of you uphill to 'Windy Wa's'. Continue uphill and then to the left with this path. This will lead you to the transmitter at the hilltop. Here go to the right of the transmitter compound through a field gate. At the end of the compound go half left across the pasture to reach the end of the fence on your left where the entrance to Cairnpapple Hill Ancient Monument site is. If you are visiting the monument (entrance fee), leave by the gate through which you entered and follow the path straight ahead. If not visiting the monument, go right along the footpath exiting the monument site. If it is raining there is a shop here where you can buy tickets to the monument and souvenirs and it could be a good place to shelter. The footpath leaving the monument site takes you to steps after about 100 metres. After descending the steps you arrive at a minor macadamised road, go left down this.

After a couple of hundred metres this road veers left to angle on to another road. As it bends, a 20 metres stretch of tarmac on your right provides a short cut to this road cutting across your front. Take this short stretch of tarmac and cross the road. A gap in the fence afront you enables you to reach a grassy path to the right of the dyke going uphill ahead of you. In spring this field is alight with the pale pink flowers of ladies smock. Once over the hill descend and cross the dyke by a gate-like structure in its wooden part, being careful of the electric fence running through this wooden part. It can give an unpleasant sting. There are one or two stiles along here with electric fencing before you reach Beecraigs Country Park. Once past the dyke go right uphill, keeping the dyke on your right. This takes you to a stile. Just before the stile is an electric fence which you can easily duck under, there are warning signs here. A sign informs you that you are entering Witch Craig Wood. Once across this stile beside a field gate go straight ahead, keeping the knoll of Witch Craig on your left. Keep along this path between a fence on your left and a dyke on your right. At the top of the hill is a stile on your right. In the top of the dyke, about five metres past the stile, is one of the original Torphichen sanctuary stones. Notice the double Bishop's or Maltese Cross carved in it. Cross the stile and follow a faint footpath left downhill, staying close to the dyke on your left. Traverse a field gate by the dyke and continue downhill. At the bottom of the hill go left through a gate and walk along for some 200

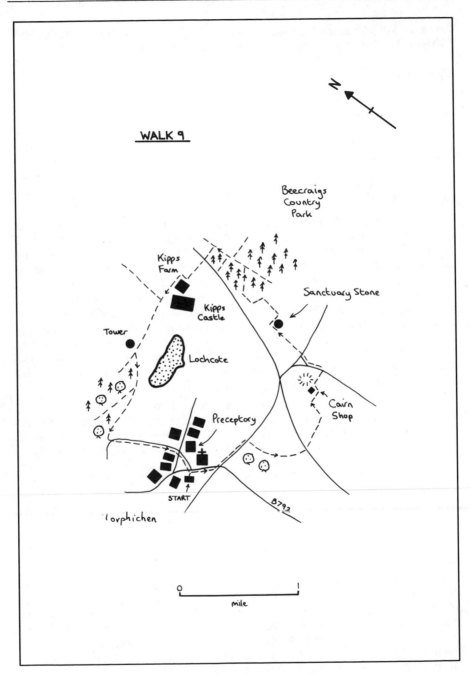

metres, keeping the fence on your right. You then see a stile on your right. Cross this and follow the footpath beyond it to the left along the field margin. At the end of the field go right along its edge. To the right of the field gate, at the end of the field, you will see a sign informing you that you have arrived at Beecraigs Country Park.

Enter Beecraigs Country Park and go straight ahead of you on the dirt road signposted for Balvormie. After about a quarter of a mile you arrive at a T-junction. Here go left where it is signposted for Balvormie. Around 300 metres along here this road bends to the right. At this point take the forest road straight ahead signposted for Balvormie. When this road bears sharply left, go straight ahead on the grassy footpath. You will see on your left a Scots Pine with nest boxes numbers 35 and 36 on it. Keep on this path past nest boxes 31 and 32, also on your left. Just keep on this path with the edge of the trees on your close left.

Go left along the next forest road then go past a forest road on the left and a footbridge and path on the right. When you come to a tarmac road, go left along this for about 20 metres. Turn right into the farm road signposted for Kipps Farm. Bear right on to the farm track at the end of the trees on your right just before the farmyard. Keep on this red earth track as it swings left. Go through farm gates as they occur and close them behind you.

On your right as the track goes left is Cockleroy Hill where the remains of a fort from the 1600s still exist. Earlier, possibly Neolithic, forts are also thought to have occupied this site in the centuries before this time. To your left are the remains of Kipps Castle built in 1625. This was the home of Sir Robert Sibbald. This interesting polymath was physician to Charles II, Geographer Royal for Scotland and West Lothian's first proper historian. In addition, along with another chap, he saved a rare plant collection in Livingston when the owner died. This plant collection became the foundation of what is today the Royal Botanical Gardens in Edinburgh.

Go along here for about three-quarters of a mile, coming level with LochCote on your left and bypassing a track to the right. LochCote was supposed to have had a crannog in it. These were natural or artificial islands which could only be reached by hidden causeways.

About 100 metres past the old stone tower of LochCote Castle on your right, just as you enter woodland, there is a fork in the track. Proceed to the left, descending towards LochCote. After around half a mile take the left-hand track as this road divides. This takes you to a tarmac road at a bend. You go straight ahead on this tarmac road in the direction of Torphichen, now on the ridge above you. When you arrive at Torphichen, go straight ahead at the four-way junction on a road which is very slightly offset to the right.

About 150 metres up here is Torphichen Preceptory on your left. Opening hours are April to September, Saturday 1100-1700 and Sunday 1400-1700. The charge when I was there was £1, last admission 30 minutes before closing, closed in winter. The kirk immediately after the Preceptory, also on the left, was granted rights of parish in 1168. The central Sanctuary Stone is to the left of the path up to the kirk. From Torphichen Church the Torphichen Inn is visible ahead in the direction you have been travelling. Be careful crossing the busy road!

# 10. Edinburgh: Leith

**Route:** Leith Docks – Royal Yacht *Britannia* – Trinity – Royal Botanic Gardens – Water of Leith Walkway

**Distance:** 4.5 miles

**Map:** OS Landranger 66, Edinburgh

**Start:** Kings Wark, Leith

**Access:** By bus – plenty of buses come here from all around Edinburgh. Ask to be put off where Bernard St. crosses the Water of Leith. For details phone 'Traveline' on 0800 232323 (Edinburgh area only) or 0131 225 3858 if calling from elsewhere. Information is also available from Lothian Region Transport on 0131 555 6363.

By car, from central Edinburgh take Leith St. at the eastern end of Princes St. This goes left away from the castle and the Scott Monument. As you pass Calton Hill on your right go straight ahead at a roundabout onto Leith Walk. Go straight ahead at a second roundabout then follow Leith Walk for about one and a half miles towards Leith Docks. Just past the Assembly Rooms on your right, Leith Walk becomes Constitution St. Go left at the next set of traffic lights into Bernard St. The Kings Wark is about 150 metres up here on your left at the junction of Bernard St. and Shore, on the nearside of the Water of Leith. You can park on Shore either side of Bernard St., or even on the bridge over the Water of Leith. The manager of the Kings Wark assures me that parking in the area is not a problem at present. But regulations may change and punishment can be heavy so I suggest that you read the parking signs carefully. In the pub I was told that some of the yellow lines are actually unenforceable as the land belongs to the Port of Leith not the city, but I would still counsel caution.

## Kings Wark

The original building was erected in 1438 by James I. He used it as a munitions factory/arsenal. It was also used as a reception centre for royal goods and guests. Anne of Denmark, wife-to-be of James VI, resided here temporarily when she first arrived in Scotland. In 1613 James VI gave the Kings Wark to Bernard Lindsay, groom of the royal bedchamber. Bernard St., on which the Kings Wark stands, is named after him. There were two conditions to this gift. One was that Bernard would build a real (royal) tennis court for the pleasure of the king and his guests. The other was that one of the building's four cellars would be set aside for storing the king's wines. In 1618 John Taylor, the water poet, came here. He was penniless, as poets often are. Bernard Lindsay filled his pockets by firing solid gold bullets at him. This seems rather a dangerous way to improve your fortunes but I expect that it is allegorical.

This building was burned down in 1695 and the present building is the sole survivor of four tenements erected on this site in 1710. It was renovated in the 1970s but this did not remove the ghost in the cellars. Billy, as he is called, was chained up here and died of thirst, in a pub! A pint of water is left out for him in the cellars at all times. What is not ghostly about this pub its that it is in the Glasgow and Edinburgh Eating and Drinking Guide and is also featured in the Edinburgh Good Food Guide.

Good food is a feature of this pub. As befits a pub beside the docks, seafood is a speciality, but do not ask for lobster. This would upset Charlie, the pub's pet lobster in his tank in the bar. It is not so unusual to have a pet lobster, Toulouse-Lautrec (the artist) used to take his pet lobster for a walk on its lead in the streets of Paris. Most other types of seafood can be found on the ever changing menu including langoustines (cousins of the lobster), mussels etc. The food shows Italian influences but also includes pub grub perennials such as steak pie. The fresh seafood comes from the Firth of Forth. There is a vegetarian choice, sandwiches, coffee and desserts. In the evening it is quite upmarket and at lunchtime it can host a few business lunches. Food is served from 1200-2200 Monday to Saturday and from 1100 to 2200 on Sundays. The early Sabbath opening is to serve breakfasts. The Kings Wark does a mean breakfast, including a vegetarian one. This time on Sundays between 1100 and 1230 opening time is the only window of opportunity to take children to this pub as it does not have a children's licence.

Opening hours are 1230-2300 on Sundays, 1200-2345 Fridays and Saturdays and 1200-2300 Monday to Thursday. There are four real ales. Only McEwans 80/- is resident. The guests when I was there were Morlands Old Speckled Hen, Flowers Original and Theakstons Bitter. Keg products listed at the bar were Beamish Red, John Smiths Extra Smooth, Miller Pilsner, Becks, Guinness and Strongbow Cider.

The Kings Wark is a listed building. The windows must be kept as they are. There is a painting on the ceiling of one bar and a real fire, in the winter, in the other. A lifebelt with Kings Wark printed on it hangs in the bar and a chart for identifying fish continues the maritime theme. A notice on the wooden bar says, 'This is our church, this is where we heal our hearts.' There are old maps on the walls and pictures of the pub in days gone by. It is a lovely old pub and mostly furbished in dark wood and stone inside. The floors are wooden so there is no problem with hikers' boots. Landlord Murray Georgeson is pleased to see walkers. This is a good pub for celebrity spotting, especially during festival time. Robert Hardy and Mel Smith have been seen in here. Footballers, politicians and media types regularly frequent this ancient inn. But it is sufficiently up-to-date to accept credit cards and American Express.

## The *Britannia*

The royal yacht *Britannia* is a popular tourist destination. Nearly half a million people visited it in its first year as a tourist attraction. It is best to buy your ticket in advance. Either telephone 0131 555 5566, hours of business 0900-1730, or call at the Edinburgh Tattoo Office, 33/34 Market St., Edinburgh, open daily from 1000-1630 each day. Admission times to the royal yacht are 1000-1630 each day.

A tour normally takes about two hours. The royal picture gallery has photographs of every generation of the royal family taken on board. Many of these have never been before on public show. The interior has been hugely refurbished since arriving in Edinburgh. There are numerous items of art from the royal collection and gifts to the Queen from heads of state all over the world. You can visit the original wheelhouse, the royal barge, the Admiral's cabin, the sun lounge, state dining and drawing rooms, the Queen's and Duke of Edinburgh's bedrooms and the engine room.

The Queen and her consort chose much of the interior decor of the ship such as curtains, wallpaper etc. The interior was created by Sir Hugh Casson. In the Admiral's suite the armchairs and settees are more than a century old, they were originally in the royal yacht *Victoria and Albert III*. The ship's wheel was previously that of the racing yacht Britannia, constructed in 1893 for the soon-to-be Edward VII.

The royal yacht *Britannia* is 125 metres long. The main mast is some 43 metres tall. The decks are planked in Burmese teak. The ship's top speed was 22 knots. This was a very quiet ship as the shouting of orders was not allowed, hand signals were used instead. The crew was 220 seamen and 24 officers. On formal royal tours, a Royal Marine band of 26 was also present. It was the final naval unit where sailors sleeping sites were hammocks. This practice continued until 1973.

*Britannia* was launched on the 16th of April 1953 from John Brown's shipyard in Clydebank. She travelled over a million miles, docking at more than 600 ports in 135 countries. She hosted nearly a 1000 royal and official visits. She was so constructed that she could be converted into a hospital ship in time of war. You can tell it is Britannia as it does not have its name on its bows like every other ship. The royal yachts have an uninterrupted history dating back three centuries to the reign of Charles II. *Britannia's* life as an ocean going vessel ended in Portsmouth on the 11th of December 1997. She was towed to Leith.

## The Walk

Leave the Kings Wark and cross Bernard St. to walk up Shore (street name) with the Water of Leith on your left. Where Turner St. bends right away from Shore, bear slightly left and ahead, keeping the river bank on your close left and passing through a cobbled area to a cobbled riverside walkway. A plaque on your right gives you details about the Port of Leith. Then go by an old harpoon gun on your left, an information board here tells you about whaling.

Cross the river by the old bridge and turn right up to the main road. Proceed left for 200 metres, passing Rennies Isle and the new Scottish Office across the water on your left. Just before the roundabout on your right is the royal yacht *Britannia*. Go straight ahead at the roundabout and past the Holiday Inn Express on your left. Come to a junction with Portland Place at traffic lights, walk to the right along Portland Place. About 100 metres up here you will find Lindsay Road going diagonally left and forward off Portland Place. There is a Lindsay Street and a Lindsay Place before Lindsay Road. Some 40 metres after Lindsay Road veers off Portland Place, a little unnamed stretch of road connects the two. On the far side of this a tarmac path descends to a disused railway line between Portland Place and Lindsay Road.

Go down here and after 100 metres, just past the first overhead bridge, go straight ahead on the red earth track, leaving the tarmac footpath to ascend to your right. This railway started off as the Edinburgh, Leith and Newhaven Railway. A parliamentary act empowering this was passed on 13th of August 1836. This section between Leith and Trinity opened in 1846. Continue along this disused railway path, now a gravel/beaten earth track. Pass under a second bridge. Go beneath a third bridge with the number 12 painted on it. The path now becomes tarmac again. About 100 metres past this third bridge bypass a signposted track to the left to Leith. Follow the sign-post pointing ahead to Cramond Brig for another 125 metres.

At this point there is a five-way junction of tarmac paths. Take the second on the left, signposted 'Canonmills ¾'. Walk up here under the first bridge crossing over the path. This is the route of the Edinburgh, Leith and Granton Railway, opened on the 31st of August 1842. It was built to service passengers using the new steam fer-ries from Burntisland in Fife to Granton. Along here you will find Indian (also called Himalayan) balsam. Part of its Latin name, like busy lizzies, is impatiens, which well describes its explosive growth. It can reach up to two metres and is characterised by Chinese lantern-shaped flowers varying in colour from dusky pink to almost white. Once you have smelt its sickly-sweet perfume you will find it distinctive ever after.

About 300 metres along this pathway, between the first and second bridges over-head, take the tarmac path going slightly right ahead up a ramp. As this terminates in a T-junction with a second tarmac path, go left here towards the second bridge over the disused railway line path. When this path ends in a T-junction with a tarmac road, turn right down the tarmac road. This is Warriston Gardens. As Warriston Gardens ends it makes a T-junction with Inverleith Row. Bear left along Inverleith Row for around 300 metres. Robert Louis Stevenson spent a lot of his childhood living in Inverleith Row. Turn right where signposted for Botanic Gardens, East Gate and en-ter the gardens. To keep on the walk all you have to do is exit the Botanic Gardens by the west (the only other) gate. So your route through these gardens can be your own choice. A map just inside the gates gives details of all the attractions you can see. The garden's opening hours are November until January 0930-1600, February and Octo-ber 0930-1700, March and September 0930-1800 and April to August 0930-1900. No dogs are allowed and their telephone number is 0131 552 7171. These botanic gardens have the largest collection of rhododendrons in the world.

For those in a hurry or uninterested in gardens here is the quick route. Follow the road around from the entrance to the right. Proceed left where the sign points for the Woodland Garden. Follow this tarmac path, ignoring tarmac and gravel paths to the left and right. It parallels the wall and road on your left. Stay with this path as it bears right, still keeping the wall and road on your left. Go past the herb garden, snack bar and botanics shop on your left to come to the west gate, also on your left. Go through the west gate onto Aboretum Drive. Hang left along Aboretum Drive. About 100 metres along the road bears left and becomes Inverleith Terrace. Cross this and go straight ahead down what is still, but is not signposted as, Arboretum Drive. Some 25 metres down here on your left is a tarmac path between two large stone posts with metal gates. This is signposted Leith 2½, Canonmills ¾. This is your path. This is the Rocheid Path. It is named after the family who bought this land in 1665. The Inverleith Society, which concerns itself with Edinburgh's amenities, looks after this path. As you walk along here look across the river on your right. The parallel streets are known as the Stockbridge Colonies. These small terraced houses were put up in the 1860s to provide pleasant housing for artisans away from the city slums. The driving force behind this social experiment was the Edinburgh Co-operative Build-ing Association. The members were in the building trades and erected the houses,

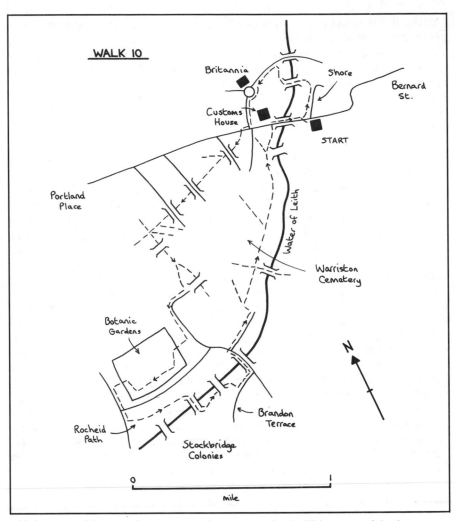

WALK 10

Britannia

Shore

Bernard St.

Customs House

START

Portland Place

Water of Leith

Warriston Cemetery

Botanic Gardens

N

Brandon Terrace

Rocheid Path

Stockbridge Colonies

0                                    1

mile

which were sold to members on an early mortgage basis. This successful scheme was emulated elsewhere in Edinburgh. A first housing scheme?

This is part of the Water of Leith Walkway. Look out for an unusual heron here, the night heron, about two-thirds the size of our own grey heron. It has the same general colour pattern as the grey heron but it is more vividly coloured. Its characteristic feature is white quills growing from the nape of its neck and lying over its blue/black feathers. The south-eastern European birds come from a free-flying colony at Edinburgh Zoo. Go along here for a quarter of a mile and turn right across the Water of Leith at the second footbridge. Then follow the path to the left with the river on your left. Just after the first bridge overhead the path leads you uphill to a T-junction with

Brandon Terrace. Go left along busy Brandon Terrace. Around 100 metres along turn left onto Howard St. at the clock on your right in the middle of the road and go over the river. Once over the river turn right immediately into Warriston Crescent. At the end of Warriston Crescent follow the sign ahead indicating 'Public Footpath to Leith'. This immediately bears to the right. As the footpath rises uphill take the steps to the right. At the top of the steps, about 10 metres in front of you, is a tarmac path. Break left along this path and then right when it forks after 10 to 20 metres.

Some 200 metres along here you pass between four ornate pillars, two on each side of you. To the left you will see the remains of Warriston Cemetery. Appropriately, two of the plants found here are terminally poisonous. White bryony is a climber with tendrils, ivy-shaped leaves, five-petalled white flowers with an orange pollen sac for each petal and red berries in autumn. Deadly nightshade has green bell-shaped flowers with a maroon tinge and black cherry-like fruits in autumn. Its poison is atropine which used to be used by medieval Italian ladies to enlarge the pupils of their eyes to make them more attractive. Talk about Dangerous Liaisons!

Keep on this tarmac path for the next half a mile or so. You pass signs pointing ahead, first Leith 1¼ and then Leith 1. At this second sign be careful to keep to the right-hand fork. Just behind the remains of an old bridge on your left is a flagged garden with seats, an old inscribed stone, memorials about the Water of Leith Walkway and views over Arthur's Seat. This is a good place to take a breather if you feel like it.

Some half to three-quarters of a mile after the little garden the tarmac cycle path swings left to end at a road. Just before it does, descend 10 metres to your right to pick up the cobbled path along the edge of the Water of Leith and turn left along it. Keep on this path between fences and over a cobbled street by a bridge. Rejoin the path once over the street, it is now beaten earth and gravel. Continue by the river on your right and over cobbles to a road bridge. On your left here is Customs House. This was

built in 1821 to exact the customs due at the port. The architect was Robert Reid. The entrance ways and stairs were built to his design and added in 1824. Fittingly, considering its proximity to the *Britannia,* it has the royal coat of arms above the entrance. Turn right across the road bridge and the Kings Wark is on its far side.

The Customs House

# 11. Edinburgh: Holyrood Park

**Route:** Duddingston Village – Samson's Ribs – Radical Road – The Dry Dam – Dunsapie Loch

**Distance:** 3.5 miles

**Map:** OS Landranger 66, Edinburgh

**Start:** Sheep Heid Inn, Duddingston Village

**Access:** By bus, There is a good bus service from the city centre, half-hourly even on Sundays. For details call 'Traveline' on 0800 232323 if inside Edinburgh, if outwith Edinburgh then ring 0131 225 3858. Or contact Lothian Buses on 0131 555 6363. Ask to be put off at the junction of Duddingston Road and Old Church Lane then walk up Old Church Lane and take the first on the right, Causeway, and The Sheep Heid is on your right.

By car, From the east end of Princes Street go left down Leith Street, opposite North Bridge on your right. Go straight ahead at the first roundabout onto Leith Walk. At the second roundabout turn right along London Road with Calton Hill on your right. Just past the Meadowbank Sports Centre on your left and Arthur's Seat on your right, go diagonally right forwards at traffic lights into Willowbrae Road, signposted for A1, Berwick-upon-Tweed. Just past the Lady Nairne pub on your right turn right at traffic lights into Duddingston Road West with the golf course on your left. Immediately past Holyrood Secondary School on your left, turn right into Old Church Lane. Just before you arrive at the church turn right into The Causeway. The car park for the Sheep Heid is ahead on your right behind the pub.

## Sheep Heid Inn. Tel: 0131 656 6951

There has been an inn here since 1360. This was rebuilt in 1670 and extensively renovated in the 1700s, so much of this pub is genuinely 200 years old at least. Mary Queen of Scots was a patron here, calling in while going to Craigmillar Castle. Around 1580 James VI, son of Mary Queen of Scots, gave the landlord a gold-plated ram's head which hung in the pub until 1888. At this time it was sold and passed behind the veils of history. There was another reason for the name of this pub: it served up boiled sheep's heads. The skulls of these sheep were used as stepping stones to cross puddles and streams around this hostelry.

But it was not only kings and queens who visited The Sheep Heid. Curlers from Duddingston Loch nearby warmed up here after a cold day's sport. It was always a popular place with Edinburgh societies and associations. The King's Bodyguard of Archers and the High Constables of Holyrood are among many who held their festivities in these premises. Edinburgh Burns Club met here for many years and the Trotter's Club still foregathers in this alehouse. The Trotters Club play skittles in what is Scotland's oldest skittle alley. Their records go back some two centuries. You can have a go on this skittle alley if you want.

Another pub facility is barbecues in summer. Food is served from 1200-1500 and 1800-2100 Monday to Thursday, Friday and Saturday 1200-2100 and on Sundays

1230-2000. Landlord William McKinnon describes the food as 'a mixture of French classical and Scottish classical'. A kind of Auld Alliance then! There is an extensive menu with vegetarian alternatives. Soup and sandwiches are available if you want a simpler meal. Local haggis and mussels are used in the cooking but not necessarily together. There are also daily specials.

Also special is one of the real ales. This is Sheep Heid which is specially brewed for this pub by Broughtons. It is a dark, slightly sweetish traditional Scottish beer. I am quite fond of these types of beers and thoroughly enjoyed this one. The other real ales are Deuchars IPA and Caledonian 80/-. In keg are Guinness, Guinness Extra Cold, Caffreys, Tennents Velvet 70/-, Tennents Smooth Draught, Tennents Lager, Grolsch and Dry Blackthorn. Opening hours are Monday to Wednesday 1100-2300, Thursday to Saturday 1100-2400 and Sunday 1230-2300.

Walkers are welcome. If you plan to arrive out of normal food serving hours and there are at least 11 of you, if you phone in advance they will be happy to lay on some food for you. Children are not a problem, I took two with me. There is a children's menu. In addition the pub has a beer garden.

Inside there is a bar downstairs and a bistro upstairs. The bar is dark and dim, having the atmosphere of its two centuries. The bar counter is two hundred years old, original apart from its top. A painting, genuine not a reproduction, of Robert Burns adorns one of the walls. Burns was a customer here. There is also a picture of the Battle of Prestonpans which took place not far away. There is also a framed menu from 1808, a sheep heid and old pictures of Duddingston and the pub in the olden days of the 19th century. The Sheep Heid is a listed building so it still has the old, small windows. The bistro is brighter with more light. It has a ram's head, bookcases, pictures, an eclectic collection of chairs and, for no known reason whatsoever, a copy of the Norwegian coat of arms.

## Arthur's Seat

Arthur's Seat is an extinct volcano. It first became active about 350 million years ago. At that time it was about twice its present height. The rocks atop Arthur's Seat are called agglomerate and they mark where the pipe of the volcano was. Arthur's Seat erupted 13 times, putting forth strong streams of molten magma. Salisbury Crags, on the other hand, are volcanic rock that never reached the surface. It was exposed as the softer rock above eroded away. This dolerite has been quarried for a long time. In 1666 it was providing London with pavements. There were three quarries on Arthur's Seat. The last closed in the 1830s as Edinburgh's citizens started to object to their disappearing skyline. About 30,000 to 40,000 tons of stone and rock was being removed every year.

After volcanic activity and weathering, the next significant influence on Arthur's Seat were the Ice Ages. The glaciers scraped the valleys of Arthur's Seat deeper. The last Ice Age ended about 10,000 years ago. About 9000 years ago Stone Age hunter/gatherers entered the area and a few of their implements have been found. Around 6000 years ago farming techniques arrived here. Some land was cleared of

The view over Edinburgh from Arthur's Seat

trees by Neolithic settlers, but the land was still wooded when the monks arrived at
Holyrood Abbey in AD1128. Roughly 3000 years ago, Bronze Age people lived
here and traces of the terraces that they cut in the hillsides remain. Archaeological remains show that bronze smiths worked here around 700BC. About two millennia
ago, the Iron Age appears to have been a bloody time, with numerous fortnified sites
above Samson's Ribs, behind Salisbury Crags and on Dunsapie Crags.

By the end of the first millennium the park around Arthur's Seat was shared by
the King and the Abbey of Kelso. Some was farming land and some was royal hunting park. Subsequent to some sacrilegious behaviour by David I, he had a vision telling him to build an abbey here so he founded Holyrood Abbey by the park and gave
the royal hunting park to the monks. The monks gradually cleared the trees on Arthur's Seat and grazed sheep there. They also built a lade (leat), dam and mill in
Hunter's Bog in the middle of Arthur's Seat to grind their grain, and built a brewery
nearby. By the 1500s all the trees had been cleared and the last record of anyone
farming here was in 1610. From then until 1977 it was solely a sheep grazing area.

During the Reformation of the 1500s the land was taken from the church and re-
verted to the Crown. Later a part of the park near Holyrood Abbey became a sanctuary for debtors. One of these was Thomas de Quincy, author of *The Confessions of an
Opium Eater*. The last debtor left here in 1880. The law making this a debtor's sanctuary has never been repealed. In the Middle Ages this park was used as an isolation
ward for plague victims. In 1788 the Wild Macraas were members of the Seaforth
Highlanders who mutinied against being sent to the Far East. Some 600 men set up
camp around the summit of Arthur's Seat. After three days they were negotiated

down. However, their fears were not groundless and few of them returned home from the Orient, most perished from disease. In 1832 60,000 people met in the parade ground section of the park to debate the Parliamentary Reform Bill.

The present layout of the park was designed by Prince Albert, husband of Queen Victoria, in the 1840s. He created St Margaret's and Dunsapie Lochs. Arthur's Seat has been a beacon hill for many hundreds of years to mark new centuries and various royal events. In both World Wars AA guns were stationed here. The author James Hogg set some scenes in the park in his books *Private Means* and *Confessions of a Justified Sinner*. Sir Arthur Conan Doyle, an Edinburgh surgeon, used the park as an inspiration for his novel *The Lost World*. In the 20s and 30s, Ronald Searle, the author of the *St Trinian's* series of books, had a niece at a school called St Trinnean's in St Leonard's Hall on the edge of the park. So, go figure!

## The Walk

Exit Sheep Heid under the inn sign and turn left past the information board about Duddingston village on your right to go straight ahead down a narrow, walled lane. At the end of the lane bear right along the tarmac road. This is closed to traffic on Sundays and is called Windy Gowl (gully). Duddingston Loch on your left is a wildlife reserve and bird sanctuary. About 200 metres along on your left is a large rock outcrop dropping steeply to Duddingston Loch. This is Hangman's Crag, so-called because the city hangman killed himself by jumping off here. Above and to your right you may see people and cars on Queen's Drive, named after Queen Victoria.

About 100 metres past the end of Duddingston Loch on your left is Murder Acre. In 1677 a riot by apprentices banned from a parade to celebrate the King's birthday was bloodily suppressed here and a number of people died. Another couple of hundred metres along this road you will see the Innocent Railway footpath on your left. This was built to bring coal into the city from the mines around Dalkeith. The journey attracted passenger demand so the company converted coal-carrying coaches for passenger transport. The railway opened in 1831 and closed in the 1960s. There are a number of stories about its name. The one I prefer is that it was called the Innocent Railway because no workmen were killed in its construction. On your right here up on the cliffs are lighter coloured hexagonal pillars of basalt, called Samson's Ribs.

Roughly a half to three-quarters of a mile from your starting point along this tarmac road is a roundabout. Go right here and walk up beside the road. At another roundabout some 50 metres further on turn right again. Follow this other tarmac road for about 150 metres and then take a broad path on your left uphill. Keep with this as it doubles back to the left to run under Salisbury Crags above you. This path is marked by a large boulder. This is the Radical Road. The trail to the quarry up here was converted into the Radical Road by unemployed weavers from the west of Scotland. Sir Walter Scott and some of his cronies were the instigators of this make-work scheme. The name Radical refers to the politics of the weavers.

Near the top of this modest ascent you will find the South Quarry on your right. This was one of three on Arthur's Seat. At the front of this quarry is an isolated rock, Hutton's Rock. The great geologist James Hutton got the quarry master to preserve it as an excellent example of how a vein of iron ore runs through rock. It was in Salisbury Crags, in a section just off the route of this walk known as Hutton's Section, that he first got the idea that igneous rock was created by magma that melted its way between strata of older rocks and set as a sill when cold. Hutton's Section is today visited by students of geology from around the world. Salisbury Crags are a dolerite sill. The presence of the yellow, five-petalled, long stemmed rock-rose and the blue, hairy spikes of viper's bugloss growing here show that limestone or chalk also exist in this spot. It is forbidden to pick flowers or to take plants or geological specimens from the park, which is an SSSI and is also scheduled as an ancient monument. These laws are enforced by the park's own police force, the Royal Park Constabulary.

Continue along this path as it runs along the bottom of Salisbury Crags. There are glorious views over Edinburgh from here. The path levels out and runs along the western side of the crags. In Sir Walter Scott's book *Heart of Midlothian* Jeannie Deans lived with her family on a farm under Salisbury Crags. Fulmars nest on Salisbury Crags. They are members of the albatross family. They resemble seagulls, being about the size of a herring gull, but they have a darker back colour than a herring gull although not as dark as a black-backed gull. Do not approach their nests as young fulmars have a defence mechanism of vomiting foul-smelling fluid all over intruders, as a number of unfortunate climbers have found out.

Stay on this path as it descends on the north side of Arthur's Seat to the tarmac road, Queen's Drive. Here, take the tarmac footpath on your right up Arthur's Seat. This runs diagonally away from Queen's drive, going gently uphill. As this tarmac footpath bends to the right, go left/straight ahead on a double beaten earth/gravel footpath. This points you to the ruins of St Anthony's Chapel. This is the oldest ecclesiastical building in Scotland. Written records report the Pope making provision for repairs to this building in 1426. The last record of anyone working or living here was in 1581. Just before the path climbs steeply to St Anthony's Chapel, take the grassy and stony path to the right. Follow this path up the dry valley known as The Dry Dam, with the peak of Arthur's Seat on your right front. There are a few of these dry valleys around Edinburgh. They were cut by glaciers or glacial melt water and then became redundant as not required by normal rainfall drainage. About 250 metres up this dry valley, slant left forward on a broad, green, grassy path. This path continues to bend left and up to a saddle on the eastern side of The Dry Dam. Cross the saddle and descend towards Dunsapie loch, with its crags above it, ahead of you.

The path terminates in a T-junction with the tarmac Queen's Drive at Dunsapie Loch, here proceed to your left along Queen's Drive with Dunsapie Loch on your right. Dunsapie is Gaelic for 'hill of wispy grass'. About 100 metres past the end of Dunsapie Loch take a narrow grass path angling right forwards towards the dyke ahead that marks the edge of Meadowfield Park. At this dyke turn right and follow it along, keeping it on your near left. Once over a small rise in the ground, bypass a stone stile on your left into the park and keep with the path as it bends right. Just after this bend the path forks, take the narrow path on the left heading into the woodland. This cuts through a neck of woodland and into the open again. On your right here is the hillside where Bonnie Prince Charlie's army of Highlanders camped in 1745.

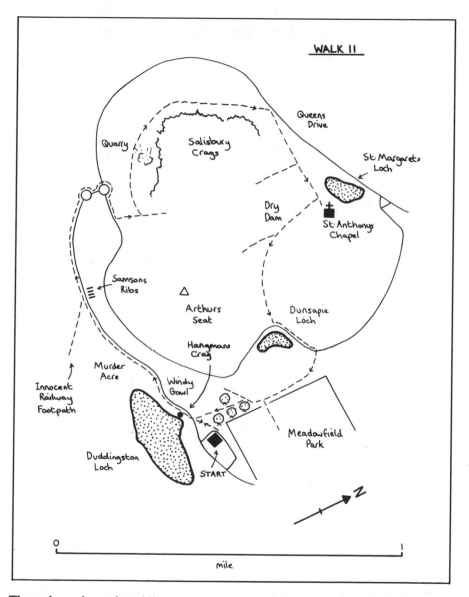

WALK 11

Queens Drive

Quarry

Salisbury Crags

St Margarets Loch

St Anthonys Chapel

Dry Dam

Samsons Ribs

Arthurs Seat

Dunsapie Loch

Hangmans Crag

Murder Acre

Windy Gowl

Innocent Railway Footpath

Meadowfield Park

Duddingston Loch

START

0                                                                                  1

mile

The path continues downhill staying quite close to the dyke and park woodlands on your left. Eventually a set of stairs appears on your left descending into Duddingston village. Duddingston means 'Dodin's town' and it has been here since the 1100s. At the foot of the steps turn left through a walled path. At the end of the path the Sheep Heid is afront you.

# 12. East Lothian: Pencaitland

**Route:** Pencaitland – Glenkinchie Distillery – Barley Mill – Saltoun Forest – West Saltoun

**Distance:** 6.5 miles

**Map:** OS Landranger 66, Edinburgh

**Start:** Winton Arms, Pencaitland

**Access:** By bus, there is a reasonable bus service from Edinburgh even on Sundays. However, be careful as some buses leave from St Andrew's Square bus station and some from the west side of St Andrew's Square. Collect a timetable from the bus shop at the bus station or phone 'Traveline' on 0800 232323 if inside the Edinburgh area, if outside Edinburgh phone 0131 225 3858. The operator is SMT Lowland and their enquiry line number is 0131 663 9233.

By car, leave Edinburgh on the A68 (T) signposted for Dalkeith. Once through Dalkeith on this road, about two and a half miles beyond it you will come across the A6093 to Pencaitland on your left. Take this. About four miles along this road you reach Pencaitland. Go straight through the western end of the village and descend into and rise out of the valley of the infant Tyne. In the eastern end of the village you will find the Winton Arms on your right. The car park is immediately before it, also on the right.

---

## Winton Arms. Tel: 01875 341278

This building was originally Winton House and part of the Winton Estate. It was erected in the early 19th century by Lady Ruthven. It was sold later in the 19th century and passed through the hands of various brewers. It was a coaching inn on the Edinburgh to Duns route. Early this century part of it was a baker's and pictures of Moirs Refreshment Rooms are up on the walls of the pub. Some 40 years ago one corner of this inn was the village shop and there are old photographs showing this adorning the interior walls of this hostelry.

However the pull between the licensed and the retail trades has been resolved in favour of the licensed trade, which is appropriate as this pub is now home to the East Lothian tug of war team. This council sponsored team go around all the Highland games, competing. In 1999 they were Scottish and British champions. They train just around the corner from the pub. The team is run by landlord Jamie McCormack.

Jamie irresistibly reminds me of the innkeeper from *Lord of the Rings*, Barliman. A very worthy, busy, bustling man but forgetful. But this can be forgiven as he is running an alehouse in transition. This used to be the local's inn but since the nearby Old Smiddy closed down and stopped servicing the through traffic, Jamie and his wife Elaine are having to diversify. They are thinking of putting in more real ale, installing a children's play area at the back and expanding the range of food.

The food, when I was there, was pies and toasties. Children are welcome and get a free glass of juice. The real ale was Caledonian 80/-. The keg was Tennents White Thistle, Tennents Velvet, Tennents Lager, Strongbow Cider, Guinness, Caffreys and Grolsch Premium. The village pub nature of this establishment is reflected in its slightly eccentric opening hours of Monday to Thursday 1430-1145, Friday 1300-0100, Saturday 1200-0100 and Sunday 1200-2400. Food serving times are not relevant here as it is simple to make a toastie or pop a pie into the microwave.

The amenities of this pub include darts, dominoes, jukebox, cigarette machine with a pool table and fruit machines in a separate room at the back, almost like being in a snooker club. Jamie and Elaine strive for and succeed in creating a friendly pub atmosphere and welcome walkers. This pub also sells Glenkinchie, *The Edinburgh Malt*, from the local distillery on the route of this walk. The bar has a wooden floor with blonde wood tables and chairs and pictures and photographs of old Pencaitland. The walls inside are of stonework and there is a stained-glass window. The comfortable lounge is carpeted.

## Glenkinchie Distillery

The Agricultural Revolution of the 1700s resulted in a great increase in barley production. In 1837 the brothers John and George Rate obtained the first licence to produce whisky here. Their own local barley was mashed with pure spring water from the Lammermuir Hills to produce Glenkinchie Whisky, a lowland malt. The brothers closed this distillery in 1853.

In 1890 a group from the local licensed trade re-opened this distillery. They kept Glenkinchie's two original lamp glass stills. These are the standard type of lowland still and are the biggest stills of any Scottish malt whisky producer. The two copper pot stills today still distil Glenkinchie single malt. The distillery closed between 1917 and 1919 due to food shortages caused by the First World War. During the Second World War the same problems restricted the distillery to producing only a little whisky every year.

In the 1950s the distillery ran the surrounding farm. Aberdeen Angus thrived on the distillery by-products and waste barley. These cattle were prize-winners at shows. The distillery also had carthorses which until the 1960s carried barley and coal from Saltoun Station until Dr Beeching's axe fell. In the summer these Clydesdales delivered whisky in Glasgow.

In 1968 malting ceased at Glenkinchie. Alistair Munro, then in charge, started collecting historical material about the distillery and distilling in general. The former malting areas became a museum in the early 1970s. A decade later tours combining the museum and the distillery began. Around 30,000 visitors call each year. The star attraction of the museum is a seven-metre-long model of a distillery on a scale of 1:6. This was shown from 1923 to 1925 at the British Empire Exhibition in the Palace of Industry.

Tours of the distillery depart every half hour between Monday and Saturday, Easter and May bank holiday weekends and weekends from July 4th to 1st of November 0930-1700 (last tour departs 1600). Outwith these dates Sundays hours are 1200-1700 (last tour 1600). There are also extended hours in August and September (last tours Monday to Friday 1900). If in doubt you can call the distillery on 01875 342004 or fax on 01875 342007.

# The Walk

Come out of the Winton Arms and turn left along the main road, A6093. Walk past a street on the left called The Glebe. A glebe is an old Scottish word for the land a minister received as part of his stipend. He would use this to grow crops or pasture livestock to supplement his income. Also note Winton South Lodge on the right with its elaborate wrought-iron gates. When I was there, there was a notice up informing people that this building was being considered for listing as a historic building. Just past this is Pencaitland parish church on your left. A plaque on the wall of the graveyard gives some details of the kirk and of the village. The kirk is very old and worth a look. It has an octagonal bell tower and an excellent ante-reformation aisle. The graveyard has some interesting gravestones with hourglasses and skull and cross-bones indicating that your time has run out. In common with other graves of the period, some tombstones give pictorial details of their occupier's previous employment i.e. one has a sledge-hammer and pickaxe on it, possibly a mason's grave.

Cross the lovely old bridge over the Tyne. Bypass a footpath on the right to Ormiston which has been created and kept open by the good work of the Scottish Rights of Way Society. Turn left at the old school on your right, up Lempockwells Road, keeping the Mercat Cross on your right. A small detour straight ahead up the A6093 for some 45 metres will bring you to the Carriage House on your left. It still has some of the old archways where the carriages stood. I have not seen one like it before. Walk past Tyneholm Cottages on the left, noting the ATs on the buildings to your right. This commemorates Arthur Trevelyn who was local laird and proprietor of Wester Pencaitland in the early 1800s. He more or less built the village and village hall in 1802. Continue up Lempockwells Road until the third turning on the right, just before the end of speed limit signs.

Turn right up this, Huntlaw Rd. About 200 metres up here a bridge crosses the road. Turn left up steps immediately before the bridge and walk ahead on the disused railway path. About 100 metres along here on your right is an upright, very weathered slab. All I could make out of the inscription were the last two lines, the most south-easterly mine in Haddingtonshire, the old name for East Lothian. If you do **not** want to visit the distillery then you continue down the railway path and rejoin the walk at the next bridge over the railway line path. Otherwise, after some 200 to 300 metres down this flower-fringed path, turn right along a narrow footpath lying across your route. Follow this narrow and slightly overgrown but distinct path into woodland. If you are wearing shorts, now might be a good time to don your waterproof trousers to protect yourself from stings and prickles. The path bends left, stay with it. In clearings in the wood here you may see red dead nettle. The leaves resemble those of nettles but are smooth, lacking the hairs of nettle cells which in reality are stings injecting formic acid into your skin. This is the same chemical that ants use. The red dead nettle has dark pink/red flowers, a white variety is also found. They are called dead nettle because they do not sting.

After two thirds of a mile or so this path ends at a stile in a T-junction with a minor road. Fifty metres up to your right you will find a sign pointing left to the Glenkinchie Distillery. Follow the sign. About 200 metres down this road follow a sign left into

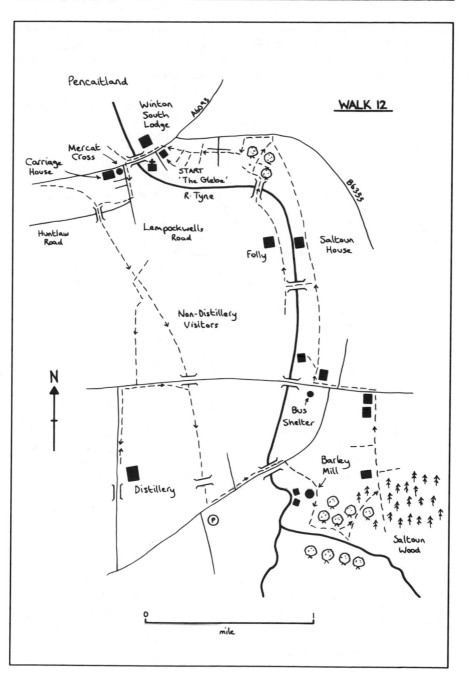

Pencaitland

Winton
South
Lodge

A6093

WALK 12

Mercat
Cross

Carriage
House

START
'The Glebe'

R. Tyne

B6355

Huntlaw
Road

Lempockwells
Road

Folly

Saltoun
House

Non-Distillery
Visitors

N

Bus
Shelter

Barley
Mill

Distillery

P

Saltoun
Wood

0        mile

the Glenkinchie Distillery. Turn right down the stairs at the bus dropping off point and follow the signs to the visitor centre. The visitor centre and tour cost £3 when I was there, but they are generous with their whisky so it is worth the money. And the ticket gets you £3 off the price of a bottle of Glenkinchie single malt!

Retrace your steps from the distillery to the junction of the woodland path and tarmac road. Continue along the tarmac road, bypassing the woodland path on your left. Some 300 metres past the junction of woodland path and tarmac road a bridge takes the road over the old railway path. Cross the bridge and on its far side a path on the left takes you down steps to the railway path. Turn left at the bottom of the steps and walk under the bridge. The large plant at the base of the bridge that looks like rhubarb is butterburr, strangely enough a member of the daisy family. From the tracks in the mud of this path it is obviously used by walkers, cyclists and horse riders. Pass under a bridge over the railway path, it appears to have a rabbit warren up the bank to the right underneath its supports. Look out for wild forget-me-not, white clover, knapweed (purple thistle-like head) and wild strawberry beside this path. **Those who have not visited the distillery rejoin the walk here.**

This path terminates in a T-junction with a minor tarmac road. Just previous to this is an information board about the Pencaitland Railway Walk that you have been traversing. Walk to your left here, keeping the car park on your right. Bypass a minor road on the left and aviaries of exotic birds to walk over a humpbacked bridge. Directly over the bridge bear right and walk up a rough track signposted for Barley Mill. Just before the sign that says 'Barley Mill Only' ahead of you, and where Barley Mill and Fletcher Cottages are on your right, go left through a gap in the dyke/fence. Then walk past Barley Mill on your right on a grassy path between hedge/dyke on your right and a fence on your left.

Barley Mill is a historic spot. Andrew Fletcher of nearby Saltoun was exiled in the 18th century. On his return he had learned of pot (pearl) barley, a well husked and de-chaffed barley that was particularly well suited to storage and cooking. He sent James Meikle to Holland to learn this process. On his return, Scotland's first barley mill was set up on this spot. It seems appropriate that it is this close to the distillery. Andrew Meikle, son of James, was another of East Lothian's numerous 'Agricultural Improvers'. He invented the threshing machine.

Still on the same path, bypass a field gate by a gap to its left and keep straight ahead along the field margin, staying close to the high hedge on your left. Proceed through another field gate, closing it behind you, and ignore a track off to the left. A faint but clear path leads you ahead through a flowering meadow towards the line of trees in front of you that marks the course of the river, while roughly paralleling another line of trees on your left. At the end of this latter line of trees, near a corner of the meadow, a much clearer path goes off left uphill into Saltoun Wood. This is your route. On your left here in July the field can be an absolute sea of blue. This is flax which is grown for cattle feed and linseed oil. Farmers' subsidies for growing the yellow rape are rapidly being reduced as I write this in 1999. Instead we can thank the Common Agricultural Policy for this colourful addition to our countryside. Farmers are currently being paid £450 per hectare to grow this crop.

This much clearer path takes you gently uphill beside the river valley. Near the top this path forks. Take the left-hand fork and follow it into a narrow belt of trees. This angles onto another broader, more clearly defined path. Angle left on to this. Keep on this path along the margin of the forest. About half a mile along this path is a T-junction with a forest track. Bear left along the forest track. At the end of the forest keep along this track, past a house on the left and a footpath on the right. Later ignore a field track to the left. This track becomes tarmac. Beside this you may see yarrow. This is a small plant, about a foot high, with feathery foliage and a cap of small, pleasantly scented, pinky white flowers. This is an achillea, like the garden flowers, and used to be used for snuff and tea.

Go past some cottages on the left and about a quarter of a mile from the end of the wood this road ends in a T-junction with another minor tarmac road. Turn left on this. At the bottom of the hill turn right up a rough track through a gap in the dyke. There is a bus shelter on the opposite side of the road here with a sign pointing to West Saltoun. Bypass an old building near the start of this rough track. Some 200 metres along this track, where it starts to curve left, downhill there is a tree stump with a wooden carving of a dog atop it. Here go right through a gap in the vegetation and left along a mown path. This ends about 15 metres short of a fence. Climb over a field gate secured with wire and directly in front of you in this fence.

Follow a first faint then more obvious path along the line of the fence on your right. When a cart track materialises on your left go ahead on this, paralleling the fence as before. At a T-junction go left over the river by a bridge. Then go straight ahead between parallel fences to a gate at the edge of the wood on front of you. As you cross the river look out for marsh marigold by the waterside. These have large, dark green, glossy, spade-shaped leaves and large flowers shaped and coloured like buttercups. About 20 metres beyond the gate is a T-junction with a grassy cart track, bear right along this track. Continue along this somewhat overgrown track and into the trees. Walk past a Gothic folly in the woodland here. This is not marked on my 1996 OS Landranger map. This track then takes you right downhill to another

The Folly

bridge over the river. Having negotiated a field gate and crossed the bridge the track then goes left and forks after around 50 metres. Walk up the right-hand fork into the wood. Stay with this rapidly improving track past a house on the left and a track coming in from the right. This track terminates in a T-junction with a tarmac road, the B6355, go left along this.

The large gates here lead to Saltoun House. In the early 18th century Andrew Fletcher of Saltoun was a notable opponent of the Union of the Parliaments. After about 250 metres on the B6355 you will see a tarmac path on your left behind two sets of off-set metal railings. Walk up this and follow it as it goes right around the edges of the housing estate. Keep on this path through houses and when you come out on a road, go straight ahead for 50 metres to its far end where you will see that the path continues. Keep on this tarmac path across a footpath cutting athwart you and bypass a path behind a field gate on your left. Ignore a tarmac path on the left through woods. This path brings you out at the old Smiddy Inn (out of business when I was there). This was the village blacksmith's. Turn diagonally left towards the main road, A6093. Then bear left along this to find the Winton Arms a few metres on your left. Notice the elaborate ironwork above the gates on Hope Cottage on your right.

# 13. East Lothian: East Linton

**Route:** East Linton – Phantassie Doocot – Preston Mill – Pencraig Wood – Over Hailes – Hailes Castle

**Distance:** 5.5 miles

**Map:** OS Landranger 67, Duns and Dunbar

**Start:** Drovers Inn, East Linton.

**Access:** By bus, there is a good service from East Linton to Edinburgh, Monday to Saturday. On Sundays the service is adequate. On weekdays there are a few limited-stop services which get there much more quickly. The limited-stop services can be boarded at various stops along Princes St. The normal bus service can be boarded at either St Andrew's Square bus station or at the west side of St Andrew's Square but not both. Check carefully where your bus departs from. Timetables can be picked up from the bus shop at St Andrew's Square bus station. Details can also be obtained from SMT/Lowland Enquiry Line on 0131 663 9233. Alternatively you can phone 'Traveline' on 0800 232323 in the Edinburgh area or on 0131 225 3858 outwith the Edinburgh area.

By car, take the A1 eastwards out of Edinburgh. About 16 miles after the A1/A720 city bypass junction you will see signs to East Linton B1377. Go left on to this road. Turn left off this, Station Road, immediately you have passed under the railway bridge. This is Bridge Street. The Drovers Inn is 50 metres up on your left. In July 99 there were no parking restrictions outside the Drovers Arms. This, however, may change. Parking restrictions are being considered. The pub has no car park.

Alternatively, there is a courtesy bus which will come and collect you from your door and take you to the pub from within a 25-mile radius. This covers Edinburgh.

---

## The Drovers Inn. Tel: 01620 860 298

This pub has been here for over 200 years. As the name implies, it served the needs of drovers on the old drove route between Haddington and East Linton. Prior to the coming of the railways (when this pub had a re-incarnation as the Railway Hotel) droving was a major industry. In these days the Highland hills and glens were covered not with sheep as now, but with black (dark brown) cattle. These resembled to-day's highland cattle except in colour. In autumn, when the grass began to fail, surplus cattle were driven south to markets, known as trysts, for sale. These trysts were in Central Scotland.

Drovers normally drove their cattle about nine miles a day and so drovers inns along drove routes are often that distance apart. Drovers' inns were often situated by drovers' 'stances', which were common (free) grazing areas. In fact, drovers' inns were often deliberately sited at drovers' stances. From Central Scotland the cattle were driven south to England. Once on better roads the cattle were frequently shod at blacksmiths. Huntingdon and Norfolk were common destinations for these cattle.

This Drovers Inn is mentioned in the Second Statistical Account of Scotland in 1835 when East Linton parish had a population of 1765 served by 11 pubs, down from 19 in the previous account. In 1888 a new clock in the church tower was named Jessie by Bob Sharpe, the son of the then landlord of the Drovers Inn, then called the Railway Hotel, in honour of his sweetheart. It did not do him any good – she later married someone else.

However, it is still a sweetheart of a pub. The AA Hotel Service recommended this pub in the 1999 'Lifestyle' guide. It is also featured in the 1999 Good Pub Guide. In the 'High Life' section of *Scotland on Sunday* on 8th February 1998, Clarissa Dickson-Wright of TV's 'Two Fat Ladies' gave this inn's food a rave write up. She also spoke very highly of the setting. She had lobster and monkfish in a stunning sauce followed by brown sugar meringues. The food is all local produce. The vegetables are all organic. I was so impressed by their flavours that I later arranged to have a regular delivery of organic fruit and vegetables at home. The meat comes from award-winning butchers Andersons, who have a shop in the village. Crab, lobster, mussels etc. come from North Berwick nearby. With coffee you can have home-made tablet and shortbread. The house speciality is roast suckling pig in honey and ginger. Food is served from 1200-1400 Monday to Saturday and on Sunday from 1230-1430. In the evenings food is on from Monday to Thursday and Sunday from 1800-2130 and on Friday and Saturday it is on from 1800-2200.

Opening hours are Monday to Saturday 1130-1430, Monday and Tuesday 1700-2300, Thursday 1700-2400, Wednesday (live music night), Friday and Saturday 1700-0100. Sunday it is open all day from 1230-2400. There are four real ales. The regulars are Adnams Broadside and Deuchars IPA. The two guests when I was there were Mansfield Cask and Oxford Varsity from Morrell. Keg pumps dispensed Cruz Campo, Carlsberg Pilsner, Belhaven Best, Dry Blackthorn and Guinness.

The bar has an eclectic collection of comfy chairs and settles. There are hop vines above the bar, a ram's head above the gents' door and a goat's head on a pillar in the bar. There is a real fire in winter and free papers. It is a lovely old atmospheric country pub. The incidental music is vintage 1930s. There are pictures for sale by local artists on the walls. The bistro beside the public bar has some lovely old furniture, an old skittles game and local scenes on the walls. There is a restaurant upstairs and a beer garden at the back. The service is friendly and helpful. They take credit cards.

Landladies Michelle and Nicole Finlay run a child and walker friendly pub. The beautifully decorated gents has today's papers pinned up above the urinal for you to read instead of the usual scurrilous graffiti.

## Preston Mill

In Scotland few places are as picturesque, as much painted or photographed as Preston Mill. It is made of beautiful, mellow, old stone and situated in an idyllic waterside location. Its pointed red-pantiled roof is reminiscent of Kentish oast houses. However, it was not built as thing of beauty but as a practical, pragmatic piece of machinery for transforming oats, barley and wheat into animal food, meal and flour.

Originally cereal grinding was done by hand in stone depressions known as querns, rather like you grind spices today in a mortar and pestle. Waterwheels have

Preston Mill

been recorded for grinding grain since the first century AD. This mill dates back to 1599. The local laird leased it to a miller who had a monopoly of grinding in the area. Even querns were banned by law. This thirlage, as it was called, was much resented as an imposition on the poor. When the grain arrived at the mill it was dried, then husked in the millstones and finally the kernels were ground. The distance between the millstones could be varied, depending on how fine or coarse the resultant meal or flour was required to be.

The mill came into the possession of the National Trust for Scotland in the 1950s. Although the machinery still turns, it no longer grinds grain. It is open Easter weekend and May to September, Monday to Saturday 1100-1300 and 1400-1700. Sunday hours are 1330-1600. In October it is open at weekends only 1330-1600. Last entry is 20 minutes before closing, morning and afternoon.

## East Linton and Preston

Linton derives from Linn Town, 'town on the waterfall/rapids'. Preston is from 'priest town'. This religious influence is attributed to St Baldred. Many names in this area recall St Baldred, such as St Baldred's Whirl, a pool in the River Tyne near Preston Chapel and St Baldred's Well. St Baldred is thought to have been a monk from Lindisfarne who worked in this area. When he died in AD756 the three parishes he ministered to, Tyningham, Auldhame and Preston, all vied for the honour of burying his body. The bishop counselled the feuding parishioners to pray. And lo and behold, next day when they returned to church they found three coffins, each with a body of St Baldred in it.

East Linton received its charter in 1127. In 1314 Edward II escaped from the Battle of Bannockburn via East Linton. In 1401 an English host under Henry Hotspur of Northumberland camped overnight at Preston. However in the morning, seeing the Scottish army from Edinburgh under the Master of Douglas unexpectedly approaching, they decamped and fled.

During the 'Rough Wooing' of the 1540s East Linton and its strategic bridge were in the hands of the English. This 'Rough Wooing' was when Henry VIII of England wished his son to become engaged to the infant Mary Queen of Scots. The Scots refused and Henry sent his armies to Scotland under his brother the Duke of Somerset, later Lord Protector of England, to enforce his will. Mary Queen of Scot's French mother, Mary of Guise, appealed to France for help. In 1549 East Linton was taken by the French who blew up the bridge.

In 1603 James VI passed through East Linton on his way to London to be crowned King of Britain. For the next 200 years the responsibility for the repair of the bridge was the subject of much dispute. In 1677 it became a toll bridge. It was eventually adequately reconstructed in 1763, some years after the 1750 Turnpike Act intended to improve the road network. In 1745 Johnny Cope passed through East Linton fleeing from his defeat at the Battle of Prestonpans by the Jacobites.

Apart from the bridge the area's main occupation was farming. This tied in with the river where water power was used to process the crops. There were flour and barley mills in East Linton. Across the water from Preston Mill was Houston Mill. Here George Rennie, the brother of John Rennie, the famed civil engineer, encouraged Andrew Meikle to invent, develop and patent the first threshing machine. Another one of East Lothian's 'agricultural improvers', George Rennie, also built a distillery in East Linton which used water power, local water and barley to create its end product. The distillery has now gone but East Linton's main business is still farming.

## The Walk

This is a walk of two halves. The first walk is a short walk of roughly one and a half miles, which could be done before lunch or after dinner. The second half is a walk of some four miles which could be done in the afternoon. Both parts of the walk start and finish at the pub.

### Part 1

Exit the Drovers arms and turn right. At the T-junction some 20 metres down, bear left along the B1377 signposted for Dunbar and Berwick-upon-Tweed. Follow this road right and left across the Tyne, passing Linn Cottage on the left. If you pause on the left of the road just before the bridge you will see the linn (waterfall or rapids) that gives East Linton its name. There are no pavements on this bridge so a modicum of care is needed. Between 100 and 150 metres past the bridge, at the end of the garage on your right, you will observe a sign on your left to Houston Mill and Houston Mill House. Go up here. If you care to continue along the B1377 past the turn off to Houston Mill for about 75 metres you will find a memorial to John Rennie, civil engineer, who was born on Phantassie Farm. This contains a baluster from his Waterloo Bridge 1817 – 1934.

After the Houston Mill sign walk some 50 metres up towards the enormous farm-stead. This is typical of many in East Lothian built towards the end of the last century at the height of this area's farming glory. Turn right along the front of the steading and left at its end. Then at the rear of the steading turn right. Shortly afterwards, as a track joins from the right, go left along it. The Phantassie Doocot is about 100 metres ahead of you. Phantassie Doocot is unusual in having a sheltered, sunny, south-fac-

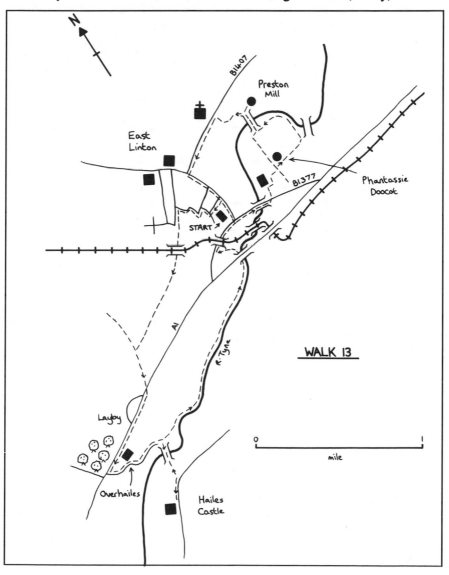

ing area at its entrance for the birds to sunbathe. This is a French style seldom seen in this country. Some 500 birds lived here. Some 50 metres before the doocot, at the end of the trees on your right, is a farm track also on the right. Go down here. Stay with this track until the footbridge over the River Tyne ahead of you.

Just before the bridge go left on the footpath that hugs the bank of the Tyne on your right. After around another quarter of a mile you arrive at another footbridge on your right, cross this. On the far side of the bridge take the right-hand path towards Preston Mill visible on the other side of the small field.

**Note:** When I was here there were two cows in this field which I thought were being a bit friendly. Later I realised that one was a bull. In Scotland it is not illegal to keep a bull in a field with a footpath through it. I feel that it should be. If you agree with me why not contact your MSP about this. If you are not happy about crossing this field then have a look at picturesque Preston Mill from the bridge and then continue in your previous direction along the river and away from the bridge for about 20 metres. There on your left you will find a road leading back to the Phantassie Doocot. From there you can retrace your steps to the Drovers Inn.

Alternatively, at the far side of the field (the one that had a bull) pass through a gate, over a bridge and into Preston Mill. There is a charge for visiting this NTS property. There is moving machinery here so please keep your children and dogs under control. Come out of Preston Mill grounds by the gate that you entered then turn right and walk along the edge of the meadow, with the fence on your right.

This leads to the end of the left-hand path from the footbridge across the Tyne. Go through the gate here and over a little footbridge. Follow the path on the other side left and right. As you approach the tarmac road a plaque on the wall on your right gives details about St Baldred. This path terminates in a T-junction with a tarmac road Turn left down the tarmac road, past the church and graveyard on your right. This church is from 1770, but the chancel at the east end is from the 13th century. This site is where St Thenew (St Enoch in Glasgow and mother of St Mungo) attended divine service. George Rennie, agricultural improver, is buried here.

As this road terminates in a T-junction, go left down High St. which becomes Bridge St. at the village green. There is an ornate fountain on the village green and lovely old houses on your left by the church. Keep down Bridge St., past the Crown Hotel on your right, to reach the Drovers Inn on your right. The Crown Hotel is an 18th-century historic building.

## Part 2

Come out of the Drovers Inn and go left up Bridge St. Around 50 metres up here turn left into Bank Rd. At a crossroads go slightly right and ahead towards the park in front of you, past the East Linton Bowling Club on your left. Once in the park, rapidly bear right along the tarmac path. Leave the park at its far end, cross School Road and bear slightly right to walk ahead along Walker Terrace. Follow this left and right to a T-junction. Turn left here and walk past McCall Gardens on your right. Then proceed across the grass afront you, keeping close to the fence on your right to find the bridge under the railway.

Once on the far side of the railway follow the well-used footpath ahead of you up-hill between the crop fields. This busy railway carries the main east coast line be-tween London and Edinburgh. Continue along this path for about half a mile, passing through four fields and crossing stiles when you come to them. I saw no side paths off this path. Behind you is the shark's fin shape of Berwick Law and the Bass Rock is a white lump to your right rear. At the sign marking the right of way (T-junction), turn left up the dirt track.

At the A1 go right along the pavement to the wood on the skyline. After about 100 metres this takes you into a lay-by off the A1, stay with the pavement. There is no pleasant diversion into the wood on your right here, it is used for archery practice, so unless it is your ambition to become a pincushion it is best to stay out of it. Follow the A1 for about a quarter of a mile after the lay-by ends until the wood on your right also ends. Cross the A1 here (carefully) and go left downhill on a tarmac road signposted for Hailes Castle. This road goes left and right through Over Hailes Farm and keeps on downhill, stay with it. Hailes Castle comes into sight in the Tyne valley below. Ahead of you as you go down here is Traprain Law. This was the ancient capital of the kingdom of Lothian and was inhabited for millennia. A treasure trove of Roman silver was discovered here in 1919. This is now in the Museum of Antiquities in Ed-inburgh. It is thought that the dwellers on Traprain Law were mainly metal workers who serviced the agricultural communities below.

At the bottom of the hill go left and take the right-hand fork labelled 'Pedestrian Route to Hailes Castle'. Go through the gate that says 'Hailes Mill' and turn right across the footbridge. This bridge crosses the Tyne by means of an eyot, or river is-land. At the far side of the bridge take the footpath straight ahead. Be careful of tall nettles here if you are wearing shorts or have bare arms. The public footpath brings you out at a small tarmac road, turn right along this although it actually looks like you are going straight ahead as the path meets the road on a bend. Keep on this road past a footpath on the left to reach Hailes Castle on the right. Entrance to the castle is free. It is open April to September 0930-1900, except Sundays when it is 1400-1900. Octo-ber to March it is open 0930-1600 except Sundays when the hours are 1400-1600. In-terpretative boards and information plaques tell you about the castle. Parts of this fortress date back to the 12th century. It had two pit dungeons. This was the ancient stronghold of the Hepburns, one of whom was Mary Queen of Scots' third husband. The castle controlled the road through the Tyne valley and the Hepburns grew rich on its tolls.

Retrace your steps to the Tyne and recross the footbridge. At the far end of the bridge you will see a sign pointing right 'Footpath to East Linton', follow this along the north bank of the Tyne. This path hugs the riverbank and leads you back to East Linton after some one and a half miles. Pass under the A1 but then this path comes to a dead end before the railway bridge across the Tyne. So bear left where the path forks at the right of way sign. This takes you a short distance up a minor road to a T-junction with the B1377. Here go right under the railway bridge. Immediately af-ter this, break left up Bridge Street, the Drovers is about 20 metres up on your left.

# 14. East Lothian: West Barns

**Route:** West Barns – Belhaven – Dunbar – Long Craigs – Belhaven Bay – John Muir
Country Park

**Distance:** 5.5 miles

**Map:** OS Landranger 67, Duns and Dunbar

**Start:** West Barns Inn

**Access:** By bus, there is a good service from Edinburgh to Dunbar on weekdays. On weekends the service, although not quite so good, is reasonable. Ask the driver to put you off at the West Barns Inn as the bus goes past its front door. Be careful as some buses leave from St Andrew's Square bus station and some depart from the west side of St Andrew's Square. There are also some limited-stop buses which are boarded from various stops in Princes St. For details pick up a leaflet at the bus shop at the bus station. Or ring 'Traveline' on 0800 232323 if in the Edinburgh area, if outwith Edinburgh call 0131 225 3858. You can also phone SMT Lowland Enquiry Line on 0131 663 9233.

By car, take the A1 eastwards out of Edinburgh. About 20 miles past its junction with the A720, city bypass, you will find signs guiding you left to Dunbar along the A1087. About a mile along this road brings you to West Barns, where the West Barns Inn is on your left. There is a small car park outside it. If this is full then go just past the pub and take the narrow road on your right **before** the post office From here signposts lead you around into a free car park across the A1087 from the West Barns Inn. There are steps from this leading to the A1087 directly opposite your hostelry.

---

## West Barns Inn. Tel: 01368 862314

The original West Barns Inn stood on the east side of the Biel Water. This was a coaching inn from the earliest days of coach travel. However this was demolished in the 1850s as the road was re-arranged and a new bridge built to accommodate the needs of a paper mill being constructed on the west side of the Biel Water. Around this time one of the local houses, in a grand old Scottish tradition, turned its lounge into a pub and traded as the West Barns Inn. At one point its licence was conditional on there always being a room ready for a traveller. This pub added another wee room used as a snug and stayed like this until the 1950s.

The nearby Belhaven Brewery acquired these premises and added a lounge which previously had been the shop next door. This lounge is now the public bar. What is now the lounge/dining room was the original bar. The fireplace in the lounge was exposed during renovation and is that from the house which became a pub in the 1850s, when the original West Barns Inn was demolished. A later owner added a skittle alley at the back, this is now a function suite.

Mine host David (Tug) Wilson was in the Royal Navy for 25 years, ending up as a Chief Petty Officer. Among the ships he served on were *HMS Eagle* (a carrier), *HMS Zulu* (a tribal class frigate) and *HMS Rothesay*, another frigate. So this explains the naval theme in the decor of both bar and lounge. Ships' clocks and barometers, the original plaque from the bridge of *HMS Rothesay*, lots of names of ships and ships' crests, items from messes, a navy rum measure, a commodore's hat, a ship's wheel, pictures of ships, model ships in the windows, ships' lamps, sailors' prayers, mariners' knots and an old diver's helmet are some of the diverse marine mementoes that make a unique atmosphere. A bell in the lounge can be rung to summon service, but you will only need to ring it once. I think that this was designed to be heard above a gale force wind.

Food is served 1200-1500, except on Sunday when it starts at 1230 and Wednesdays when no food is served at all. Evenings food is available from 1800-2100 except Wednesdays. On Wednesdays toasties only are available. There are no snacks served outwith these hours. The fish could not be more local as the trout and salmon (smoked) come from the Belhaven Trout Company across the road. There is a good selection of home-cooked food including vegetarian. There are high chairs for children should you need them.

Opening hours are 1100-2300 Monday to Wednesday, 1100-2400 Thursday, 1100-0100 Friday and Saturday and 1230-2400 on Sunday. There are two real ales. Appropriately near the home of Belhaven, both are Belhaven. These are Belhaven 80/- and Belhaven Five Nations. The keg products include Belhaven Light, Belhaven Best, Guinness, Stella Artois, Tennents Lager and Strongbow. There is a beer garden where walkers can take their ale.

In winter there are two real fires, the one in the lounge is the original one from the house that became a pub in the 1850s. Sweets are on sale. Every early Sunday evening there is live Scottish accordion and fiddle music. There is also live music on Saturday nights. Credit cards are accepted.

## John Muir Country Park

This 733-hectare country park was established in 1976. It is named after John Muir who was born in Dunbar in 1838 and emigrated to the USA in 1849. After various adventures he settled in California and became pre-eminent in the fields of geology, nature writing and climbing. He was noted for tramping through the Sierras of California for days at a time carrying nothing more than a tin mug and a pocketful of tea. He became a friend of President Theodore Roosevelt and used this friendship to establish America's and indeed the world's first National Parks, including Yosemite. He died in 1914 and is remembered by Muir Woods where his favourite giant redwoods or sequoias predominate. It is not stretching things too far to call him the Father of Conservation.

The country park has a range of environmental types: cliffs, meadowland, dunes, salt-marsh, woodland and heathland. Over 400 species of plant grow here. Sea aster (like a garden michaelmas daisy) and thrift or sea pink with its masses of pink flowers in the spring are typical of the salt-marsh. Biting stonecrop grows on the shore, its thick fleshy leaves reducing water loss in this arid environment. It has five-petalled yellow flowers in summer. The biting aspect of its name refers to the sharp taste of the leaves. On the dunes a characteristic plant is birdsfoot trefoil. Known as bacon and eggs because of its red/orange/yellow flowers, the seed pods resemble a bird's foot. On the edge of the wood, meadow cranesbill is common. This member of the geranium family has a five-petalled blue/purple flower in summer. Its name derives from the shape of its fruiting bodies which resemble the beak of a crane.

## Dunbar Castle

This castle is known to have existed as far back as AD858 when it was razed by Kenneth II. In 1072 Malcolm Canmore gave it to Patrick, Earl of Northumberland, a member of his family. Thus the Cospatrick Earls of March and Dunbar began. This was one the earliest castles to be equipped with cannons and is the oldest of all surviving castles in Europe to have been so equipped. In 1296 Edward I of England took this castle. In 1314 his son Edward II fled from here after his defeat at Bannockburn.

In 1338 the Countess of March and Dunbar, Black Agnes, was being besieged by the English and running out of supplies. Troops from the Bass Rock then sailed ships into Dunbar harbour at night, past blockading English vessels, and resupplied them. The Bass Rock troops then returned undetected. Next morning Black Agnes sent an invitation to breakfast to the English commanders, Arundel and Salisbury. Discouraged, the English lifted the siege and left.

The Cospatrick Earls of March and Dunbar played both ends against the middle once too often and were deprived of the castle in the 15th century. It then remained a royal stronghold until the reign of Mary Queen of Scots in the 1560s. She made her third husband the Earl of Bothwell the castellan. The Confederate Lords who removed Mary Queen of Scots from power then partially destroyed the castle and removed its guns to Edinburgh Castle.

The ruins of Dunbar Castle

In the 1650s Oliver Cromwell had this castle virtually levelled to the ground. The stones were used to build the harbourage facilities of Dunbar. It was known as Cromwell's Harbour. Today only a shattered outline of the castle remains to mark eight centuries of turbulent history. The ruins are unsafe to visit.

## The Walk

This is a butterfly-shaped walk. The body of the butterfly stretches from the pub that you start from to the footbridge over the Biel Water and the walks are around the peripheries of the butterfly's wings. So you could do one wing or both, perhaps one in the morning and one in the afternoon or one in the afternoon and one in the evening. You can also do this walk all at once There are lots of choices.

To do the western wing of this walk only, do not cross the footbridge over the Biel Water when you return to it after the John Muir Country Park. Instead walk up the west side of the Biel Water, away from the sea on the footpath to where you left it on your way out. Then retrace your steps to the pub. To do the eastern wing of this walk on its own, reverse directions from the end of the walk section and when you reach the footbridge over the Biel Water for the second time do not cross it but retrace your steps to the pub.

Anyone intending to complete the walk in one session should follow these directions. Turn right out of the West Barns Inn along the A1087. After about 50 metres cross the Biel Water on the road bridge. Just before the bridge on your left is the Belhaven Trout Company, which has a smokery and shop. The shop sells fresh and smoked trout and smoked salmon. Opening hours are 1000-1700 seven days a week. Immediately over the bridge you will find a gap in the dyke on your right. This leads to a well-marked footpath. Walk up this footpath on the right-hand, western, side of the Biel Water. After roughly 150 metres you arrive at a grassy cart track going left away from the Biel Water through crop fields. This is your route. After the field you emerge on a piece of tarmac with the car park for the John Muir Country Park on your left front. Go straight ahead on the grassy path, keeping the car park on your left. Bypass a path to the left. Walk past the barbecue pits on your right towards the shark's fin shape of the public conveniences showing above the grassy dunes.

When you reach the information board about the park on your left walk past this and the children's play area on your left, ignoring a path going left. There are peacock butterflies around here, so-called because of the eye marking on each forewing. About 20 metres past the information board bear left into the pine plantation, following the white arrow and horse's hoof signs on a post. Here you will see the first of many plants of viper's bugloss. It has five-petalled blue bell-shaped flowers and hairy stems with black spots on them. It is a plant of dry, bare spaces, which likes light soils, especially chalk and gravel. It does not occur all that frequently in Scotland, but when it does, it does in profusion.

Follow this broad path left and right through an open glade. Stay with this path, being guided by the horse's hoof signs for some three-quarters of a mile and bypassing paths to left and right. The edge of the plantation is about 30 metres to your left. This pine wood has a good under-storey of, for example, elder trees three to four metres tall. This allows more life into the forest as birds can feed on the berries of the elder trees. This is typical of seaside pine forest.

At the end of the trees is another interpretative board and the estuary of the River Tyne ahead of you. When I was there a man was exercising a trotting horse in its racing rig on the firm sands of this estuary. This sport is quite popular in this part of Scotland. At the board turn right before the footbridge and follow the coastline with the pines on your right. In the grass here you will find pink mounds of wild thyme. Brush a little in your fingers to get the characteristic scent. Continue along this path at the edge of the pines and sometimes among them with the sea to your left. After a couple of hundred metres go left at a fork. Stick with this path as it bends gradually right, ignoring paths to the right, and keeping close company with the coast. At the end of the forest walk along a sandy path with forest on your right and sand dunes on your left. The sea fades away into salt-marsh and mud flats behind the dunes. Look out for the burnet moth here that's featured on the front of John Muir Country Park literature. This day-flying moth has green wings with six red spots on each one. A patch of deciduous woodland on the left here is sea buckthorn. It has grey/green narrow leaves like those of willows. Orange berries in summer and, surprisingly, thorns! This salt tolerant plant has the ability to fix loose flowing soil in place. For this reason it is often used by conservationists along with marram grass, a similar type of plant, to hold dunes in position. Ignore paths to left and right. This is a glorious spot full of flowers and fragrance.

As the pines end on your right, keep directly forwards. Walk past the public toilets on your left and immediately past the barbecue pits also on your left. Take a grassy path half left ahead. Stay on this path along the top of the little ridge and pass paths left and right. This broadens out into a dirt track. When this track bears right into fields, your route lies ahead along the crest of the little ridge. At a gap in the ridge, drop down on its seaward side where a wall appears on your right. Then re-ascend the ridge and the path now leads you around to the right between the Biel Water on your left and the wall on your right. Follow this path along the right-hand (western) side of the Biel Water for about a quarter of a mile then cross the footbridge over the Biel Water. Go left on the track on the left-hand, eastern, side of the river. (Left-hand and right-hand in context of the Biel Water refer to it as seen from the sea.)

Follow this track around to the right. This leads you onto a kind of causeway between a loch on your right and Belhaven Bay on your left. This should really be called Bielhaven Bay so the beer should be called Bielhaven, but you would get some funny looks if you went into a pub and asked for a pint of Bielhaven. The oystercatchers along here are reasonably tame, which allows a quite close inspection. Despite their name they do not catch oysters but feed on smaller shellfish such as mussels. They have two ways of doing this, either by hammering the mollusc against rocks to shatter its shell or by using their beaks like a jemmy to force the two half shells apart. Studies have shown that each individual oystercatcher uses the method that its parents taught it. On your left here is the Bass Rock like a giant wedding cake in the sea. frosted white with gannets and their guano. In spring/summer at least

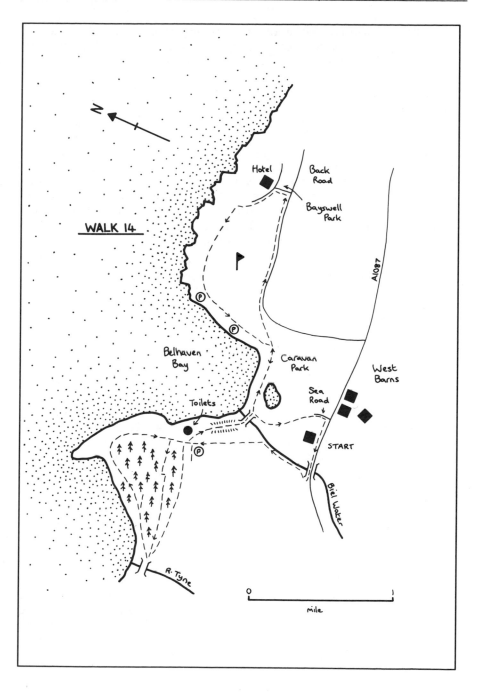

WALK 14

Hotel

Back
Road

Bayswell
Park

A1087

Belhaven
Bay

Caravan
Park

West
Barns

Toilets

Sea
Road

START

P

P

P

Biel Water

R. Tyne

0                    1

mile

13,000 pairs of gannets nest here. The proper name for these birds is *Sula Bassana*. The sula refers to one of their common names – the solan goose. The bassana refers to the Bass Rock. Some two thirds of the world's gannets nest in the UK. This colony is recorded as being here as far back as 1518.

Go past the loch and then a caravan site on your right. This site is where a local brewery and distillery used to be. Around 100 metres before this track makes a T-junction with a tarmac road, go left over a step stile. Bear half right through the park, missing two gaps in the hedge on your right to arrive at a third. Here you will see a sign pointing right to Winterfield Park and the town centre. Follow this sign up Back Road. Walk along this road for around three-quarters of a mile past the roads to the tennis courts and putting greens, both on your left. Then go sharply left up Bayswell Park. Some 50 metres up here, at a T-junction with the Bayswell Park Hotel opposite, you break left and stay with this road as it veers to the right. This takes you to a path with a wall on your left and the sea on your right. On your right here are the ruins of Dunbar Castle at the edge of Dunbar Harbour.

**The next stretch is along the top of dangerous cliffs so keep your children and dogs under control. You will be perfectly safe as long as you stay on the path.**

Straight ahead of you as you walk on the edge of the cliffs is Traprain Law, the obvious rounded hill, the capital of the ancient Kingdom of Lothian. Walk along the clifftops for the next half a mile or so. There are interpretative boards looking like giant mushrooms that supply information about the geology and wildlife of the area. There are terns along here. They look like wee white gulls but they have white tail streamers. This gives them the nickname of sea swallows. Below on isolated skerries are dark green cormorants holding their wings out to dry.

At the end of the concrete path go left through a gap in the railings, down steps and follow the path along the edge of the shore. Walk around the periphery of the golf course. The small grey/brown birds flitting about the shore here are rock pipits, distinguished by the longitudinal whiteish feathers on the outer edges of their tails.

Eventually this path brings you out at a small tarmac car park. Stroll straight through this and bypass the picnic table to the left. Then proceed through a gap in the fence at the end of a brick path and hang left on a grassy path, accompanying the railings on your left. This leads to another car park. Wander to the opposite side of this and down a rough track which peters out after some 30 metres. Then keep the picnic tables on your right and aim ahead for a gap in the bushes. Once through this head diagonally right to find the step stile. Over this go right along the causeway and retrace your steps to the footbridge over the Biel Water.

Walk past the footbridge and along a path on the eastern, left-hand side of the Biel Water. This soon bears away from the river on a rough road between mortared dykes, drystone dykes appear to be uncommon in this area of East Lothian. This leads straight on to a tarmac road, Sea Road. This terminates in a T-junction with the main road, A1087. Here go right along the A1087. The West Barns Inn is about 125 metres along this on your right.

# 15. West Lothian: Almondell Country Park

**Route:** Linhouse Water – Murieston Water – Visitor Centre – Old Railway Viaduct

**Distance:** 6.5 miles

**Map:** OS Landranger 65, Falkirk and Linlithgow

**Start:** Torphichen Arms, Mid Calder

**Access:** By bus, there is a reasonable bus service from Edinburgh to Mid Calder. On weekdays it is approximately two buses an hour. On Sundays it is an hourly service. Ask to be put off at the Torphichen (said 'torficken') Arms. For bus information ring SMT Lowland Enquiry Line on 0131 663 9233. You can also call 'Traveline' on 0800 232323 if calling from Edinburgh or on 0131 225 3858 if calling from outside Edinburgh. Alternatively, collect a timetable from the bus shop at St Andrew's Square bus station.

By car, take the A71 out of Edinburgh for Livingston. About four and a quarter miles past the A71's junction with the A720, city bypass, turn right off the A71 onto the B7015. Approximately two and a quarter miles along this road, having passed through the village of East Calder, you cross a bridge over the Linhouse Water. Roughly 50 metres after this bridge you will see the Torphichen Arms on your left, a tall white building. The car park is immediately past the pub on your left.

## Torphichen Arms. Tel: 01506 880020

This came into existence as a coaching inn in 1763, when a turnpike (toll) road was established through the village of Mid Calder. Previously runners had taken the mail by a different route through Blackburn, West Lothian. Mid Calder was the first stop for coaches leaving Edinburgh to various destinations. A pend (enclosed yard) across the road previously contained the stables. This is now private housing.

The inn would have done good business from coaches. In 1838 the Revd John Summers noted the frequency of services. Besides the mail and daily coaches between Glasgow and Edinburgh, a daily coach also ran between Edinburgh and Ayr. On alternate days a coach ran from Edinburgh to Hamilton. In addition to which there was a daily coach service from Edinburgh to Lanark in the summer months which went to an every other day service in winter. A coach also went from Mid Calder to Edinburgh each Wednesday.

When this coaching inn opened it was known as the Lemon Tree. Earlier this century it was called the Top Shop. The present name refers to the local laird, Lord Torphichen. It has vaulted cellars, now boxed in, which before the advent of washing machines were used as a washhouse. The ceilings inside the bar were also high, giving the pub an airy feel. What it will be like I cannot say as it was due for internal renovation when I was there. All I can say is that it had a certain seedy splendour. The outside has had a recent face-lift and is very attractive.

Also attractive is the fact that there are five real ales on tap, of which three are guests. The regulars are Caledonian 80/- and Burtons. Keg products include Calders 70/-, Calders Cream Ale, Calders Special, Carlsberg Lager, Stella Artois and Guinness. Opening hours are Monday to Saturday 1100-2400 and on Sunday from 1230-2400. They have a children's certificate until 2000.

Food is served on weekdays from 1200 to 1430, Friday and Saturday from 1200-2000 and on Sunday from 1230 to 2000. The food is good standard pub fare. If you are an OAP they do reduced price pensioner meals. Should you be a party of ten or more and wish food outside their normal serving hours, if you phone a week in advance then they will be happy to lay on food for you. Pizzas and toasties are available all the time.

Landlady Helen Hill welcomes walkers and walking and cycling groups already use this pub. There is a beer garden, fruit machines and pool table. Pre-renovation there were pictures of Mid Calder in earlier days on the wall.

## The Bridges of Almondell

Almondell is the old name for the valley of the River Almond. Nowadays this part of it is Almondell and Calderwood Country Park. This country park is 92 hectares in extent. This became a designated country park in 1971. Previously the Almondell portion of it was owned by the Earl of Buchan.

Much of the interesting history of this park revolves around the Erskine family who owned this land for centuries. In 1790 Henry Erskine, who was Lord Advocate of Scotland, designed and had erected a country house here. He should have stuck to the law. The house was poorly designed and put up and caused continual problems. In 1969 it was blown up by the Army as it was in a very dangerous condition. The old coach house and stable block is now the visitor centre.

Henry Erskine's brother, the 11th Earl of Buchan, lived a couple of miles away in Broxburn. In 1776 he built a scale model of the solar system in the grounds of his house. The calculations enabling him to do this were carved on a stone column. The scale model has been lost but the crumbling stone column was rescued and repaired and today stands outside the visitor centre. This pillar has a dedication on it to James Buchanan, professor of mathematics at Glasgow University, engraved personally by the Earl. The north face gives the column's latitude and longitude, height above sea level and distances from various places. On the east face is a précis of the mathematics and arithmetic that he used to establish the correct distances on his scale model of the solar system. The scale was 12 283 miles and 28/100 to an inch. The model contained the sun and all the planets as far out as Saturn, including rings. These were all the planets known in those days. The earth was 198 metres from the sun in the model.

Also unique to Almondell is its collection of bridges. There must be few, if indeed any other, places where you can walk across such a selection of footbridges in such a short space of time and distance:

* The **Nelson Mandela Bridge** is a 19-metre-high, cable-stayed, A-frame suspension bridge erected by the Royal Engineers in 1970. The parts were flown in by helicopter. This bridge has been awarded civic trust and structural steel design awards.

* The **Dell Bridge** was built in 1784 under the auspices of the 11th Earl of Buchan's wife. This bridge and nearby Fraser Stone commemorate her ancestor, Sir Simon Fraser, who helped Robert the Bruce in the Wars of Independence.

* The **Naysmith Bridge** was erected by Alexander Naysmith, the celebrated painter. Naysmith, who painted the only portrait of Robert Burns that has provenance, should have stuck to painting. This bridge, although very attractive, was unstable until renovated in 1997. This was, needless to say, his only bridge.

* The **Aqueduct** was built in 1820 by the engineer Hugh Baird, who built the Union Canal. Among his workers were Burke and Hare, the bodysnatchers. This aqueduct carries the canal feeder across the river to fill up the canal where it crosses the Almond Valley. The feeder needs to cross the river here to hold the high ground as the river is some 23 metres below the canal aqueduct. The canal needs some 10,000,000 litres of water a day to keep it topped up. The Cobbinshaw Reservoir, some ten miles away in the Pentlands, was created to be a reserve water supply for the Union Canal. You can walk across this cast-iron trough bridge which is cantilevered on stone supports. The nearest any of us will get to walking on water!

* The **Viaduct** was built in 1885 by the North British Railway Company. It has nine arches, is 23 metres above the river and is made of brick. Perhaps the same type of bricks were later transported across it from the brickworks in nearby Camps. It was always a freight-only railway and supplied the quarries, limeworks and the local shale oil industry. The line closed in 1956 but the bridge is still accessible to pedestrians.

## The Walk

This walk forms a figure of eight with the pub at the centre. This opens up lots of possibilities. You could do one loop in the morning and one in the afternoon or one loop in the afternoon and one in a summer's evening etc., etc. You could do one loop one day and the other on another day or just choose to do one loop only. The choice is yours.

## First Loop

Come out of the Torphichen Arms and turn right towards the road bridge. After about 20 metres turn right downhill on a footpath. This path forks but rejoins at the bottom of the hill so take whichever one you fancy. At the bottom ignore the footbridge to the left and go straight ahead across the other footbridge. You are now walking on the tongue of land between the Linhouse Water on your left and the Murieston Water on your right. About 20 metres along on your left, the houses across the Linhouse Water have lovely, terraced gardens. Keep on the beaten earth footpath leading away from the footbridge you have just crossed to pass a couple of ponds on your right. Ignore minor grassy footpaths going off to the left and right. In the spring this area has great drifts of azure from the bluebells in the grass.

For the next mile and a quarter you just follow this path, keeping the valley of the Linhouse Water on your left. It periodically disappears behind mounds but then re-appears. The only point where you might feel lost is where the path bears right across an open area. This is about 300 metres after the footbridge. Just follow the path towards the right-hand of the two pylons visible ahead of you and you will rejoin the valley of the Linhouse Water. The pylons roughly mark your halfway point before you turn back.

This is Calderwood and it is fascinating to find such a large area of wild wood in an industrial area such as this. The shale mines have many horizontal shafts criss-crossing the ground under here. Calderwood is deliberately left to be natural. This trees here include gean (wild cherry) and hazel, so you may be able to eat as you go. Natural unprocessed hazelnuts on a tree look rather like hops.

As you approach a line of telegraph poles cutting directly across your line of travel, look for a beaten earth footpath going right just before a line of trees. This will be about 30 metres before the telegraph poles. Go along this path until it starts to bear left about 150 metres along. Go right at this point along the obvious path keeping the valley of the Murieston Water on your left. Again, just keep the river valley on your left for the next mile or so. The riverbank is sometimes nearby and sometimes fades away to the left but never goes very far away or for very long. The line of pylons again represent a halfway point. The path becomes broader and better defined as you go along it. As the houses of the village of Mid Calder come into sight ahead the path forks, Take the right-hand path over the little knoll. Once over the knoll follow the path straight ahead towards the road whose traffic you can now glimpse and hear. Where this path terminates in a T-junction with a beaten earth path turn left down towards the river valley, ignoring minor paths to the left and right of you. Stay on the path as it goes left to the footbridge. Cross the bridge and go uphill (either path as before) to the road. Turn right along the road. The Torphichen Arms is on your left here should you require refreshment. For those doing the walk without stopping, follow the instructions in the second loop from the point where they bypass the footpath to the right immediately after departing the Torphichen Arms.

## Second Loop

Come out of the Torphichen Arms and turn right towards the road bridge, walking

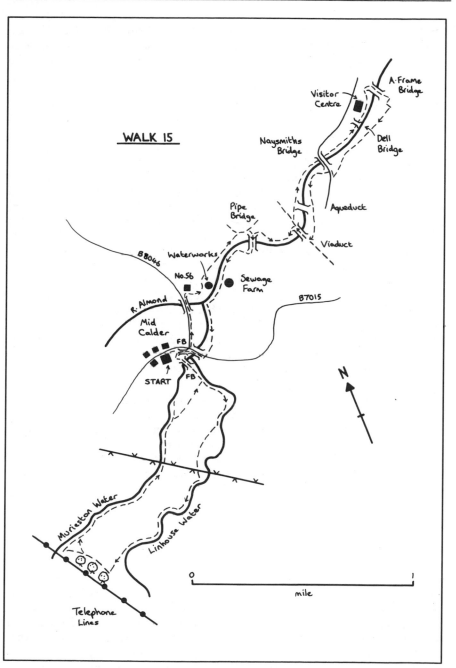

WALK 15

A·Frame Bridge

Visitor Centre

Naysmiths Bridge

Dell Bridge

Pipe Bridge

Aqueduct

Waterworks

Viaduct

B8046

No.56

Sewage Farm

R. Almond

B7015

Mid Calder

FB

START

FB

N

Murieston Water

Linhouse Water

Telephone Lines

0                                   1

mile

past a footpath descending to the right. About 20 metres before the road bridge take the road on the left signposted for Pumpherston and Uphall, B 8046. Cross the River Almond by the road bridge and immediately after the bridge turn right down the drive just before number 56. At the end of the drive you will find a sign saying 'Powies Path to Pumpherston', a nice bit of alliteration. Follow this. Keep on this somewhat overgrown, but discernible, footpath to the left of the waterworks installation and through what looks like giant rhubarb but is actually butterbur, a member of the daisy family. At the top of the wee brae, turn right along the edge of the field. Continue along the field margin for about a quarter of a mile with the trees on your near right. At a T-junction with a farm track go right along the track. The cart track then bears left and about 40 metres after this bend there is a gate on your right with a footpath leading down from it. Follow this down steps. Walk past the footbridge on your right, keeping the River Almond and the canal feeder on your right. Keep on this path as it twists right and left via a pedestrian bridge over the canal feeder. This path now takes you up the riverside and under the railway viaduct to the visitor centre. On the way you bypass the canal feeder bridge (unless you want to walk on water) and the Naysmith Bridge which is very attractive. Stay walking along the footpath by the river, ignoring the tarmac road coming off Naysmith Bridge. A couple of hundred metres past Naysmith Bridge you cross the Dell Bridge. Shortly after this you arrive at the visitor centre. Opening hours are Monday, Tuesday and Thursday 0930-1700; Wednesday 0930-1600; Saturday 1000-1700 and Sunday 1000-1730. It is closed on Fridays. The telephone number is 01506 882254. There is an interesting selection of information about the park and wildlife. However, the main attraction is the astronomical pillar – details about which can be found in the Bridges of Almondell introduction to this walk.

Continue up the riverside past the toilets and walled gardens on your left. Some of the fruit trees and bushes here once satisfied the Erskine family's appetites. Soon after this turn right across the unique, A-frame Nelson Mandela bridge. About 30 metres after crossing the bridge go uphill to the right on a path with steps and railings. This path takes you left and right uphill. Then follow this broad, beaten earth path along the top of the Almond Valley with the river on your right. At the minor tarmac road across the path turn right downhill towards Naysmith Bridge. Just on the nearside of Naysmith Bridge take the tarmac footpath on the left. Then bear left on to a gravel path along the edge of the trees. In the spring this path is almost smothered in wild garlic, also called ramsons, these are edible. Ramsbottom in Lancashire gets its name from being shortened from Ramsonbottom, 'valley of the wild garlic'.

Where the canal feeder crosses the river, go left **across** the canal feeder on a little bridge, still staying on the river's left bank. Follow this path leftish up steps and stay on it up and down and over a footbridge, still keeping the river on your right until you reach the old railway viaduct. Turn right across the viaduct. At the far end of the viaduct take the steps on your left descending into the Almond valley. At the bottom of the steps walk to the right away from the viaduct, the river should now be on your left. Then go over the footbridge over the canal feeder and turn right.

Along here you may come across great willowherb. Its large pink flowers can be an inch in diameter and its faint fragrance gets it the name 'codlins and cream'. A codlin was an old type of apple of tapering shape. Further along here cross another footbridge back over the canal feeder and then go left over a large footbridge to cross both the canal feeder and river. Having crossed the bridge, go right to follow a well-delineated footpath with the river on your right. Bypass the sewage works on your left, not at all odiferous. Just before the next footbridge go left downhill on steps with rails beside them. Keep along the riverside between the river on your right and a fence on your left. This path is not too clear at first but there is nowhere else to go. As you approach the road bridge over the river the path becomes clearer. The river here is no longer the Almond, that has veered off on the far side of the water, this is the Linhouse Water.

About 20 metres before the road bridge, the path forks. Take the right-hand fork and descend the steps to the river's edge. **Take care as these are not the best of steps.** At the bottom follow the path ahead under the road bridge and along the riverside for about 20 metres then ascend a footbridge up stone steps to cross the river. At the track about 10 metres past the footbridge turn right uphill on it. At the road at the top of this the Torphichen Arms is on your near left.

# 16. Edinburgh: Currie

**Route:** Currie Brig – Blinkbonny – Lymphoy – Malleny House – Balerno – Water of Leith Walkway

**Distance:** 4 miles

**Map:** OS Landranger 66, Edinburgh or OS Landranger 65, Falkirk and Linlithgow

**Start:** Riccarton Arms, Currie

**Access** : By bus, both First Edinburgh (0131 663 9233) and Lothian Regional Transport (0131 555 6363) run frequent services through Currie to Balerno. Alternatively, ring 'Traveline' on 0800 232323 if in the Edinburgh area, if outside the Edinburgh area ring 0131 225 3858. Ask to be put off at Currie Brig. The Riccarton Arms is just across the road.

By car, take the A70 (Slateford Road/Lanark Road) out of Edinburgh. Once over the A720 city bypass it is about a mile and a half to the Riccarton Arms. Go through Juniper Green into Currie and the Riccarton Arms is on your right opposite a set of railings on your left. The car park entrance is on your right immediately before the pub.

---

## Riccarton Arms Hotel, Currie. Tel: 0131 449 2230

This is one of the oldest structures in Currie. It is over a century old and a listed building. It started life as a farm, Wester Currie Farm. It was also called Riccarton Farm House. This name comes from the local estate. The Riccarton estate used to own the land to the north of the Water of Leith.

This farm functioned both as a farm and as an inn. Around 1870 it became a full-time inn and gave up farming. At this point contemporary accounts record 15 natural history students getting a hearty breakfast at the Riccarton Arms. It was a coaching inn and had a bell on the wall outside to signal your arrival with. The stables were across what is now the car park. Horse hitching hooks are still on the wall of a storeroom. These coaches went to Lanark among other places. Today they serve the needs of walkers as the Water of Leith Walkway passes within 100 metres of their door.

Walkers will find good food here, mainly Scottish fare but with Italian, Mexican and Cajun also on the menu. Seafood is a speciality. All the vegetables used are local. The whole range of food is covered: starters, main courses, sweets, jacket potatoes, sandwiches and pizzas. Vegetarians are not forgotten. The food is all home cooked apart from the pizzas, which go from freezer to microwave. Food serving times are 1200-1500 and 1800-2100 Monday to Saturday. Sunday's hours are 1230-1500 and 1800-2100. Outside these hours only pizzas are available. However, if you are a party of at least five and you intend to arrive out of normal food serving hours, if you phone them a couple of days in advance they will lay something on for you.

Opening hours are Monday to Thursday 1100-2300, Friday 1100-2400, Saturday 1100-2345 and Sunday 1230-2300. They pride themselves on the excellence of their cask conditioned ale. In fact, if you are not completely satisfied with your pint landlord Steven Bremner will exchange your ale for another **and** refund your money. I had no opportunity to take them up on this offer. There are three real ales, Caledonian 80/-, Deuchars IPA and Marstons Pedigree. Kegs include Calders 70/-, Carlsberg Lager, Calders Cream, Stella Artois and Guinness.

It is a lovely old country pub and well worth a visit. There is some attractive wrought-iron work and leaded lights by the bar. Other decor includes numerous certificates won by the staff for bar management and customer relations. Behind the fruit machine is a picture of Gibson Craig, a local laird from two centuries ago. Other facilities include a flagged darts area and a cigarette machine. There is jazz on the last Thursday of every month. There is a real fire in winter. Children are welcome and there is a beer garden. Credit cards are accepted.

## The Water of Leith

At the onset of the Ice Age the glaciers rumbled remorselessly south and east from the Highlands. As they hit the solid mass of the Pentlands they were deflected north and south. Thus they scooped out the deep valley that the Water of Leith runs down today. Glacial melt water running off at the end of the Ice Age deepened this valley still further and so the steeply descending, clear running stream that is today's Water of Leith was produced.

It is as clear water today as it was in 1617 when an Act of the Scottish Parliament defined a pint jug as that holding three pounds and seven ounces troy weight of water of the pure water of the Water of Leith. However, sewerage and industrial effluent led Robert Louis Stevenson in the 19th century to describe it as, 'That dirty Water of Leith'. In 1894 the first Royal Commission on Water Pollution found it to be the worst river in Britain for pollution. Since 1896 much work has been put into cleaning the river and today the Water of Leith measures eight or nine on the Trent Biotic index. This measures the diversity of life found in water and has a maximum score of ten. Another mark of the health of the river is the number of fish it supports. These apex predators of streams signify much healthy life at the base of the pyramid of prey and predation. You can get trout of up to three pounds in weight from the Water of Leith.

There are 12 miles of free fishing between Leith and Balerno. The fishing is administered by the Honorary Bailiffs of the Water of Leith whose office dates back to at least 1606. These bailiffs raise funds to restock the river with fish. In olden times, millers along the river trapped salmon and sea trout by their mills to feed their families and/or supplement their incomes.

The Water of Leith, trapped in its narrow valley and falling rapidly (between Balerno and Juniper Green in six miles it falls 130 metres), is ideal for milling. In 1854 the power generated in this six-mile section alone was 450 horsepower. There were once 80 to 90 mills along this river. However, the narrow valley prevented large scale industrialisation. In the Middle Ages the mills were mainly corn and waulk (paper processing) mills. In the 19th century there were 39 mills along the course of the river, these processed mainly corn but also pepper, snuff, spices, paper and barley.

The average catchment area rainfall is 37 inches. Roughly half of this is removed by the river. The rest is accounted for by abstraction, transpiration (plant sweating) and evaporation.

## The Walk

Depart the Riccarton Arms and turn left along the main road outside it, the A70. About 50 metres along here cross the road and descend right down Kirkgate. At the bottom ahead of you, just inside the grounds of a private dwelling, are the ruins of the kiln of the mill that once was here. Currie first developed as a milling hamlet in the 1300s. The mill this kiln served was here from at least 1506. This mill produced oatmeal, the staple foodstuff of the day.

Bear left across Currie Brig, traversing the Water of Leith. This very old bridge dates back to 1378. In November 1666 across this bridge rode Tam Dalziel o' the Binns, the Beast of Muscovie, and his troops to defeat the Covenanters at the Battle of Rullion Green on the other side of the Pentlands, according to contemporary accounts. The bridge's forbidding appearance gave rise to the local saying 'As dark as Currie Brig'.

Continue under the old railway line footpath bridge and where the road forks go straight ahead, ascending by stairs a path into the churchyard. Currie Kirk dates back to 1785. Before this a church was here in memorial of St Kentigern in 1296. Previous to that a list of church authorities here goes back to 1140. Ante-dating even this, the Celtic Church had a cell here in AD570 dedicated to St Kentigern (St Mungo). There are many Celtic tombstones here.

At the church follow

The old kiln of Currie Mill

the path right and left uphill. Bypass a branch of this footpath going right to a tarmac road and ascend through the graveyard. Pass through a gap in a wall and at the far end of the graveyard this path terminates in a T-junction with a minor tarmac road. Go left on this road. Keep on this quiet country lane between hedges as it goes left downhill at Moidart House on your left. Go past where Braeburn Drive comes in from the right. About 100 metres after this the road bends to the right. Here go left on a path flanked by fences that descends a set of steps. This is immediately before a sign pointing left to the Water of Leith Walkway. Around 100 metres down here turn left over a footbridge and follow the path along the contour of the hillside. This footbridge crosses Poet's Glen, named after local poet James Thompson who was contemporaneous with Robert Burns.

Follow this thin path for roughly 200 metres and then take one of the narrow paths on your right down to the broad tarmac path of the Water of Leith Walkway on your right. Bear left along the walkway. The Cockburn Association (1875) tries to improve and preserve the valley of the Water of Leith. It was influential in getting the Water of Leith Walkway laid out. In 1976 the Water of Leith Walkway Trust was formed to enable the path.

Continue along what becomes a wide, beaten earth path. Just before this crosses a tarmac road by a footbridge, take the steps down to the right. Turn left along the tarmac road under the bridge and where the road splits, go on the road to the right of Currie Kirk. Some 20 metres past where this road bends left uphill at Currie Baptist Church on the corner on your right, take the dirt road on the right marked 'Lymhoy Estate, No Parking'.

Go along here past footpaths to the left and right. On your right just along here is a memorial to General Sir Thomas Scott of Malleny. Walk along this road for roughly a mile and a half and past Lymphoy Stables on your right. Ignore footpaths left and right and stick with the track. At the end of this track a cart track goes left and two dirt roads go to the right. Take the first of the dirt roads on the right. Down here past Riccarton Croft the road becomes tarmac. Past the Croft, some 100 metres on your left is the entrance to Malleny Gardens. Malleny House goes back to at least 1478. The Scotts of Malleny were here for around six generations. The gardens are under the care of the National Trust for Scotland and are open to the public. The house specialities are rhododendrons and shrub roses. The best displays are in the second half of the year.

After Malleny Gardens, walk down the rough road over the Bavelaw Burn and past the grounds of Currie RFC on your right. This track bends left to terminate in a T-junction with a tarmac road, Bavelaw Green. A track goes right/ahead just before this T-junction, ignore it. Proceed to the right along Bavelaw Green for approximately 100 metres until it ends at a T-junction with Bridge Rd. Go right here. Pass by Balerno Community High School on your right. About 50 metres past the school, on your left is a sign pointing right for Water of Leith Walkway. Descend the broad, beaten earth/gravel footpath. On your right here, bounded by walkway, river and school, is a wildlife garden laid out by the pupils and community.

Proceed on past a set of steps on your left. Stick with this path with the river on

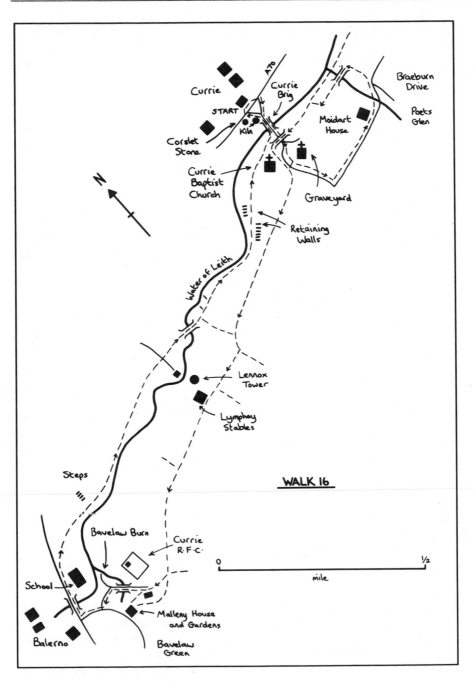

Currie

A70

Currie Brig

START

Kiln

Corslet Stone

Currie Baptist Church

Moidart House

Braeburn Drive

Poets Glen

Graveyard

Retaining Walls

N

Water of Leith

Lennox Tower

Lymphoy Stables

Steps

WALK 16

Bavelaw Burn

Currie R.F.C.

School

Malleny House and Gardens

Balerno

Bavelaw Green

0                                    ½

mile

your right. You may see grey wagtails here. These blackbird-sized birds have grey backs and yellow chests. The name wagtail is very apt. This is thought to be a means of communication that overcomes the noise of running water. Also along here you will find wood sorrel. This has three leaves like clover, but the leaves are double-lobed. It is delicious. In autumn you may find edible fungi in this section of the walk. These include oyster mushrooms, growing out of wood, that you often see on supermarket shelves and the blueish purple edible wood blewit. It is best not to pick any fungi unless accompanied by an expert, people die this way every year.

About a quarter of a mile along the Water of Leith Walkway you cross a tarmac road. On your right here is a piggery, this was previously a distillery and as far back as 1376 there was a fulling mill here. Fulling was the process of cleansing and thickening cloth. Across the river in the trees you might see the ruins of Lennox Tower. Mary Queen of Scots often visited here. Her second husband, Lord Darnley, was a son of the Earl of Lennox. James VI, 'the wisest fool in Christendom', came here for the hunting. Later it passed into the hands of George Heriot, the king's banker, a weel-kent Edinburgh name.

A signpost here points ahead, 'Currie ½'. Follow this and cross the Water of Leith on a footbridge. Bypass a footpath to the right and keep straight ahead on the obvious track in front of you. Ignore two paths to the left and some 200 to 300 metres along here you arrive at the old, stone retaining walls of the railway. Dougal Haston, the famous Scottish climber who was raised in Currie, practised climbing here. This railway line was opened in 1874 to supply raw materials to and transport finished products away from the numerous mills along the river's course. Following its opening one mill tripled its monthly output of paper. It also carried passengers until 1949. It was closed by the Beeching axe in 1967.

Shortly after this you cross a footbridge. At the end of the bridge hairpin left down steps and go right across the Water of Leith on Currie Brig. Then go left uphill by the old kiln to the main road. Just to your left on the A70 is the Corslet Stone, an inscription on it gives details. The Riccarton Arms is just across the main A70.

# 17. Edinburgh: Braid Hills

**Route:** Oxgangs – Cockmylane – Braidburn Valley Park – Hermitage of Braid – Blackford Hill – Royal Observatory – Howe of Dean Path – Braid Hills – Buckstone – Caiystone

**Distance:** 4.5 miles

**Map:** OS Landranger 66, Edinburgh

**Start:** Hunters' Tryst, Oxgangs

**Access:** By bus, there is a good service of a number of buses which stop outside Hunters' Tryst. Ask to be put off there. For timetable details ring 'Traveline' on 0800 232323 if in the Edinburgh area, if outwith the Edinburgh area then call 0131 225 3858. Or you can phone Lothian Buses on 0131 555 6363.

By car, from the centre of Edinburgh take the A702, Lothian Road, at the west end of Princes Street. Follow this A702 for about three miles through Bruntsfield and Morningside. It has a number of names, eventually ending up as Comiston Road. At Fairmilehead, the last set of traffic lights before the A702 crosses the A720 city bypass at the Lothianburn Interchange. Turn right here onto Oxgangs Road. Roughly a quarter of a mile along here, at the first roundabout, turn right into Oxgangs Road North. Immediately past the roundabout on your left is Hunters' Tryst. Just after the pub, also on the left, is the car park entrance.

---

## Hunters' Tryst. Tel: 0131 445 3132

This opened again as an inn in 1969 after being non-licensed premises from 1862 until 1969. In that time it was a dairy, a farm, a piggery and a breeding stud for trotting horses. The name derives from the fact that this was where Scottish Kings and their courtiers met before going hunting in the Pentlands. This inn is first recorded in 1747 by General Roy, the Scot who founded the Ordnance Survey. In the period between 1747 and 1862, one set of owners were the sisters Betty and Katie McCone. The Edinburgh business people of the day closed early on Saturday afternoon and went to small pubs in the country to eat a teatime meal. The Hunters' Tryst of that day was one of these. They were recorded as serving delicious meals.

In the early 1800s Hunters' Tryst was where members of the Six Foot High Club met. This club was established in 1826. Not all the members were six feet tall although all were gentlemen. Exceptions were made for high achievers such as local literati Sir Walter Scott and James Hogg, the Ettrick Shepherd. Members could be recognised by their attire of dark green tailcoat, tile hat, white Kerseymere waistcoat and black trousers. This club became the Honour Guard of Scotland's Hereditary High Constable in 1828. This was mainly a sporting club. The *Edinburgh Courant*. of 1828 records events such as shot putting, hammer throwing, one-mile steeplechase and hop, step and leap (sic).

Robert Louis Stevenson in *Edinburgh, Picturesque Notes*, describes how in the mid-1800s Hunters' Tryst was tormented by the Devil. Satan danced on the roof, smashed down dishes, shook the building and made unholy noises. This last gives the clue. Some dozen or so years after Stevenson wrote this the explanation was found. The water pipes from Bonaly Reservoir run right past Hunters' Tryst. Dry weather would damage the wooden pipes allowing air in which, when expelled, created these eerie sounds. Robert Louis Stevenson did not forget Hunters' Tryst. While living in Samoa he located a scene from his novel *St Ives* at Hunters' Tryst. A Frenchman, Saint Yves, having escaped from Edinburgh Castle, stumbles inadvertently on an all-night session of the Six Foot High Club. He is then, in boozy good fellowship, granted temporary membership of the club.

However you do not need membership to enjoy their facilities today. These include a wacky warehouse (this is a child friendly pub) and a small beer garden. The resident real ales are Caledonian 80/- and Deuchars IPA as well as an occasional guest such as Tetleys. Keg products on sale comprise Calders 70/-, Calders Cream, Carlsberg Lager, Castlemaine 4X, Stella Artois, Guinness and Dry Blackthorn. Opening hours are Monday to Thursday 1100-2300, Friday and Saturday 1100-2400 and Sunday 1230-2300.

Food is served from 1200-2200 Monday to Saturday and from 1230 to 2200 on Sundays. As the pub is part of Bass Leisure Retail, it is the standard menu of all the pubs in the chain. However, there is an extensive choice from steaks to sandwiches and the menu caters to the tastes of vegetarians and children. It is good food, well presented and served. Manager/joint licensee Bob Crawford is happy to meet and greet walkers in his establishment.

## Hermitage of Braid

History first notes this area in the late 12th century. Sir Henry de Braid, Sheriff of Edinburgh, owned these lands. The family residence is thought to have been a castle, probably on crags, a secure defensive position in these turbulent times. This family had passed into obscurity by the 14th century.

The lands around the Hermitage of Braid were next recorded as being held by Sir Robert Fairley, a supporter of Mary Queen of Scots, in the late 16th century. Sir Robert, by contemporary accounts, killed a soldier with a two-handed sword. The soldier was one of a party looting a mill here and belonged to an anti-Mary Queen of Scots faction. This was a corn mill and later at the end of the 17th century it was briefly a paper mill.

In 1631 William Dick, Provost of Edinburgh, purchased these lands. This multi-millionaire is portrayed in Scott's *Heart of Midlothian* as showering silver from his window to help the Scottish Covenanting Army. However when this army was beaten by Cromwell, Cromwell had a double grudge against William Dick. Not only had he been supporting Cromwell's foes in Scotland, he had also been lending fortunes to Cromwell's English enemies, the Royalists. So Cromwell defaulted these loans and fined William Dick an enormous amount. He died in poverty in Westminster debtors' gaol.

In 1676 the Brown family bought these lands and held them for over a century. It was during their stewardship that the manor house here was rebuilt and became called the Hermitage. In 1772 it was sold to Charles Gordon. In 1775 he erected the existing Hermitage. The architect, Robert Burn, created a house on the Adam pattern. Gordon was a skinflint. When the flow of the Braid Burn was altered, Charles Gordon sued the town council for lost income from his mill. It transpired that the mill had been knocked down on his orders ten years before! He used to stay in bed all day to avoid parting with any cash.

By 1868 the Gordon family had left and the Hermitage was being rented. The first occupier was Sir John Shelton, a noted writer. He gathered other writers about him and notable visitors to the Hermitage in this era included Robert Browning, Thomas Carlyle, Thomas Huxley and Dantë Gabriel Rosetti. The next distinguished tenant was Edinburgh professor C.G. Barkla, Nobel Laureate for Physics in 1917. In 1938 local man John McDougal bought this estate and philanthropically gave it to the people of Edinburgh as a public park, which it remains as to this day.

## The Walk

This is a stone walk. I did not plan it this way, it just happened. You will encounter a number of either single or groups of historic stones along this route.

Turn left along Oxgangs Road at the roundabout at Hunters' Tryst. Then around 100 metres along here go left down Caiystone Drive. Walk another 100 metres or so down here, crossing Caiystone Terrace to reach a T-junction with Caiystone Gardens. Here bear diagonally left to pick up a footpath some 10 metres along on the other side of Caiystone Gardens. Go through the overlapping iron gates and proceed down this footpath, between fences. This path is called Cockmylane, which means unfenced cart track. About 100 metres down here bypass a footpath to the right, this gateway used to be the back entrance to Comiston House. About 150 metres further on go through overlapping iron gates and ahead on a tarmac footpath. Keep with this path as it becomes beaten earth/gravel and veers right and left into an open space. A small stone structure here used to be the cistern that gathered water from local springs.

When the path splits take the left-hand fork, which debouches onto Greenbank Crescent. Turn right and walk across the bridge over the Braid Burn. Immediately over the bridge go right on to a broad, beaten earth/gravel path which is signposted for Braidburn Valley Park. Follow this path, keeping the Braid Burn on your right as you pass two footbridges on your right. At the third footbridge on your right, if you turn and look right and slightly behind you uphill you will see two small concrete blocks. These are marked 5 and 7, the numbers indicating the subsurface water supply pipes. The 5 is the diameter in inches of the pipe which substituted the original three-inch diameter pipe from Comiston in 1704. The 7 is the diameter in inches of the adjacent water main from Swanston.

Continue on the path through Braidburn Valley Park until the path, and park, end at a T-junction with Greenbank Crescent. Walk right along Greenbank Crescent to the main road, Comiston Road. Cross this and go directly forward down Braidburn Terrace. About 100 metres down here turn left down Braid Road. Around 150 metres down this road, outside number 66, are the Hanging Stones, embedded in the road and surrounded by brick. On this spot on 23 November 1814 Mr Lock, a carrier from Biggar, was assaulted and robbed of some £5. Thomas Kelly and Henry O'Neil were convicted of this crime. Judge David Boyle condemned them to be hung where the robbery was committed as an example to others. They were duly executed here on the 25 January 1815. These two stones mark where this act of judicial murder took place.

Retrace your steps to Braidburn Terrace and walk across it. Some 20 metres past Braidburn Terrace go left into the Hermitage of Braid Park. Another 20 metres or so into the park go left through a kissing gate to an earthen footpath just to the left of the information board. The old house you have just passed on your left is the old tollhouse which was previously situated at the foot of Morningside Road. In 1888 the entire house was relocated here.

About a quarter of a mile along this path beside the Braid Burn, on your right, is a set of hidden steps accessed just past the end of a dyke on your left. Go up here to find the doocot, an information board tells you all about it. Then return to the riverside path and go left along it. When you come to the Hermitage go to its right on a path between it and the Braid Burn. Follow this uphill, taking the left-hand fork where it splits. Then take the second footpath on the left (just after the first one, also on the left, which doubles back). Cross a ditch by a gap in the fence on your left and climb up the bank. Then turn right and walk through grassland towards Blackford Hill ahead of you. Aim for the gap in the dyke on your front. Go through the gate in the dyke and turn left along the broad path. After some 50 metres take the right-hand fork uphill. Follow this, contouring around Blackford Hill and ignoring a path to the right. When this path starts to descend to the left above the pond, bear right across the turf to a well-marked path. This pond is used for skating and curling in winter. Stay with this path as it bears to the right and becomes grassy. Follow it over the shoulder of Blackford Hill and between the transmitters on your right and the domes of the Royal Observatory on your left. Once over the shoulder of the hill, break left as the path forks and then turn left along the tarmac transmitter road in the direction of the observatory. The Royal Observatory has a visitor centre, open 1000-1700 Monday to Saturday and 1200-1700 on Sundays, phone 0131 668 8405 for further details.

Go right into the visitors car park and out on its far side on a well-worn path. This path shortly becomes grassy. After some 100 metres, a rock ahead forces you right on to another broad, well-defined path. After roughly 200 metres along this path double back left down into the valley of the Braid Burn. Pass through a kissing gate and then turn left along a broad path before the footbridge over the burn. Walk along here with the burn on your right. At the entrance to the quarry on your left along here is the Agassiz Rock, which is named after the Swiss geologist Louis Agassiz. He was the first to state that the scratches in this rock were made by glacial action. This was later confirmed by modern science. This whole valley was gouged out by glaciers and their melt water.

Approximately 300 metres along here, having passed the quarry on your left, a footbridge on your right is signposted Howe of Dean Path. Cross here. Then follow

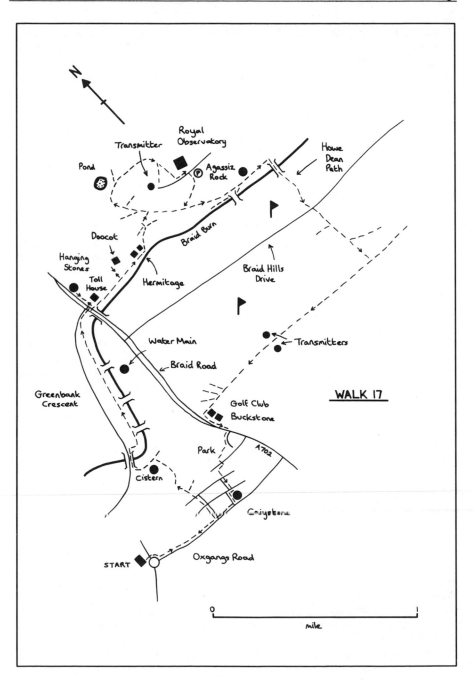

N

Royal
Observatory

Transmitter

Pond

Agassiz
Rock

Howe
Dean
Path

Braid Burn

Doocot

Hanging
Stones

Toll
House

Hermitage

Braid Hills
Drive

Water Main

Braid Road

Transmitters

Greenbank
Crescent

WALK 17

Golf Club
Buckstone

Park

A702

Cistern

Caiystane

START        Oxgangs Road

0                                                      1

mile

the path directly ahead up the little valley. At the top of the stairs go left to the road, Braid Hills Drive. Go straight across Braid Hills Drive and onto the track on the other side going ahead. Follow this track for roughly 200 metres, ignoring a track to the right. When the track veers left, go forward on the narrow path uphill through the gorse. Then follow the mown path through the rough and ahead to find a red earth road cutting across your path. Turn right along this. Keep on this red earth track for a mile or so as it bends between transmitters and goes along the top of the Braid Hills, giving glorious views over Edinburgh. As it descends, keep breaking left at the forks until it terminates in a T-junction with a tarmac road, Braid Road. Go left along here. Around 200 metres along this road, just past the entrance to the golf club on your left, is the Buckstone. This is set back from the road in a little alcove-type setting, half facing the opposite direction. Keep looking over your shoulder. A plaque above gives details about it.

About 100 metres beyond the Buckstone, follow the road around to the left and at the T-junction turn left up Buckstone Terrace. After some 35 metres turn right into East Comiston. Follow the pavement on the right into Fairmilehead Park. Here go

The Caiy Stone

straight ahead across the grass, heading for the far left-hand corner of the park. As a tarmac footpath cuts across your line of travel, go left on this. This takes you out of the park onto Comes Road. Here go right and then quickly turn left into Comes Park. Take the path bearing diagonally left at the end of Comes Park. This brings you out into Caiystone Hill. Go directly forward uphill on this, bearing left when Caiystone Gardens is on the right. At the top of Caiystone Hill slant right across Caiystone Avenue to go down Caiystone View. Here you can view the Caiy Stone, marking the site of a Pictish battle. At the end of Caiystone View turn right along Oxgangs Road for around 200 metres to find Hunters' Tryst at a roundabout.

# 18. Edinburgh: Lothianburn

**Route:** Lothianburn – Hillend Ski-Centre – Caerketton Hill – Allermuir Hill – Howden Burn – Stevenson's Cottage – Swanston

**Distance:** 4.5 miles

**Map:** OS Landranger 66, Edinburgh

**Start:** The Steading, Lothianburn

**Access:** By bus, a Lothian bus from the city centre turns round and returns to the city at the entrance to Hillend Ski-Centre. Get off here and walk back down towards the city for about 75 metres and the Steading is on your left. Otherwise a number of bus companies run buses past The Steading: Stagecoach, McEwans and First Edinburgh. Ask to be put off at the first stop after the road crosses the A720, city bypass. You will then see The Steading across the road. For information on all these buses ring 'Traveline' on 0800 232323 in the Edinburgh area or on 131 225 3858 if ringing from outside Edinburgh. Lothian Regional Transport can be reached on 0131 555 6363, McEwans on 01387 710357, Stagecoach on 01387 253496 and First Edinburgh on 0131 663 9233.

By car, take the A702, Lothian Road, out of Edinburgh at the west end of Princes St. Once over the Lothianburn Interchange on the A720, city bypass, the Steading is some 200 metres along on your right. The car park entrance is immediately preceding the pub on your right. Should it be full there is overflow parking just inside the entrance to the Hillend Ski-Centre, around 75 metres past the pub also on your right.

## The Steading. Tel: 0131 445 1128

This building was erected between 1766 and 1773. It was called Lothianburn. The building directly across the road from The Steading, now confusingly called Lothianburn, was called Loudenburn. By 1841 the pub was a coaching inn, The Lothian Inn, and the landlord was John Kay. In 1851 the landlord of this pub was James Hamilton. By 1861 it had become the Lothianburn Dairy, which it remained until 1935. Later it became a pub again. The name The Steading is believed to come from the fact that this was a farm steading belonging to the big house at Hillend where the ski-centre is now.

The owner from 1982 to 1999, R.D. Simpson, lived in a rundown house attached to the pub for the first few years. In 1986 the bar was lengthened and part of it turned into a restaurant. The restaurant was extended in 1987, utilising the now semi-derelict house. In 1989 the first of the conservatories, with a glorious view of the Pentlands, was added. Subsequently a second was built, with a no-smoking bar and more car parking.

These are quite rambling and extensive premises. The smoking bar has a real fire in winter. There is a picture of The Steading when it was the Lothianburn Dairy. There are old maps of Edinburgh and wooden floors. This is the only part of this inn to accept dogs and they must be kept on a lead. There are free newspapers. This bar is comfortably old fashioned with red sandstone blocks, dark wood and light plaster.

The non-smoking bar and restaurants are more up to date although brass work including warming pans offsets the modernity. The modern, clean and comfortable conservatories have their views over the Pentlands to commend them in good weather. In very good weather there is a beer garden where you can eat or drink.

You can eat (or drink) in either of the conservatories, in either smoking or non-smoking restaurant areas or in the bars. There are some children's items and children or not-too-hungry adults can have a reduced price, reduced size portion, roughly three quarters of the size of a normal meal. A full range of food is available, starters, main meals, desserts, jacket potatoes, sandwiches, snacks, steaks and grills, rice, pasta and salads. Vegetarians are catered for. The meat comes from the local butcher's 100 metres away and the food is fresh and almost all home cooked. Tea, chocolate and a good selection of coffees are served. Desserts include carrot cake and millionaire's shortbread. There are also daily specials. Food is on between 1000-2200 seven days a week.

Opening hours are 1100-2400 Monday to Saturday and Sunday's hours are 1230-2400. This pub appears in CAMRA's Good Beer Guide for 1995, 1997,1999 and 2000. There were six real ales on sale when I was there. The five resident real ales were Burton Ale, Belhaven 80/- (at the price of 70/-), Orkney Dark Island, Deuchars IPA and Timothy Taylors Landlord. The guest was Thomas Hardy Country Bitter. Keg pumps were Stella Artois, Caffreys, Tennents Lager, Belhaven Lager, Guinness, Guinness Extra-cold, Belhaven Best and Strongbow Cider.

As you can see the Pentlands towering over the pub it is no surprise to find that landlord William Storrie already regularly entertains parties of walkers. The Steading is also a haven for those with offspring. It takes credit cards, American Express, Delta and Switch.

## Robert Louis Stevenson

Robert Louis Stevenson was born in 1850 in Edinburgh. His paternal ancestors were lighthouse builders. They erected the Bell Rock lighthouse among others. The family were wealthy which gave Robert the financial support to ride out the inevitable lean years that preface many writers' careers. Originally the family lived in Edinburgh, but from when Stevenson was in his mid-teens to mid-twenties the family lived at Swanston on the edge of the Pentlands.

Robert Louis Stevenson was frail and thin and prone to over excitability. Despite this he was able to walk to and from Swanston to attend university in Edinburgh. He was also fit to roam the hills with local people, absorbing their lore as he did so. These experiences served him well in his writing career, indeed he was still setting scenes in the Edinburgh and Pentlands areas in novels he was writing when he died.

At university he studied engineering at first and then law. He did not take either very seriously, being a skiver and prankster by all accounts, but he scraped through his exams to acquire a law degree. However, he never practised as a lawyer. Instead, using family money and small amounts earned writing he travelled extensively. In France in 1876 he met his wife-to-be Fanny Osbourne. She was an American. In

1879 *Travels with a Donkey* was published. Stevenson married Fanny in San Francisco in 1880.

In summer 1881, while holidaying in Braemar, he started *Treasure Island*, first published in instalments in the magazine *Young Folks*. In 1883 he lived in the south of France for a year, ever afterwards calling it the only time in his life that he was truly happy. From 1884 to 1887 Robert and Fanny lived in Bournemouth. In 1886 *Dr Jekyll and Mr Hyde* was published. This is based on the true Edinburgh story of Deacon Brodie, a respectable man by day, he was a villain by night. The same year *Kidnapped* appeared in *Young Folks* magazine.

In 1887 Stevenson went to the USA and then on to the South Seas. *The Master of Ballantrae* came out in 1889. By Christmas that year the family had moved to Samoa where they settled, buying an estate. He still travelled, visiting Australia in 1893. *Catriona*, a sequel to *Kidnapped*, was written in 1892. He died in 1894, leaving some unfinished novels such as *Weir of Hermiston* and *St Ives*.

# The Walk

This walk can be made less of a climb by using the ski lift. To check if it is open you can phone 0131 445 4433. As the ski lift may not always be open I have given you both routes. Leave The Steading on the main road, A702. Turn right along this. About 30 metres along here you come to the entrance to Midlothian Ski-Centre on your right, go in here.

## Using the Ski Lift

Follow the tarmac road up to the ski-centre. Take the ski lift to the top. With your back to the artificial ski slope, take the path on your left contouring along the hillside with a fence on your right for about 300 metres. You will arrive at a stile on your right with a signpost. This points right uphill for Caerketton and back the way you have come for Swanston. Now pick up your directions again at 'After the Ski Lift'.

## Avoiding the Ski Lift

As you enter the gate at Midlothian Ski-Centre you will see two signs on your left. Both point the same way, diagonally left forward. One indicates Capital View Walk (CVW), waymarked with a blue arrow with a white castle within it, and the other is a Scottish Rights of Way Society sign to Caerketton, Swanston and Boghall. Follow these signs through the car park, up a set of steps and on to the obvious path at the far side of the car park. After a couple of hundred metres you arrive at a junction of paths, go ahead where the sign points to Caerketton. Keep on this path up steps and around to the left between bracken and gorse. When you reach a broad, grassy path athwart your path, go left along it for about 10 metres. Then bear right uphill at the CVW waymark. Some 100 metres uphill the path splits. Fork left here, ignoring the CVW waymarker pointing right. At the next fork hang a right, bypassing the CVW waymarker indicating left. This brings you to a fence cutting across your line of travel with a stile in it and a signpost informing you that ahead uphill is to Caerketton and to the right Swanston, CVW. Continue with the following directions.

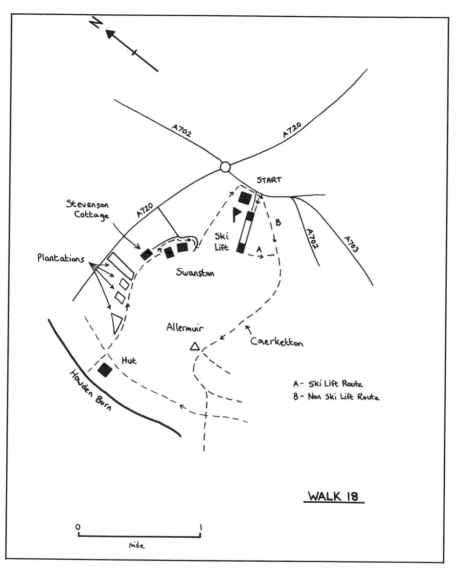

WALK 18

## After the Ski Lift

Cross the stile and climb uphill beside the fence on your left. Generations of walkers have created natural steps here. At the top of the hill follow the fence around to the right on what is now a broad path. The slope begins to ease. It is now simple walking along the ridge, keeping the fence on your close left.

The first cairns that you come to are not Caerketton proper but a minor summit of it. If you look 90 degrees left at this point you will see a line of hilltops. In order, nearest to furthest, these are Turnhouse Hill, Carnethy Hill, Scald Law, East Kip, West Kip and South Black Hill. Sir Walter Scott considered that this was the finest thing that he had ever seen. You are now walking along the boundary between the City of Edinburgh and Midlothian. Down on your right you will see a famous pine plantation in the shape of a cross. This was planted by Sir Henry Trotter of Mortonhall, the landowner, in 1776. Perhaps it is this shape to remember the Knights Templar whose arms carried a Maltese cross. It is believed that they had lands here. Ascend gently on this path to the top of Caerketton Hill.

From the top of Caerketton stick with the path along the ridge with the fence on your left for about half a mile. This path descends into the saddle between Caerketton and Allermuir Hills and climbs up to the top of Allermuir Hill. Allermuir means 'moor where the alders grow'. At the top of Allermuir Hill a view indicator tells you which sights you are seeing. The views are tremendous.

Leave the view indicator and take the stile straight ahead, not the one on the left. Keep walking with the fence nearby on your left. About 200 metres down from the summit of Allermuir, follow the path as it clings to the fence as the fence turns 90 degrees to the left. About 100 metres after this sharp turn take the broad grassy path bearing right down into the valley of the Howden Burn. This path broadens into a cart track and eventually reaches a four-way junction with a red dirt road. At this point follow the sign pointing right to Dreghorn. Keep on this road as you descend the valley of the Howden Burn.

You may hear red grouse here calling 'Go back, go back, go back'. These are the only birds that are only found in Britain. The heather you see growing by the roadside is their staple diet. It must be glorious here when it flowers.

Walk down this valley for the best part of a mile until it broadens and flattens. There is a little hut at a junction of paths here. Follow the sign pointing right to Dreghorn. A couple of hundred metres along here take the path on the right that goes along the right-hand side of a small, triangular, fenced-in plantation. At the end of the plantation drop left downhill for about 50 metres to gain a roughly parallel path and go right along this. This, not always obvious, path travels between gorse on the right and three plantations on the left. The first two plantations are small and squareish and the third and final one is a long, narrow belt of trees falling down towards Edinburgh. As you pass through the rough pasture the path becomes more defined and heads towards the edge of the plantations. Stay on this now broad, grassy path along the border of the woods on your left.

At the start of the long, narrow plantation on your left, bear right and then left to walk along the top, right-hand fringe of this woodland. At the far end of the wood cross the dyke by a stone stile to the right of the field gate. At the junction directly after the field gate go straight ahead down the track in front of you. Roughly a quarter of a mile down this track a wall comes in from the left and runs along the left-hand side of the road. Behind this wall, the white building is the cottage where Robert Louis Stevenson lived with his parents for around a decade from 1867. He attended university in Edinburgh (engineering) while he was here. He used it in a setting in his

Sir Walter Scott considered these hills the finest thing that he had ever seen.

novel *St Ives* when, subsequent to escaping from Edinburgh Castle, a Frenchman arrives here. The locals considered Stevenson eccentric: a long-haired lad, frequently abstracted, and wearing absurd (but absolutely characteristic) velvet jackets.

This house was created in 1761 by the Edinburgh Corporation Water Trust for housing the water workers. The springs at Swanston supplied around one and a half million litres of water a day to Edinburgh.

Less than 100 metres past Swanston Cottage you arrive at Swanston Farm. Turn sharp left through the farmyard. At the other side of it go right on to the minor road. This terminates at a T-junction with the road into Swanston village. Bear right along this road into the village. It was through this village in November 1666 that the shattered remnants of the Covenanting army passed in retreat after their defeat at the Battle of Rullion Green on the eastern flank of the Pentlands. Swanston was well known for its support of Covenanters so they could be sure of some help here.

Just past the entrance to Swanston Golf Club on your right, bear left into the car park. At the far end of the car park take the beaten earth/gravel path and follow it up a wee brae, past a house on the left and across a footbridge. This path finishes at a little bit of tarmac. At the far end of the bit of tarmac a sign indicates left to Lothianburn. This is your way. Roughly 50 metres up this tarmac road bends left. At this point go directly ahead on a track where a CVW sign and waymarker shows the way to Lothianburn. Walk on this track for about half a mile, with the golf course on your right, until it terminates in a T-junction the A702. Proceed to the right along this road for approximately 150 metres and The Steading is on your right.

# 19. Midlothian: Glencorse

**Route:** Flotterstone – Visitor Centre – Old Filter Beds – Glencorse Reservoir – Kirk Burn – Castlelaw Fort and Souterrain

**Distance:** 5 miles

**Map:** OS Landranger 66, Edinburgh

**Start:** Flotterstone Inn, Flotterstone

**Access:** By bus, there are three separate operators running bus services to the Flotterstone Inn. None of these services is very good but taken together they just about make an acceptable service Monday to Saturday. It might be an idea not to get a return ticket unless you can be sure that the service you get back will be run by the same operator. Ask to be put off at the Flotterstone Inn, it is well known. For travel details contact 'Traveline' on 0800 232323 if in the Edinburgh area or ring 0131 225 3858 if outwith the Edinburgh area. The individual operators numbers are First Edinburgh 0131 663 9233, McEwans 01387 710357 and Stagecoach Western 01387 253496. On Sundays there are only four services. However on summer Sundays the Pentland Rover service runs around the perimeter of the northern Pentlands. So perhaps you might be able to get a Lothian bus to the edge of the city and travel from there on a Pentland Rover. Lothian bus details on 'Traveline' as above or on 0131 555 6363. The Pentland Rover timetable can be obtained by phoning 0131 445 5969.

By car, leave Edinburgh on the A702, the road to Biggar. Once across the Lothianburn Interchange with the A720, city bypass, you will encounter a fork in the road. Keep right on the A702(T) as the A703 drops off to the left. After about two and a half miles along this you will find the Flotterstone Inn on your right. It is signposted. It is set at the apex of a half moon shape in the old road. You can park in the half moon. Or you can turn right off the old road with the inn on your left to find its car park just past the pub on your left. If this is full then you can proceed up past the pub to find a free Pentland Hills Regional Park car park some 50 metres past the pub on your right.

## Flotterstone Inn. Tel: 01968 673717

This building dates back to the 1600s and was originally workmen's cottages. Later it was a toll-house for the bridge/road. Over the years, as thirsty and hungry hikers came down off the Pentlands here, free enterprise led the occupiers to start selling them lemonade etc. By the 1950s it was a tea-room and by the 1960s it was a pub. The name Flotterstone means 'flat stones'.

If any pub can be said to a walkers' pub then this is it as it was created to serve the needs of walkers. In December chilled walkers can warm up with mulled wine. There are also two real fires in winter. Also warming is the food. The beef is all Scottish and steaks are a speciality. The food ranges from hors d'oeuvre through Sunday roasts and classic pub food like steak pie to snacks. This is all local food and all home cooked. Vegetarians are catered for. Food is available all day, 1200-2200 seven days a week. There is a children's menu, this is a child friendly pub.

Opening hours for beer are Monday to Thursday and Sunday 1200-2300, on Fri-

The Flotterstone Inn

days and Saturdays it is 1200 – 2400. The real ale is Boddingtons. Foaming from kegs are Beamish Red, the ubiquitous Guinness, Miller Pilsner, John Smiths Extra Smooth, McEwans 80/-, McEwans 70/-, McEwans Export, McEwans Lager, Theakstons Best Bitter and Strongbow Cider. Coffee and wine by the glass are also available.

The bar has lovely stonework with medium dark wood and cream-coloured wallpaper. Other decor comprises carpets, tables, comfy chairs, plates, Toby jugs and pictures. There is a television and fruit machine. A sign says that beer is the best long drink in the world, I concur. Dogs were in while I was there. Leaded windows with small square sections add to the atmosphere. The dining room has the same ambience of stonework and wood. It also has old pictures of Edinburgh and details of brewing kit such as hydrometers and beer extractors. The beautiful bar here has horse brasses above it. There is a beer garden outside. Landlord Paul Brodie accepts credit cards but there is a 50p surcharge if this is for less than £10.

## Rullion Green

The spark that set the fire that was to lead to the Battle of Rullion Green was an inflammatory remark. On the 14th of November 1666 soldiers threatened to roast over a fire a man who had not paid his fines for not attending the Episcopalian Church foisted on Scotland by Charles II. Outraged Covenanters rescued this man, wounding a soldier. Then, emboldened by the capture of their local tormentor in Dumfries, began a rambling procession up into and across Central Scotland. They succeeded at first because much of the army was fighting abroad.

However fencibles (local militia) were roused, armed and equipped and sent after them under the command of Tam Dalziel o' the Binns. He was called the Beast of Muscovie because of his battle hardening in the Russian Wars. He had refused to shave after the execution of Charles I as a mark of mourning. The Covenanters had gained many fewer adherents to their cause than they hoped. On the 28th of November this fated-to-fail insurrection had had its fortnight and the rebels were cornered at Rullion Green.

The rebels numbered some 900 men and the government forces 2600. However, as the rebels held the high ground the outcome was by no means assured. Near to dusk Dalziel attacked the right (western) side of the rebels. These attacks were twice repulsed, but the experienced soldier Dalziel persisted. The third attack gained the high ground for the establishment troops and then Dalziel pushed his centre and left into the attack. The Covenanters broke and fled.

Dalziel's losses were minimal and but for approaching night the rebel's losses would have been much more. They lost some 50 men killed and 80 taken prisoner. Among these latter some were executed and many were transported to the West Indies as indentured servants (effectively slaves), a probable but prolonged death sentence. Rullion Green is a scene used in Sir Walter Scott's novel *Guy Mannering*.

## The Walk

Come out of the Flotterstone Inn and turn left to walk up the minor road into Glencorse with your back to the main road. The old bridge at the main road is where the Covenanters crossed to reach the battle field of Rullion Green in 1666. About 50 metres up this road on your right is a visitor centre giving details of the Pentland Hills Regional Park. On leaving the visitor centre turn right just outside its door and take the path through the trees parallel to the minor road up Glencorse. Around 50 metres along this path follow it directly over a farm track cutting across the path, as guided by the purple Pentland Path arrow.

Some 200 metres further along this path you will see a plaque on the dyke on your right. This commemorates C.T.R. Wilson, Nobel Laureate in physics and inventor of the cloud chamber. He was born in this valley. Shortly afterwards the path rejoins the road, here bear right along it. About 50 metres further along the road is a choice of two paths on the left. Take the first of these, which is on the near side of the footbridge and is signposted for Glencorse Reservoir by the old filter-beds. Walk diagonally left and forward, keeping the burn on your left. Pass through a gate ahead and some 50 metres past this look up and ahead. You will see a semi-circular group of trees with a green field in front of it. This is the left-most of the three clumps of trees on the hill ahead and above you. This green field was the site of the Battle of Rullion Green in 1666. Keep with this track between fences as it bears right. Another sign confirms that this is the way to Glencorse Reservoir by the old filter-beds.

In the summer you will find knapweed beside the track here. This has a purple

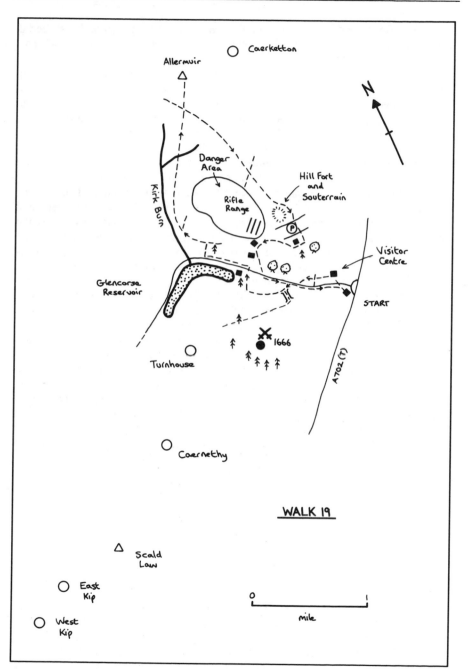

Caerketton

Allermuir

Danger Area

Kirk Burn

Rifle Range

Hill Fort and Souterrain

P

Visitor Centre

Glencorse Reservoir

START

A702 (T)

Turnhouse

1666

Coernethy

WALK 19

Scald Law

East Kip

West Kip

0 _____ 1
mile

thistle-like flower and long, narrow, undivided leaves. This particular knapweed is black knapweed, originally called knobweed or hardhead because of its dark-coloured, hard, knob-like buds.

Continue with this now more grassy dirt track flanked by fences and among gorse, ignoring a stile on the left. Bypass two field gates by small gates to their right. Note that this is sheep country with consensual access by landowners, so dogs on leads please. Approximately 100 metres past the second gate a notice board gives details of the Pentland Hills Ranger Service tree nursery. About 50 metres past this another board informs you about Flotterstone's wildlife garden. Follow this road as it bears right and up through big old pines. Pass through a wee gate to the right of a large white gate. Bear left along the tarmac road up Glencorse here.

This road runs along the route by which Tam Dalziel o' the Binns and his soldiers rode to the Battle of Rullion Green. There is very little traffic along this dead end road. There are fantail doves at Glen Cottage on your left immediately before the start of the Glencorse Reservoir. Beside this road in late summer/early autumn you will see the ball-shaped, spiky, mauve flowers of water mint. This has spearhead-shaped leaves. If in doubt gently rub the leaves and smell your fingers, the smell of mint will confirm it. On Glencorse Reservoir there are goosanders. These long, narrow ducks have an elongated bill with a little downturn at the end. They are part of the sawbill family as their beaks have serrated edges for securing struggling slippery fish. Their presence indicates a healthy eco-system as they need a steady supply of small fish. The male is a striking bird with a mainly white body and dark green head and neck. The female is mainly grey with a rust red head and neck.

Nearly half a mile along this tarmac road with the Glencorse Reservoir on your left, you arrive at a narrow plantation of pines on your right. Just past this plantation is a stile and a sign pointing up the footpath indicating Castlelaw. Ascend this footpath. Approximately 200 metres up here this path terminates in a T-junction with a track. Break left along the track, ignoring the sign pointing right to Castlelaw. If you pause for breath here and look across the reservoir the hill nearest you is Turnhouse Hill and behind it going away from you in nearest to furthest order are Caernethy Hill, Scald Law, East Kip and West Kip. This line of hills was considered by Sir Walter Scott to be the finest thing he had ever seen. Law is an old Scottish word for a rounded hill.

Follow the track right around the shoulder of the hill into the valley of the Kirk Burn. The Kirk Burn gets its name from St Catherine's Chapel, which stood at the mouth of this burn until the rising waters of the reservoir engulfed it. This chapel was built by William St Clair, an ancestor of the Earls of Roslin. While hunting with Robert the Bruce the party put up a white hart, St Clair bet his life against the lands of Glencorse that his two hounds Help and Hold could catch the stag. When they succeeded the erection of this chapel was a mark of his gratitude to God.

Here the track forks, take the left-hand one, which immediately degenerates into a well-worn footpath. As you walk up this valley in summer you will see the yellow, four-petalled flowers of tormentil hugging the ground to avoid the ravages of the wind. Here you will also see members of the W.B.B. bird family, wee brown birds.

These are meadow pipits. They can be identified as they fly away from you by the longitudinal white stripes on the outer edges of their tails.

After around a mile along this valley the path starts to be marked by white-painted posts. However this path is well defined. Another quarter of a mile or so further on this path crosses a broad dirt road. At this point turn right onto the dirt road. The two hills ahead of you at this junction are Allermuir on the left, which the path you have been walking on ascends, and Caerketton on the right. 'Caer' is an old Celtic word meaning 'castle' or 'fort'. So there was probably some kind of fortified building on Caerketton.

Stick with this dirt road around Castlelaw on your right and downhill for about a mile. Do **not** ascend any of the tracks on your right towards the transmitter on Castlelaw. This is a military training area and is dangerous. Instead enjoy glorious views over Midlothian as you descend the eastern shoulder of Castlelaw. Pass over a grassy track crossing this dirt road. Down here you will find creeping thistle by the roadside. You can recognise it by its grey-green leaves, rosette shape and habit of pressing itself to the ground. It has small, lilac-coloured flowers in summer. This perennial is hard to eliminate and is one of the biggest pests on our soils.

Shortly after this the firing ranges come into view on your right. Continuing with a military theme, a hill fort is ahead of you. The dirt road swings left around the fort. You can go in and visit it. An information board gives details. There is also a souterrain here. These were stone-lined passages into the hillside used for storage, mainly of food. As you enter this souterrain you can feel the drop in temperature which would have made it good for storing food. It would also make a handy shelter during a shower.

Keep with the dirt road around the hill fort to the gate at its end. Negotiate this by a kissing gate to its left then cross the tarmac road and walk through the car park. At the far end of the car park cross the next tarmac road, bearing slightly left to pick up a footpath signed for Glencorse and Flotterstone. This starts at a gate with a purple Pentland Path arrow. This path bears right through a wood around the farm on your right. At the end of the wood follow the purple Pentland Path arrow and signs to Glencorse through a kissing gate to the left of a field gate. Walk along the hillside here for about 100 metres and go through a field gate by a kissing gate on its right. At the isolated building here go left where the sign points for Flotterstone. At first there is no path here. Keep to the left of what looks like a brick outhouse and you will soon find a purple Pentland Path arrow. This guides you to a path downhill by the ruins of a dyke. This ends in a T-junction with the tarmac road up Glencorse. Break left along this road. Continue along it for roughly half a mile and it will bring you to the Flotterstone Inn on your right.

# 20. Midlothian: Roslin

**Route:** Roslin – Mountmarle – Hewan – Roslin Glen – Rosslyn Castle – Jacob's Ladder – Rosslyn Chapel

**Distance:** 5 miles

**Map:** OS Landranger 66, Edinburgh

**Start:** Old Original Roslin Hotel

**Access:** By bus, Monday to Saturday a frequent direct bus service to Roslin runs from Princes Street. However there are only two direct buses on a Sunday. On Sundays you may have to get the bus to Loanhead, an hourly service. This departs from the north side of St Andrew's Square. There is an adequate connecting service to Roslin. The necessary telephone numbers for information are 'Traveline' on 0800 232323 (Edinburgh area) or 0131 225 3858 (outside Edinburgh) and First Edinburgh 0131 663 9233.

By car, from the Straiton interchange on the A720, city bypass, take the A701 towards Penicuik. About one and a half miles along here go left onto the B7006 at a roundabout. This is signed for Roslin. Around a mile along here, at Roslin Cross, the Penicuik Road swings sharply right. The Old Original Rosslyn Hotel is on your left here. Street parking was unrestricted when I was there. To reach the pub's car park go left up Manse Rd at Roslin Cross. About 20 metres up here on your left is the car park entrance for the pub. The car park is behind the pub.

---

## The Old Original Rosslyn Hotel. Tel: 0131 440 2384

The original Rosslyn Inn dates back to 1660 and was located beside Rosslyn Chapel. Today it is the curator's house and a plaque marks it. William and Dorothy Wordsworth left this inn early one morning to visit Sir Walter Scott at nearby Lasswade. Dr Johnson and Boswell took tea and dined here on their way to Penicuik House. Robert Burns and Naysmith (the portrait painter whose picture of Burns is the only authenticated one) had breakfast here after a ramble on the Pentlands. The poet rewarded the landlady by writing two verses for her and inscribing them on a pewter plate. In 1827 the landlord of this inn fell out with the local landowners, the St Clairs, and moved the pub into the village which the St Clairs did not own. The building was then called the Star Inn and had been a pub since 1821. In those days licences applied to people, not premises. The old inn beside the Rosslyn Chapel continued until 1863/4.

The present site was a coaching inn. Coach travel to Roslin started around the beginning of the 19th century. In 1805 Sir Walter Scott published *The Lay of the Last Minstrel* part of which, *The Dirge of Rosabel*, was believed to have been set, in Scott's mind, in the glen of the North Esk at Roslin. Suddenly Roslin was a tourist attraction and beds, stables etc. were needed for the visitors and their coaches. These regular four-in-hand services had brightly equipped horses. The driver wore a red coat with a black velvet collar, broad-brimmed silk hat, gaiters, breeches and white gloves. The coachman was similarly clothed and had a big brass horn which he sounded vigorously.

By 1843 there were five miles of turnpike (toll) road in the parish and the Great Dumfries Road ran through it for about a mile. Coach services calling at this inn included the Dumfries mail coach, the Peebles coach and sundry coach services from Edinburgh. Records from the 1860s and 1870s show this inn employing ostlers (stablemen at inns), coachmen, housemaids, cooks etc. In 1871 it was described as a terminal dwelling place, partly of two storeys and partly of one storey, known as the Original Rosslyn (Inn) Hotel. From 1829 to 1890 it was under the control of the Ainslie family and afterwards it had a series of owners. In the 1920s rumour has it that there was a murder in the car park. The Harris family took over in 1973. Landlord Graham Harris commissioned professional historians to find out about the pub's past. This information can be read in bound form at the inn if you ask for it.

Today this is an excellent pub. It has awards from the British Hospitality Association 1991-7, and in 1997 was AA recommended as QQQ. Graham and Marion Harris run a hiker-friendly hostelry that also welcomes children. They take credit and debit cards. There is a beer garden at the back and picnic tables at the front.

Opening hours are 1200-2300 seven days a week. There is one real ale, Belhaven Export. The keg barrels pump Guinness, Tennents Velvet, Tennents Lager, Tennents 80/-, Belhaven Best and Strongbow. The bar is floored in wood with a stone fire surround. It is nicely furbished with plates, lamps, bottles, jugs and old brewery/drink oddments. It has a fruit machine, cigarette machine, jukebox and television. A machine dispenses hot pistachio nuts.

The dining room is lovely and much plusher with dried flowers, pictures of Roslin Glen, old clocks and a Chinese screen. You can also eat in a comfortable lounge bar with dark wood beams, exposed floor and pictures of Burns and the old inn at the Chapel. Food is served 1200-1400 and 1700-2200 Monday to Saturday. Hours are 1200-2200 Saturday and Sunday. 1600-1800 on Sunday is that grand old Scottish institution high tea. Food ranges from snacks through light meals to full meals. You can have whatever you want says mine host, up to fillet steak. While there is plenty for the carnivore in duck, fish, lamb etc., there are also up to five vegetarian choices in the main courses. House specialities are specialist coffees and local haggis from Mr Anderson in Rosewell. This is dipped in oatmeal, deep fried and served with a sweet onion and whisky sauce. And talking of sweets, the distinctive dessert here is home-made pavlova.

## The Battle of Roslin

This was one of the more important battles of the Wars of Independence. On the 24th February 1303, a Scots army of 8000 men under the command of Sir Simon Fraser and John Comyn marched during the night from Carlops, about eight miles away, to Roslin. The English were an army of over 30,000 led by Sir John de Seagrave. He foolishly committed his divisions piecemeal. His first division encountered the Scots in the pre-dawn darkness just south of Roslin, in the glen of the North Esk. Using local knowledge the Scots caused heavy casualties to their enemies. Later this day a tired but invigorated Scots army met the English near where the Dryden Tower stands today, about a mile north of Roslin. Scottish archers (now there's a rarity) caused havoc in the English lines and this division was driven down a steep-sided valley to defeat. Today this valley is known as the Killburn. Local tradition has it that the waters ran red with blood. The third division was manoeuvred between the Scots and the valley of the North Esk at Hewan about a mile and a half north-east of Roslin. The English were forced into the deep ravine of the North Esk and many were killed. The name Hewan comes from much hewing, as with battle-axe or sword. Other local names recall these battles such as Shinbones Fields and Stinking Rig. This latter is a ridge of high ground or long, narrow hill where many of the dead rotted under a thin covering of soil.

## Rosslyn Chapel

This was built in 1446 by William St Clair, Prince of Orkney. It was dedicated to St Matthew in 1450 as a collegiate church – one that is dedicated to saying masses in perpetuity for the soul of its founder and family. Most of the planned enormous cruciform building was never erected. With the onset of the Reformation it was gradually abandoned and used as a stable by the roundheads of General Monk as they besieged Rosslyn Castle. In 1736 repairs started under a St Clair family member. In 1807 Dorothy Wordsworth considered the internal stonework most impressive. In 1915 the famous Scottish architect Robert Lorimer inspected it and considered it to be in fairly good condition. In the 1940s it was almost abandoned as church attendances plummeted. Subsequently it has been preserved as an ancient monument.

The carving and sculptures here are astonishingly beautiful and quite unique. There is no place like Rosslyn Chapel in the country. Carvings of sweetcorn give credence to the theory that Prince Henry the Orcadian landed in America a century before Columbus. It has the highest number of 'Green Men' in any medieval structure. These are symbols of good luck. The high point of Rosslyn Chapel is the Apprentice Pillar. This incredibly detailed and intricately carved pillar is supposed to have been done by an apprentice while the master mason was away. On returning, the master mason was so enraged by his apprentice's forwardness and consumed by jealousy of his ability that he slew the apprentice with his mallet. The chapel is open 1000-1700 Monday to Saturday and 1200-1645 on Sundays. There is an admission charge. For further details phone 0131 440 2159.

## The Walk

Exit the Old Original Rosslyn Hotel and turn left for about 20 metres to reach the cross. At the cross turn left along Manse Road, signposted for the Battle of Roslin cairn. Confusingly, a road to the left here is labelled Manse Road but keep straight ahead. Walk past the 'No Entry' signs and through the bollards. Keep on past the 'No Through Road' sign, the Dryden Farm sign and past a footpath on the left. Part of Dryden Estate is Killburn, named after a part of the Battle of Roslin. The large building on your left here is the Roslin Institute where Dolly the Sheep, the world's first cloned animal, was created. Walk past a road across the disused railway line on your right, the bridge is numbered 16. This is Mountmarle. Here, one of the English captains, Marle, was given the advice by his own men, 'Mount Marle and ride.'

Go past a footpath on the left and immediately past this is the Battle of Roslin cairn on your left. An information board here gives details of the battle and of James Lockhart Wishart of Dryden, which is just to the left here.

Walk past Dryden Farm. Behind it on a hill is Dryden Tower, which was erected to commemorate one site of the Battle of Roslin. It is a three-storey Gothic tower from the 19th century. Beyond the farm the road in front of you becomes a dirt road, keep ahead on this. There are good views of the Pentlands to your left. Pass through the abutments of an old railway bridge. The valley of the North Esk comes into sight on your right. When the track comes to an end, continue ahead on a broad beaten earth/tarmac footpath with trees on your left and a hedge on your right. Bypass two footpaths to the left and follow the path around to the right and downhill. This is Hewan where the third part of the Battle of Roslin took place.

As the path starts to descend steeply take the first path on the right at the end of the field. There appear to be the ruins of a stile here but access to this path is open. After about 150 metres this path terminates in a T-junction with another path. Turn right here. Proceed along this path with the North Esk on your left and the field on your right. This path descends towards the river by steps and crosses a narrow ridge. **Care is needed here.** Once across the ridge descend for 100 metres into an open space. A path goes straight ahead here, a rudimentary path goes left and another path goes right and doubles back down to the river's bank. This latter one is the path for you.

When you reach the river go right over a low fence, an easy step-over. Follow the path with the River North Esk on your left. This has been a public right of way since 1847. A court case that went to the House of Lords decided this. This right of way runs from Polton behind you, to Roslin, through the glen. A peregrine falcon flew over my head here. The peregrine falcon is half as big again as a city-square pigeon. The female, as in all falcons, is larger than the male. It has a light underside, dark back and a characteristic black Mexican moustache on its face. These can stoop spectacularly on folded wings at up to 200mph on prey species such as pigeons, jackdaws and ducks in flight. They strike their prey with their feet, stunning them. These falcons are quite common nowadays, having recovered well after the banning of DDT which made their eggs shells thin and easily broken. While they normally nest on cliff faces, some have nested in cities such as Toronto.

Walk down this beaten earth path paralleling the river for the next two miles, bypassing paths to the left and right of you. You may well think that you have gone too far and have passed Roslin on your way back. I did. But persevere and you will eventually come out into an open grassy space with Rosslyn Chapel above and to your right. Cross footbridges and stiles when you come to them. The path rises and falls but just keep the river on your left. This was a favourite walk of Sir Walter Scott. And Dorothy Wordworth thought that Roslin Glen was one of the finest places she had ever seen. About halfway along this part of the walk you will glimpse Hawthornden Castle on the other side of the river through the trees. This dates back to the 15th century. The celebrated poet William Drummond lived here in the 1800s and his work attracted many visitors to walk here. After Hawthornden Castle there are a couple of places where walkers could go astray. After the path turns right and zigzags uphill, at the top take the path to the left not the one through the dyke ahead. Subsequent to this take the left-hand path at a T-junction.

At last a small drop down a buried dyke deposits you on a grassy path through a meadow with Rosslyn Chapel above and to the right. Contour along the hillside and forward with this grassy path, which ends at a dyke with some top stones removed so that you can scramble over it. A sign here informs you about Gardeners Brae Nature Reserve that you have just passed through. Once over the dyke, turn left down the dirt road beyond it. You will arrive at a bridge. Your route is down the steps to the right and on the nearside of the bridge. Rosslyn Castle remains are on the far side of the bridge and can be visited for free. The original castle was begun by Henry, first Earl of Orkney, around 1330.

The ruins of Rosslyn Castle

Descend the steps and keep directly forwards on the path at the bottom to cross the North Esk by a footbridge. On the other side of the river bear left along a mown grass path for about 100 metres. At a fork take the right-hand option for about 15 metres then go right again on to a gravel cart track. This terminates in a T-junction with the B7003 after some 100 metres. Proceed right along the B7003. After nearly 150 metres this takes you across the North Esk on a bridge. Immediately over the bridge turn sharply right where the sign says 'footpath and chapel'. Climb the steps to re-encounter the B7003 at the top of them. These steps (76) were built in 1913 by the local scouts for the weavers etc. at the carpet factory. They were kept in good order by the employees of the carpet factory until it closed in 1968. In 1988 the Heritage Society renovated the steps, which are called Jacob's Ladder. The river water powered the carpet factory from 1868 onwards. Richard Whytock's factory also created the velvet table covers that made Roslin famous. Before the factory there were bleach fields down here dating back to at least 1719.

Turn right along the B7003 for about 50 metres, where a blue sign guides you right to Roslin. Take this footpath going right through the trees. This path splits, but as the parallel footpaths soon merge again it does not matter which one you take. This path takes you past the graveyard on your right and to a T-junction with a tarmac road at the top of the hill. Bypass a track on your right before this. At the top of the hill go

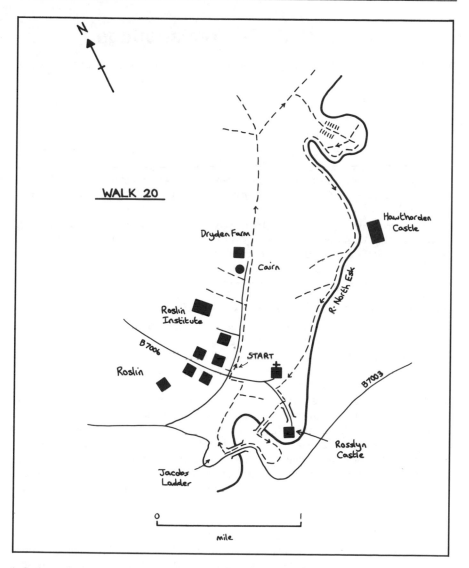

left along the road and Roslin Cross is about 200 metres ahead of you. The Old Original Rosslyn Hotel is on the opposite side of the cross.

If you turn right at the T-junction at the top of the hill instead of left you will find Rosslyn Chapel with its famous Apprentice Pillar some 50 metres along. The entrance fee when I was there was £3.50. Opening hours are Monday to Saturday 1000-1700 and on Sunday 1200-1645. There are also the old Roslin Inn site and Roslin's old stables to visit.

# 21. Midlothian: Lothianbridge

**Route:** Lothianbridge – Newbattle Abbey – Maiden Bridge – Ice House – Lady of Lothian Walk

**Distance:** 3 miles

**Map:** OS Landranger 66, Edinburgh

**Start:** Sun Inn, Lothianbridge

**Access:** By bus, Monday to Saturday services going past the door of the Sun Inn are roughly hourly. On Sundays this service is roughly two-hourly. These buses run from St Andrew's Square bus station. For timetable details call 'Traveline' on 0800 232323 in the Edinburgh area or 0131 225 3858 if outwith Edinburgh. Or phone SMT Lowland on 0131 663 9233.

By car, leave Edinburgh by the A7. About two and a half miles beyond the A720, city bypass, on the A7 is the Sun Inn. It is just beyond the Hardanger roundabout. You come round a left-hand bend with a large railway viaduct on your right. At this point the Sun Inn is on your left. The car park entrance is just past the pub, also on your left.

---

## Sun Inn. Tel: 0131 663 2456; Fax 0131 663 5800

This was originally a house which belonged to a flour mill across the road dating back to the 16th or 17th century. It became a pub some 50 years ago, taking its name from a much older pub on the Newbattle Road. In those days Newbattle Road was the main road and this older Sun Inn was the first and busy staging post on the main road south from Edinburgh. There is a picture on the wall inside the pub of an old coach and horses outside it. This coaching inn had one peculiarity, you had to show your money before you were allowed entrance. There was a small hole in the side of the building through which you had to insert your hand with your money displayed on it before the doors opened for you. It was called the Sun Inn because the sunburst was the motif of the local landowners, the Earls of Lothian. Fortunately today's Sun Inn is more relaxed about entry. This shows in the guest list which is a 'Who's Who' of Edinburgh prominenti. I cannot imagine the likes of Donald Dewar, Michael Forsyth, Malcolm Rifkind and Robin Cook eating here if asked to show their money first.

Landlady Sheila Tydesley today welcomes all. Walkers already use this pub. It has also won an award from the *Edinburgh Evening News* for its reception and treatment of children. Lots of the staff are young mothers who are used to children. Children of all ages will also love the pub's train set. It runs above head height behind the bar, through the lounge and public and above the door. There is an exact scale model of the Sun Inn in this train set made by a customer. The railway theme is continued on the walls where pictures show the *Waverly Engine* crossing the viaduct outside. There are also details of engines and the viaduct on the walls and goods invoices from Great Western Railways. The walls also have pictures by local artists for sale, including some of local scenes. The scenery theme continues behind the bar where there is a photo-montage of Vertsberg, Germany. Mr Tydesley, now deceased, did a lot of business in Germany. There is also a papier-mâché model of a German scene.

The scene inside the pub is of velvet banquettes with wooden (upholstered) chairs and tables. There are flowers on the tables and plants on the windowsills. The bar is warmed by a real fire in winter. For summer there is a beer garden/patio with five acres of gardens. The inn also provides accommodation and local information. There is a non-smoking dining room in the bar or, if you are a smoker, you can eat in the bar. There is a good selection of well-cooked, home-made food including vegetarian. There are daily specials on the blackboard. Food is served from, on weekdays, 1200-1430 and 1700-2130. Friday and Saturday the food hours are 1200-2130 and on Sundays from 1230 to 2130. Credit cards are accepted.

Opening hours are 1100-2300 Monday to Saturday, Sunday it is from 1230-2300. There are normally two real ales. One is resident, Deuchars IPA, and the other is a guest which was Culloden from the Tomintoul Brewery when I was there. Keg products include Tennents Lager, Tennents Special, Caffreys, Dry Blackthorn, Belhaven Best and Guinness.

## Newbattle Abbey

Newbattle Abbey was founded by the Cistercian order of monks in 1140. This was one of the Benedictine orders of monks founded in 1098 at Citeaux in France and was a re-modelled form of the Cluniac order founded at Cluny in 910. It was less austere than the Cluniacs. These, nevertheless, busy monks introduced many new businesses and techniques to the area as they did elsewhere. They had coal mines in Lanarkshire, farmed sheep and produced salt at Prestonpans, Priest Town of the Salt Pans.

The initial part of the abbey built was the lay brothers quarters in the west range. The church was built in the late 1100s. The present structures give a good idea of how the original abbey would have looked. An archaeological dig in the late 19th century found that the present buildings were laid out on the outlines of the ancient abbey remains.

In 1385 English raiders burnt part of the church. As abbeys were rich they were particularly hard hit by such things. This was then reconstructed, including a four part sleeping area with groined roof. This is still an integral part of the present day structure. Subsequent to the Reformation part of the cloister was converted into a country house with a beautiful courtyard around 1580. It was then in the possession of the final commendator, Mark Kerr, who had had a well-timed and politic change of religious beliefs. So he was able to keep and convert the premises.

Rich lands around enabled following lairds to lavish money on the interior decor. This included the Lothian sunburst coat of arms on the first floor. In the 1700s turrets, battlements and spires were added in a flight of Gothic fancy. In 1836 an attic was added on with more fancy stonework by William Burn, the famous architect. In 1858 David Bryce built a family wing at the rear which was extended in 1875. Fur-

The gates of Newbattle Abbey

ther building work was carried out later. Thomas Banner, the noted interior designer, added a fabulous double-height dining room in 1870 which is still preserved in the present day structure. This had painted (pictures) ceilings and damask walls and held the Lothian family's picture collection This building today is a residential college.

## The Walk

Leave the Sun Inn via the car park. Turn right at the bottom of the car park where you will see railway memorabilia. Follow the path around to the left. Take the right-hand path at the fork and continue straight ahead to the river. Ignore an earth footpath to the right and cross the river by the footbridge. There are dippers in the river here. These are small, dark brown birds, the size of a robin, with a white patch on their chests. They bob characteristically up and down, which gives them their name. Special waterproof oil from a gland makes their frequent underwater forays possible. While under water they walk on the river bottom while foraging for aquatic invertebrates and fly larvae. They can do this because they have a special solid skeleton unlike the hollow skeleton of most birds.

Once across the bridge bear right and walk along ,keeping the River South Esk on your near right. As you walk along this beaten earth path you will see the remains of the lade (water channel) that powered some of the mills along this water. After about half a mile this path bends left away from the river and then right onto a dirt road at Barondale Cottages. At the far end of this dirt road it terminates in a T-junction with

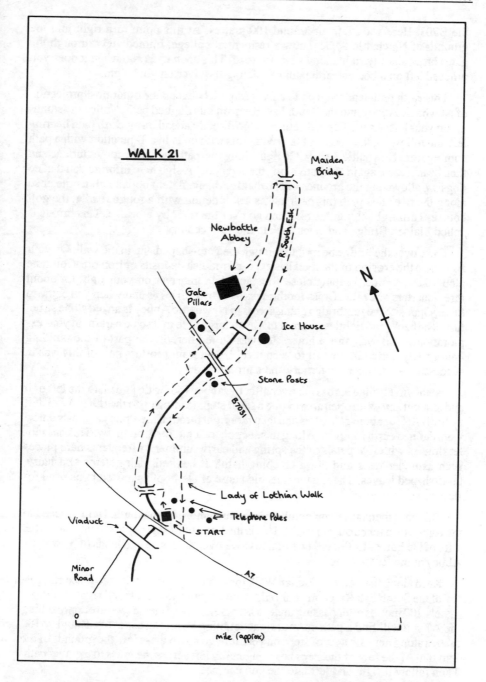

WALK 21

Maiden Bridge

R. South Esk

Newbattle Abbey

Gate Pillars

Ice House

N

Stone Posts

B7051

Lady of Lothian Walk

Telephone Poles

START

Viaduct

Minor Road

A7

0 — 1
mile (approx)

the B703. Here walk left for around 100 metres. At this point turn right into the grounds of Newbattle Abbey, now a residential college. Immediately through the gates break sharply right along a tarmac road. This soon ends and when it does you proceed left on a beaten earth path paralleling the river on your right.

This earth path leads you on to a flagged path between the outermost projection of Newbattle Abbey and the South Esk. Keep on this flagged path. Notice the sundials on your left. As the flagged path ends, go directly ahead on an earth path bearing left and following the course of the river. This path ends in a T-junction with a path coming from Newbattle Abbey. Go right along this path, which becomes tarmac and then beaten earth again as it runs along the riverside. A sign here informs you that no dogs are allowed in the grounds of Newbattle Abbey. After another half a mile or so along the river this path this path makes a T-junction with a rough road at the golf course. Turn right along this road and go over the river by a bridge. This bridge is called Maiden Bridge and dates back to the 15th century.

Once over the bridge bear right through the gate-shaped gap in the wall. On your right here the erosion of the river has exposed reddish deposits of iron ore. Continue along the riverside, keeping close company with the river on your right for about three-quarters of a mile. Cross footbridges over tributaries as and when you come to them. Opposite the footbridge going across to Newbattle Abbey is an old stone structure. The back, and lightless, part of this has a large hole in it so be careful in your explorations. This was an ice house. Ice was stored here in the part of the building deliberately buried in the soil to keep it cold. The front roofless part of this was in succession an orangery, a fernery and a grotto.

At the first bridge across the river after the abbey footbridge go up to the left of it and straight across an open area to find a set of steps leading up to the B703. Walk left up the B703 for about 50 metres and then turn right through the stone gateposts onto a well-defined earth footpath. Along this section look out for ground ivy. This has violet flowers with five petals in the spring and early summer. It frequents bare places such as under trees and has a creeping habit. It has red, hairy stems and hairy, hoof-shaped leaves. These gave it its old name of ale-hoof as it used to be used for flavouring beer.

This path then takes you uphill on to a much more formal path. Here proceed to the right with a fence on your right. This is the Lady of Lothian Walk, named after the wife of the Earl of Lothian. The Lothians took over the house and lands of Newbattle Abbey at the Reformation.

Keep along the Lady of Lothian Walk for about half a mile with the fence and valley of the South Esk River on your right. Bypass paths to the left and right. Approximately 200 metres after passing under a set of telephone lines as you are approaching the A7 you will find a path on your right doubling back. Descend this. Roughly 100 metres along here are a set of steps on your left, go down these into the grounds of the Sun Inn. At the foot of the steps bear diagonally left across the grass to a gravel path. Then follow it right and left into the pub car park.

# 22. Scottish Borders: Carlops

**Route:** Carlops – Fairliehope – North Esk Reservoir – Spittal Farm – Amazondean Farm – Habbies Howe – Kitleyknowe

**Distance:** 5 miles

**Map:** OS Landranger 65, Falkirk and Linlithgow or OS 72, Upper Clyde Valley

**Start:** Allan Ramsay Hotel, Carlops

**Access:** By bus, three different operators run buses from Edinburgh through Carlops. None of these services is very frequent but taken together they just about form an adequate service, Monday to Saturday. It might be wise not to purchase a return ticket as you cannot be sure that your return bus will be run by the same operator. Ask to be let off at Carlops, the Allan Ramsay is on the main road through this small village. For travel times ring 'Traveline' on 0800 232323 if in the Edinburgh area, if outside the Edinburgh area ring 0131 225 3858. The bus companies individual numbers are First Edinburgh on 0131 663 9233, McEwans on 01387 710357 and Stagecoach Western on 01387 253496.

On Sundays there are only four services all day. However on summer Sundays the Pentland Rover service runs around the northern perimeter of the Pentlands so perhaps you could get a Lothian bus to the edge of the city and pick up the Pentland Rover from there. Bus times available from the 'Traveline' number shown above or from Lothian Regional Transport on 0131 555 6363. The Pentland Rover number is 0131 445 5969.

By car, take the A702 out of Edinburgh. Just under a mile after the Lothianburn Interchange with the A720, city bypass, bear right at a fork as the A703 descends to the left. Keep on the A702(T) and about eight or nine miles down this road you arrive in Carlops. The Allan Ramsay is on your right. There is car parking in front of it. There is also other car parking behind it reached by turning right immediately after the hotel. This is signposted. There is also a free car park around 100 metres past the pub on your left.

---

## Allan Ramsay Hotel. Tel: 01968 660258

This is a two-storey structure built in 1792 for a Mr Alexander. Around the end of the 18th century it became an inn as the weaving trade declined. Rooms were added to accommodate tourists who wanted to visit Carlops, which was by then famed as the setting for Allan Ramsay's play *The Gentle Shepherd*. There is a portrait of the poet over its entrance.

It was also a coaching inn. Coaches stopped here while running between Edinburgh and Carlisle. For many years Croall's stagecoach changed horses here as it plied its way from Edinburgh to Blythe Bridge and Dumfries.

Today the Allan Ramsay still serves travellers. There is a good selection of reasonably priced food. It is all home cooked. The home-made steak pie is a speciality. When I was there I asked for a basket of chips, what I got would have fed a starving African family for a week. Perhaps one basket of chips between two or three might be better. At the time of my visit in 1999 they were offering a three-course meal (or two starters and one main course) plus coffee for £7.95. I was pleased to find them offering real Scottish morning rolls, not the soft tasteless pap that falsely masquerades as a roll all too often nowadays. Food is served 1200-2100 Monday to Thursday, 1200-2130 Friday and Saturday and 1230-2130 on Sundays.

Opening hours are 1030-2400 Monday to Saturday and Sunday 1230-2400. There are between two and four real ales depending on the time of year, four in high summer and two in the depths of winter. The resident was Deuchars IPA and the guests were Belhaven 80/- and Sandy Hunters. This pub is in the CAMRA *Good Beer Guide* for 1995 and 1997. On keg were Belhaven Best, Guinness, Dry Blackthorn and Tennents Lager. Interestingly, sloe gin was for sale behind the bar.

The bar itself is topped with old pennies (1d) under glass. It is a lovely old country pub with a low ceiling, internal stonework, dark wood and cream-coloured plaster. A post-horn and an old flintlock pistol echo its past. As does a bill from the early 19th century, for food and drink in this pub, framed on a wall. Pictures of the pub and local area in olden days adorn the walls. There is also an incredibly detailed map of the village. Other interesting items include pictures of British Army officers of the 19th century in full dress uniform and stained glass by the toilets which is an emblem of a British Army regiment. A carved Whitbread horse's head and an old machine from Bordeaux for corking wine bottles are fitting objects for an old pub like this.

The pub is child and walker friendly. Landlord Tony Swift assures me that credit cards are accepted. There is a beer garden and real fires in winter.

## Carlops

Carlops was originally a Pictish settlement. There are traces of their prehistoric military installations in the hillsides around. The Romans were here, as the presence of a Roman road running through the village testifies.

The modern village of Carlops was established in 1784 as a weaving centre and to quarry stone and other minerals. Just to the south of Carlops stood two outcrops of red porphyry close together. One theory for the origin of the name Carlops is that it was shortened from 'carmine lips', named after these two near contiguous poutings of red rock. Porphyry is an igneous rock, produced by volcanoes, with large crystals in a fine-grained mass. It is much prized for ornaments. It was admired by the ancient Egyptians who had red and white crystals in their porphyry. Limestone was also mined and refined into lime locally. Limestone is a form of chalk, calcium carbonate. This was burned with coal in kilns for around a week at high temperatures of around 900 degrees centigrade to produce quicklime, calcium oxide. Water was then added to this to make lime, calcium hydroxide. This was a dangerous step as much heat was produced and the water boiled. The lime produced was used as fertiliser, mortar and as a waterproof covering for houses.

Carlops has two famous 'sons'. One was George Meikle Kemp, the architect responsible for the Scott Monument in Edinburgh. The other was Allan Ramsay, the Edinburgh poet, who made Carlops famous with his major work, *The Gentle Shep-*

*herd*, in 1725. This takes place in and around Carlops. An operetta was made of this in 1729. This is a rustic comedy like *Tam o' Shanter* and indeed Robert Burns admired the word work of this play. Lots of local names are derived from or mentioned in this play, including Rogers Rig, Scroggy Brae and just off the route of this walk Peggyslea and Patieshill. The walk goes through Habbies Howe or, as Ramsay wrote, Habbys How, Halberts Hollow, a famous site in this work. This play had an amazing effect on Carlops as it became popular and deluged with hordes of visitors.

One of the 'carmine lips' that gave Carlops its name

## The Walk

Depart the Allan Ramsay and turn right along the main road, A702(T). About 100 metres along here on your right is a narrow road just past Carlops Village Hall. A Scottish Rights of Way Society (SRWS) sign points up here guiding walkers to Buteland by the Borestone. Follow the sign right up this narrow road. Across the road from this sign is Carmine Lips, one of the red rocky outcrops that is believed to have given Carlops its name. The other one has been quarried away. The two originally were quite close together. As you walk along this narrow road look to your left. There are what appear to be desert dunes in shape but covered in green. This is Carlops Dean and the lumps and humps are glacial moraines. The glaciers scraped and scoured the hills and dumped the soil and stones here when they retreated.

Around 100 metres up here the road bears left to Carlopshill Farm. At this point go straight ahead on the rough road, following a purple Pentland Path arrow on a fence post. Walk up this rough road for approximately three-quarters of a mile past Fairliehope Farm and bypassing a footpath on the right to Carlops via Patieshill. Keep on this road for roughly another mile along the valley of the Carlops Burn until you descend right to the isolated house at the North Esk Reservoir. On this section before the reservoir ignore a path on the right to Carlops and a SRWS sign pointing left to Buteland. Just follow the signs ahead for Nine Mile Burn. This is so called because it is nine Scots miles from Edinburgh, 11.75 English miles. This reservoir is a natural lochan deepened and extended by an earth dam. It was built as a compensation pond. This means that its supplies kept enough water in the North Esk River to power the pepper mills of Penicuik, despite abstraction elsewhere.

Follow the right of way signs to bypass the isolated house on your right. Walk past a sign to Buteland on the left and cross the dam, signposted for Nine Mile Burn. In the middle of the dam you cross from Borders Region into Lothian Region. At the far end of the dam cross a stile and turn left uphill towards the signpost, as guided by a purple Pentland Path arrow. At the signpost turn right uphill as indicated by the sign. It indicates Nine Mile Burn and has a purple Pentland Path arrow. Cross a path running along the contour line and head diagonally right ahead uphill, using the line of the dam as straight ahead to measure your diagonal from. Stay with this faint but discernible path up the north side of this tributary of the Carlops Burn. This next little bit can be tricky. You are heading for the saddle between Patieshill on your right and Spittal Hill, whose shoulder you are walking on and whose summit is on your left. If you lose the path it should not be a problem. Just keep up this small valley between the hills until you hit the line of the fence. Then cast left along it until you find a field gate and cart track a little way along it. Turn right along the track and proceed through the gate.

Should you make the mistake of going too far left and too steeply uphill the line of the track and fence will be across your path. Simply turn right along the track and follow it to the field gate.

This gate is marked with a purple Pentland Path arrow. Follow this track down to Spittal Farm. 'Spittal' is an Anglo-Saxon word meaning 'hospital'. The hospital here was founded by the monks from Newhall in the valley of the North Esk below the farm. These monks were Cistercians of the Benedictine order. On your left in the next valley to the north is a monk's road where monks went on pilgrimage to other sacred sites in Scotland such as St Andrew's, Dunfermline and Holyrood Abbey in Edinburgh. Some of the gates along this track have stiles beside them marked with purple Pentland Path arrows. At Spittal Farm go through the farmyard and follow the track downhill as it winds left and right. This track becomes tarmac and terminates in a T-junction with as minor tarmac road. A signpost here guides you right to Carlops. This road follows the line of the old Roman road and coach road.

Stay with this quiet country road for half a mile or so until it bends sharply to the left to the A702(T). Bypass a tarmac road on the right as it bends. Go directly across the main road and down the farm road for Amazondean Farm. 'Dean' is a Scottish word for a 'narrow valley', especially one with trees. Immediately past the sign for Amazondean Farm, where the road swerves abruptly left, go straight ahead on a

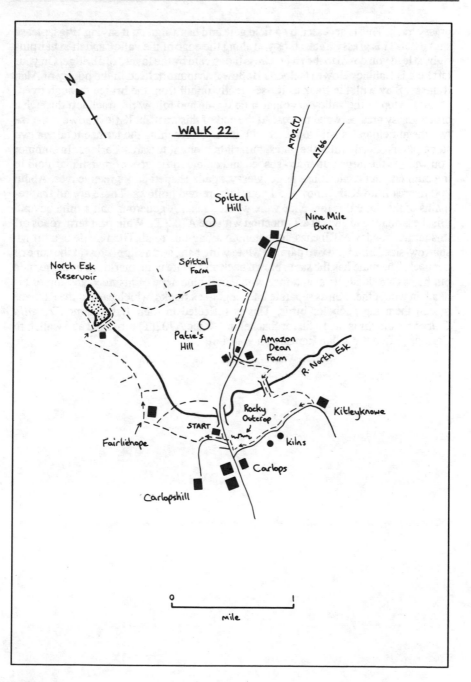

WALK 22

A702(T)

A766

Spittal
Hill

Nine Mile
Burn

North Esk
Reservoir

Spittal
Farm

Patie's
Hill

Amazon
Dean
Farm

R. North Esk

Rocky
Outcrop

Kitleyknowe

START

kilns

Fairliehope

Carlops

Carlopshill

N

0                    1
mile

grassy track. This is accessed by a field gate and has a sign on it saying 'Pigs, please shut gate'. This grassy track takes you along the edge of the valley and then hairpins right to lead you down to the river. Cross the stream by the lovely old bridge. On your left here is Habbies Howe (Halberts Hollow), as immortalised in the poetry of Alan Ramsay. Stay with the track as it rises gently uphill from the bridge through trees.

At the top of the valley negotiate a field gate and follow the track left through a broad grassy area between fences. At the end of this track, at Kitleyknowe, traverse two metal field gates held together with wire. On reaching the tarmac road via two stone pillars shortly after the gates, turn right along it towards Carlops. In summer you will see the large buttercup-shaped and coloured flowers of marsh marigold in the burn on your right. It has large, glossy, spade-shaped dark green leaves. About 200 metres from Kitleyknowe, on your left are two hollows. These are all that remains of the limekilns that once were worked here. A generous half a mile beyond this the tarmac road ends at a T-junction with the A702(T). Walk past farm roads off this tarmac road. Chaffinches are common along this road. The female is a brown sparrow-sized bird with two parallel white wing bars, and a slight crest at the nape of her neck. The male has the same brown back and white wing markings as the female but he has a reddish chest and face with a dull blue nape of his neck and top of his head. In winter these birds separate into single-sex flocks, which caused the Romans to call them the bachelor birds. This is reflected in their Latin name *Fringilla Coloebs*. *Coloebs* is the Latin for 'bachelor'. At the A702(T) turn right and walk into Carlops to find the Allan Ramsay on your left.

# 23. Scottish Borders: West Linton

**Route:** West Linton – Roman Road – Hardgatehead – Ingraston – Garvald – Ferniehaugh – Nether Cairn – Upper Cairn – North Slipperfield

**Distance:** 10 miles

**Map:** OS Landranger 72, Upper Clyde Valley.

**Start:** Gordon Arms, West Linton

**Access:** By bus, three disparate companies run services to West Linton. None of these services is frequent, but taken together they just about make a passable service, Monday to Saturday. It may be prudent not to acquire a return ticket as you cannot be sure on what operator's bus you will be going back. Ask to be put off at West Linton. The pub is on the main road through West Linton, A702, and is in the middle of the village and easy to find. On Sundays there are only four buses all day. But on summer Sundays the Pentland Rover service circles the northern half of the Pentlands so perhaps you could get a Lothian bus to the city boundary and pick up a Pentland Rover from there. Lothian bus times are available on 'Traveline' (see below) or on 0131 555 6363. The Pentland Rover number is 0131 445 5969

For timetables call 'Traveline' on 0800 232323 if calling from the Edinburgh area, if calling from elsewhere ring 0131 225 3858. The companies' numbers are First Edinburgh 0131 663 9233, McEwans 01387 710357 and Stagecoach Western 01387 253496.

By car, leave Edinburgh by the A702, Lothian Rd. Once across the Lothianburn Interchange with the A720, city bypass, keep going on the A702. The A703 drops off to the left at a fork, here bear right on the A702(T). Continue along this road for the next 11 miles or so. On reaching West Linton, drive past the sign pointing into West Linton village and stay on the A702(T). The Gordon Arms is just past this on the main road on your left. There is parking outside it for one or two cars. The car park entrance is on your left immediately before the pub.

---

## The Gordon Arms. Tel: 01968 660208

The road that became the A72, that the Gordon Arms stands on, was built in 1834. This replaced the old coach/Roman road that you perambulate along on this walk. The Gordon Arms was erected around this time as a coaching inn. It serviced coaches between Edinburgh, Biggar and Lanark. The garage across the road was formerly the stables for this inn. This is why it used to be called the Gordon Garage. A horse-drawn hearse was kept here.

Gordon Jardine, grand-daughter and daughter of the previous owners of this inn, whose unusual first name is in honour of the pub, gave me some reminiscences of life here in the 40s and 50s. They had Golf Club dinners and the Rotary Club dinners that the hotel still hosts. In those days lots of people came out of Edinburgh and stayed at the Gordon Arms for an extended summer break of up to two months. A couple of old ladies were permanent paying guests. She remembers an old, built-in bath of beaten tin that was comfortable and always warm. Where the car park is now, was then a garden. Her grandfather kept monkeys in it. These monkeys were fascinated by knee-caps and used to reach out and wiggle them if you got too close, and particularly if you were a small boy in short trousers. It makes me shiver to think of it.

You won't shiver in the Gordon Arms today though, there are real fires in winter. It is a lovely old country pub with extensive stonework inside. There is an eclectic collection of sofas, settles and chairs. The decor comprises old bookcases and books, old clocks, brass work, candles and ornaments. A separate dining room is pleasantly furbished in the same general style. There are pictures of the area in olden times and of the Gordon Arms in days gone by on the walls. Behind the bar, a framed newspaper article headlined Guns, Grouse and more Grouse is about a regular. Murdo is a gamekeeper in a local estate.

So it is no surprise to find local game on the menu, but the house speciality is chargrilled steaks. The steaks are from grass-fed, BSE-free herds. They are from the Earl of Buccleuch's herd, which is equivalent to Aberdeen Angus in quality. These steaks are hung for 28 days to mature instead of the normal 14 days. The chargrill is a proper one where the steaks are cooked on hot lava rock. All the beef is Scottish. Fresh fish and seafood comes from Pittenweem. When lobster is available, lobster thermidor is also. All the food is fresh and home cooked. On Sundays you can have a big breakfast: eggs Benedict, eggs Florentine, smoked salmon Florentine or house omelettes with the Sunday papers. With each Sunday roast meal you receive a free child's meal with ice cream and a soft drink, no age limits apply. There are also vegetarian choices. Food is served 1200-1500 and 1700-2100 Monday to Thursday, Fridays 1200-1500 and 1700-2200, Saturdays 1200-2200 and Sundays 1130-2100. Outside these hours a choice of snacks is available; sandwiches, baked potatoes, pizza, nachos etc. The food is served both in the dining room and the bar.

While I was in the bar there was a border collie sitting on a bar stool at the bar. He did not get served but you will. There are two real ales. The resident is Deuchars IPA. When I was there the guest was Old Mellow Traditional Bitter from Old Mill. Keg pumps dispensed Belhaven Best, Guinness, Tennents Lager, Dry Blackthorn and Stella Artois. Opening hours are 1100-2400 Monday to Saturday and on Sundays 1200-2400.

Landlady Fiona Ingram is happy to be hostess to walkers and children. In nice weather they can sit in the beer garden. Other amenities include cigarettes behind the bar and a jukebox. Credit cards are welcome, there is a cash-back facility.

## West Linton

This area was anciently inhabited. A Roman road passes within half a mile of the village. And from times before this there are numerous remains and traces of Bronze Age and Iron Age peoples. However West Linton, or Linton Roderick (or Rotherick) as it was known then, first claimed recorded history's attention in the 12th century. Then church records show it as a vicarage of the Abbey of Kelso. Linton means 'linn town' or 'town at the waterfall or rapids'. While on the subject of water, West Linton is situated on the base of an old loch of some 15 square miles in size. Situation is the

Restored Bronze Age cemetery near West Linton

reason for West Linton's existence as it is at the junction of the old Roman road from Edinburgh to the Clyde Valley and the old drove road from the Highlands to England via Cauldstane Slap in the Pentlands.

Cattle and sheep markets were West Linton's bread and butter for many a year. The local inns and stables made money out of this trade. Money was also dug out of the ground locally in the form of silver. Closed in 1753, this mine is said to have provided the money for Mary of Guise, wife of James V, to pay her forces. Another way canny West Lintonites used to find money coming out of the ground was in the waters of two local wells. Rumbling Tam, which you will see in the course of this walk, had its supposedly curative waters sold for a halfpenny a glass; while across the river St Mungo's Well provided 'healing' water for one penny a glass.

As well as silver, coal was mined here and stone quarried. This village's most famous character was a sculptor, James Gifford. Numerous examples of his work remain, including much in the graveyard at the kirk. You will see the Gifford panel on this walk, created to honour his marriage. His most notable sculpture of his wife and children used to stand in the centre of the village, but because of pollution and vandalism it is currently locked away in the village hall.

James Gifford was a staunch Covenanter and in 1666 is thought to have fought at the Battle of Rullion Green. Covenanters hid from retribution after this battle at Harbour Craig near West Linton. Covenanters also used to gather to worship in secret at the Garral, a saddle in the hills between North Muir and Mendick Hill, which we pass through in the course of this walk.

In 1690 the inhabitants sent a welcome to William of Orange describing themselves as 'The Substantial Metropolitan of Tweedale'. Not surprisingly, West Linton at this time was infamous for its poor but prideful petty lords, around a third of whom were on parish relief. Nevertheless, it is said that Queen Victoria considered two places for her Scottish Estate, the other was Balmoral. After the sheep tryst closed around the mid-19th century and trains and buses replaced coaches, West Linton declined from the 'Substantial Metropolitan' to the small market town that it is today.

## The Walk

Exit the Gordon Arms on to the A702(T) and walk left along this, bypassing a tarmac road into West Linton. Just before the bridge parapet on your left is a set of steps leading down to a paved footpath, descend these. Bear diagonally right over the grass at the foot of the steps towards the right-hand end of the row of houses. About 10 metres from the door of the Tan House you will find a small set of steps on your right between two leylandii bushes and leading down to the river. Here Rumbling Tam, a well of supposedly curative power, today flows into the river. In times gone by glasses of its water were sold for a halfpenny.

Return to the paved path and at its far end from the main road turn left for about 10 metres. Then go right across some gravel into a narrow lane. This is Teapot Lane, named because of the public tap here from which the local women got the water for their drink of tea. At the T-junction at the terminus of Teapot Lane go right, this leads you out into Raemartin Square. On your right was the Hall House where the local laird lived. Rent and feu duty had to be paid on Term Days through a small hole in the wall between 1200 and 1300. Go left through the square to Main St. Here look across the road to where the Gifford Carving is on a wall. A notable local sculptor, James Gifford carved this to commemorate a marriage. Walk down Main Street to the clock and here turn right up this nameless street. Just before you reach the clock, diagonally on your left is the gable end of the old school from the last century with its carving of St Andrew and his cross. Go up this little road and across the footbridge at its end. You can see where the ford used to be. Once over the bridge proceed straight ahead up Chapel Brae to the A702(T).

Cross the main road, bearing slightly right into Medwyn Road signposted for West Linton Golf Club and Baddinsgill. Walk up here for roughly half a mile past Medwyn Park and Medwyn Drive on the right. The fields on the left were the site of the Linton Trysts. These large sheep fairs were held annually until 1856 when they were relocated in Lanark. West Linton is at the end of an old drove road across the Pentlands. A local type of sheep had their wool woven into hodden grey, a tough fabric. The Linton sheep had grey wool so they did not need dyeing. This road follows the route of the old drove road. Just before the golf course on the left look right to see Medwyn House in the trees. This was an old coaching inn. The golf course road and the path off it that you will be walking on follow the routes of the old Roman road and coach road.

Turn left up the golf course road, also signposted for Slipperfield Farm. About

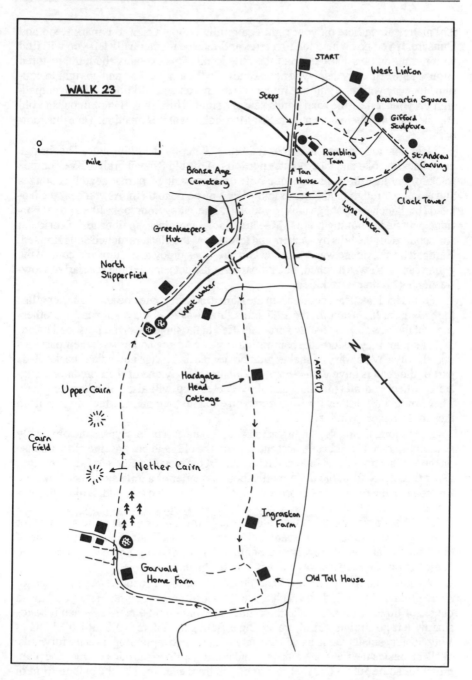

WALK 23

START

West Linton

Raemartin Square

Steps

Gifford Sculpture

St. Andrew Carving

Rumbling Tam

0        mile        1

Bronze Age Cemetery

Tan House

Lyne Water

Clock Tower

Greenkeepers Hut

North Slipperfield

West Water

N

Upper Cairn

Hardgate Head Cottage

A702 (T)

Cairn Field

Nether Cairn

Ingraston Farm

Garvald Home Farm

Old Toll House

250 metres along here on your right is a public footpath sign to Lanark Road and Dunsyre. If you go up here for 10 metres and then bear diagonally left you will find an information board at the top of the little knoll. This explains about the restored Bronze Age cemetery displayed here. Return to the tarmac road and go right to continue the way you were going. Around 100 metres on you will find a public footpath sign on your left as the road bends sharply right. This reads 'Dolphinton, the old Biggar road, 4'. There is a house called Mendickfoot at this junction. Take this footpath.

Negotiate a field gate and cross the West Water by the old bridge. This bridge dates back to 1620 and incorporates portions of the old Roman bridge. Keep on this track for another three-quarters of a mile or so, crossing a tarmac road by cottages and passing through field gates as and when you come to them. As you near the isolated Hardgatehead Cottage look to your left. The valley floor looks like a pot of porridge petrified at boiling point. These are glacial moraines, spoil heaps of rock and soil scoured off the hills by glaciers and left here as the glaciers melted and retreated. Hardgatehead Cottage was where the Gowrie Conspiracy to capture and control the young James VI was hatched. The kidnapping did not succeed and the Earl of Gowrie and his brother were killed.

From Hardgatehead, continue up the same track for some one and a quarter miles to the farm at Ingraston. In the 1700s this farm was run by the Alexander brothers (no, not the singers) and the two brothers died at the same moment, poisoned by adders. Perhaps they disturbed a pair of fighting or courting adders with their passions raised. Anyway be wary of snakes with heavy black zigzags down their backs. This part of the road is alive with rabbits. So unsurprisingly one of their predators, buzzards, wheel and mew in the skies above here. You will also see wheatears here. Their white rump as they fly away from you explains their name, which derives from the Anglo-Saxon 'white arse'.

Keep along the track past Ingraston for just under a mile. Bypass the obviously new dirt road on the right and descend left via the old sand pit. Past the old tollhouse on the left this track turns right and left to end at the metalled Garvald Rd. Turn right along this, away from the main road. About a quarter of a mile along here take the first road on the right, at the quarry on your left, signposted Garvald. Follow this tarmac road around to the left where another Garvald sign guides you. Just over half a mile further on you arrive at Garvald Home Farm. This appears to be a centre for mentally retarded adults. The road/track terminates in a T-junction at the far side of the farm. Break right here where a Scottish Rights of Way Society sign points to West Linton, four miles away via a public footpath.

Walk on this first unsurfaced and then later surfaced road between two sets of stone pillars. You will then reach a small lochan on your right. Here you have a choice of three dirt roads. Take the centre one for about 50 metres. When it bends sharply left go straight ahead, traversing a field gate. There is a Scottish Rights of Way Society small plaque beside the gate with an arrow pointing directly forwards. Walk up beside the trees on your right and continue along the edge of this pine plantation for some 500 to 600 metres. When the trees end, keep on the path in front of you paralleling the edge of the cleugh on your right. On your left here you will see the Nether Cairn. This massive cairn is believed to be in its original state. Some half a mile further on, on your left is the Upper Cairn. This has been extensively plundered for stone but is still very large. Also along this path in springtime you may see the rare mountain pansy. This is a recognisable pansy of five-petalled, yellow flowers up to an inch in diameter. Please do not pick this endangered species.

Along here, if you look up to your left you will see a field of cairns on North Muir. There are also small cairns beside the path. What the purpose of these cairns was or what they signify no one seems to know but there are a lot of them here. Shortly after the Upper Cairn this path enlarges to a cart track. Pass through field gates on this track as and when you come to them. About half a mile beyond the Upper Cairn a track comes in from the right, go straight ahead here over the plank bridge. This area is the Garral where Covenanters once held services in the 17th century. A further half a mile beyond this a tarmac road comes in from the left from the West Water Reservoir. Go right on to this and proceed on it towards North Slipperfield Farm. Walk through the farm and then through the golf course on this road for roughly half a mile. Where the golf course starts there is a drinking water fountain on your left at a tee beside the road. I feel that the golfers would not grudge you a drink if you are thirsty.

Some 50 metres past the green keeper's hut on your left, a greenish shed with a white base, is an unsignposted grassy track going diagonally left across the golf course. This is a public footpath. Where this well-maintained track veers left towards the green take the less kempt track straight ahead. This takes you around to the right and ends at a tarmac road. Turn left along this. After some 250 metres this makes a T-junction with another tarmac road. Here go right down this, Medwyn Road, for about half a mile until you reach the A702(T). Bear left along the main road. The Gordon Arms is about 100 metres on, on your right.

# 24. Scottish Borders: Leadburn

**Route:** Leadburn – Nether Falla – Cowieslinn – Spylaw Cottage – Easter Deans

**Distance:** 6.5 miles

**Map:** OS Landranger 66, Edinburgh or OS Landranger 73, Peebles and Galashiels

**Start:** Leadburn Inn

**Access:** By bus, there are regular bus services to the Leadburn Inn from Edinburgh. Weekdays and Saturdays the bus services are adequate, but on Sundays the service is a bit sparse. Ask to be put off at the Leadburn Inn. For details phone 'Traveline' on 0800 232323 in the Edinburgh area or on 0131 225 3858 if phoning from outside Edinburgh. Alternatively call SMT Lowland on 0131 663 9233.

By car, leave Edinburgh by the A702, Lothian Rd, at the west end of Princes St. A short while after crossing the A720 (city bypass) at the Lothianburn Interchange, take the A703 descending to the left. About one and a half miles along here go right at a roundabout onto the A701 for Penicuik. In Penicuik, where this road forks, take the left-hand fork, which is the A701 for Peebles and Biggar. Leadburn is about three miles beyond this junction at a St Andrew's cross-shaped meeting of roads. The Leadburn Inn is on your left just previous to this junction. The entrance to the car park is immediately before the pub on your left.

---

## Leadburn Inn. Tel: 01968 672 952

You will not find many pubs that prominently display in their bars unflattering comments about themselves. This is one that does. The quotation in question is from a book by John Buchan, *John Barret of Burns*. This describes the surroundings of the inn as godforsaken, evil and dour black peat bog. It depicts the inn as having damp and mouldy rooms with chimneys likely to fall down at any moment. But he relieves the gloom by saying that he had an excellent meal here.

It must be remembered that this is fiction. It is also worth noting that only an establishment brim full of confidence in their quality and service would have the self-belief to publicly display such a notice. Their confidence is not misplaced. They are members of the Edinburgh and Scottish Tourist Boards and approved by the latter. They display a Les Routiers sign and are featured in the Best of Scotland Pub Guide.

The Leadburn Inn dates back to 1777 when a Mr Thompson was licensed for 'The Privilege and Liberty of Brewing, Baking, Vending and Retailing Ales'. The Thompson family ran this inn for around two centuries. Originally it was a drovers' inn, then it became a coaching inn and finally a railway inn. Latterly the racing cyclists of Edinburgh's Waverly Club used to breakfast here.

The food is excellent, the house speciality is steak pie. However the chef keeps his recipes to himself so I cannot give any hints as to what any special ingredients might be. There is an excellent choice of reasonably priced food, including traditional fish suppers. There are a number of vegetarian starters and main courses. The starters include nachos. You can also have sandwiches, including baguettes, with hot or cold fillings. The snack menu in the bar includes old favourites like pie (or bridie) beans and chips as well as more modern delicacies such as vegetable korma in a sesame seed bun and standbys such as toasties, baked potatoes etc. There is a children's menu with mini pizza and such like. Food is served Monday to Friday 1200-1430 and 1730-2100 Monday to Thursday. Friday evenings food serving times are 1730-2200. Saturday and Sunday food is available from 1200-2200.

Opening hours are Monday to Thursday and Sunday 1100-2300. Friday and Saturday doors are open from 1100-2400. Real ales are seven in number. The residents are Southerness and Cuil Hill from the Gillfoot Brewery in Dumfries and Galloway. The guests when I was there were Black Sheep from Masham, Deuchars IPA, Inde Coope Burton Ale and Aviemore Brewery's Ruthven and Wolf of Badenoch.. Keg products included Calders Premium Cream Ale, Calders 70/-, Castlemaine 4X, Guinness and Dry Blackthorn.

There are a number of places you can eat or drink. The bar is flagged in stone and has a panoramic picture window looking out to the Pentlands. It is heated, in the winter, by a Jotil wood burning stove in the middle of the floor. A board gives details of James Hogg, the Ettrick Shepherd. The old character in a picture beside this was a captain in the Boer War, a civil servant in Burma and the oldest customer, until he died aged 95. We should be so lucky. The lovely old embossed and embellished till is a replica, it has a digital display. A selection of fishing flies are also on display. There is a lovely conservatory area with plants where you can eat or drink. The restaurant/lounge bar is plush and comfortable with a lovely, randomly shelved, dark wood wall unit with a beautiful display of jugs, plates etc. Additionally there is an old railway dining car at the back to eat in as well as a beer garden outside.

There are the usual amenities, cigarette machine, fruit machine and dart board. Landlord Mr Dempsey has hearty hospitality for hikers. The pub is child friendly. They take credit cards but not Switch. Sometimes they have folk music sessions.

# Leadburn

The reason for Leadburn's existence is in its crossroads. It was once also a railway junction. In this walk you wander along the remains and routes of the two railway lines that once joined here. In fact, if you go up the A6094 to Hardgate for about 100 metres you will find the remains of Leadburn Railway Station on your right preserved as a picnic site.

In the Victorian age of railway building an Act of Parliament had to grant the right to build a railway. Such an act was passed on the 8th of July 1853, authorising the building of a railway to Peebles, Scottish Borders. This single-track railway ran from the North British Railway's (NBR) line near Dalkeith some six or so miles south-east of Edinburgh for 18.5 miles to Peebles. The line was opened on the 4th of July 1855. The Peeble's railway engines took the train to the junction with the NBR line between Hawick and Edinburgh. From there NBR engines pulled the train into Edinburgh. The first train of three returns each day departed Peebles 0745 reaching

Edinburgh at 0945. In its first two months the business made a profit of £1000, a vast sum in those days. Many companies were asking for sidings for their own businesses. Later a Peebles Express left Peebles at 0844 and arrived in Edinburgh at 0937, having called at Leadburn among other places.

In 1857 the signaller at the junction of the NBR and Peebles railways was John Latta, a cobbler. He mended shoes in the signal box while working part-time as a signal man. This arrangement ceased after an accident injured four people.

The railway prospered. Among its innovative schemes were free season tickets for outsiders who built a house near Peebles and commuted to the Edinburgh area. They also gave free season tickets to the founders of a spa in Peebles. Travellers were collected at the station by the spa's horse-drawn omnibus. On the 1st of August 1876 the NBR took over the Peebles railway.

Even though a subsidised coach running west from Leadburn Station was in difficulties, this did not deter enthusiasts from proposing a ten-mile stretch of railway from Leadburn west to Dolphinton. On 3 June 1862 an Act of Parliament enabled this. The LLD (Leadburn, Linton and Dolphinton) Railway was born. Thomas Bauch was the engineer here as he was on the Peebles line. During a test train trial on the LLD in 1863 an iron girder on a bridge broke. The bridge was found to be too slightly built. Thus,

Footpath on the remains of the North British Railway between Dalkeith and Peebles

perhaps, foreshadowing the Tay Rail Bridge disaster of 1880 with its horrendous loss of life. Thomas Bauch was the engineer for this bridge also. Another accident on this line followed an hour's drinking in the Leadburn Inn. This led to a series of minor accidents which culminated in a runaway wagon from this line reaching the Peebles to Edinburgh line where it crashed head first into a passenger train. There was a fatality. The LLD was taken over by the NBR on 31 July 1865.

On 1 March 1867 the Caledonian Railway opened a spur line into Dolphinton from the east starting at Carstairs, a major rail junction. However a combined station was never established, leaving passengers to walk over a quarter of a mile between stations.

The railways opening up gave access to markets and supplies for the textile mills of the sheep farming Tweed Valley area. Soon tweed was exported all over the world. These trains also took local cattle to market. Tourists used these trains to visit the Scott country of the borders.

On 1 April 1933 passenger services ceased to call at Dolphinton. Freight trains stopped soon thereafter. The Peebles line succumbed to Dr Beeching on 5 February 1962. It is ironic then that while prospecting for another walk in the area on a disused railway line and viaduct, I had to abandon the idea when I was told that it was being surveyed with a view to reopening it to ease rail congestion.

## The Walk

Leave the Leadburn Inn by the exit near the stove in the public bar. Once on the main road, A701, turn left along this. Cross the A6904 to Hardgate and walk along the left-hand side of the A703. The A701, confusingly, dog-legs right at this crossroads. Proceed on the pavement on the left of the A703 for approximately 100 metres. Immediately before the Scottish Borders sign on your left you will see a grassy path on your right across the road. This runs diagonally forward up a bank. Go up here. The A703 is a busy road.

At the top of the bank bear left along the old railway line path towards the trees. At the fork about 150 metres along this path take the left-hand option. Near the junction of these paths in summer/early autumn you will find the spiky blue/purple flowers of sheep's scabious. The Latin name contains the word *Montana*, indicating that this is the mountain version of scabious. Which could explain why it is sheep's scabious. This plant likes dry grassland and acidic soil. After around a mile, having bypassed a path to the right and gone directly across a metalled road, you reach a gate at the end of the wood. Hikers' footprints in the mud and horse-apples indicate who uses this ride through the woods.

Having passed the gate, follow this track straight ahead across the moor. On your left front are the Moorfoot Hills. Keep straight ahead on this broad, grassy track for a mile or so and eventually it becomes a farm track beside a plantation of pines on your near right. The RSPB is reporting a shortage of lapwings but down here I saw a flock of 100 or so, so it must be a problem of other places. This is a bird of moorlands, meadows and marshes. It is recognisable by the crest at the back of its head, ol-

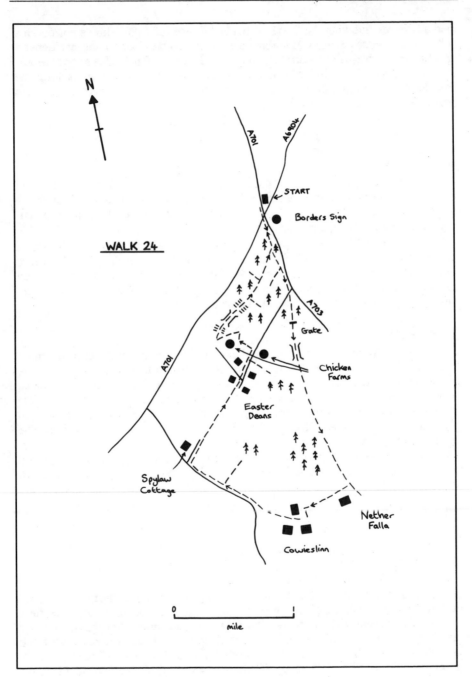

ive-green back, white belly and face and black upper chest. It is about the size of a gull. Nesting in the very early spring they will dive-bomb you if you stray near their nests. About the same time of year they make tumbling, aerobatic courtship flights.

Roughly half a mile further on, turn right through a field gate to an earth track immediately before the isolated cottage of Nether Falla. Go along this track for about 300 metres, passing through field gates and closing them behind you, as and when you come to them. This track then bends sharply left into Cowieslinn Farm. Just before the farm are two tracks on the right. Take the first of these. Roughly a quarter of a mile along this track it ends at a bend on a tarmac road. Go right/straight ahead on this road. Between a half and three-quarters of a mile along this quiet road, having walked past a forest track heading into trees on the right, take the minor road to the right at the top of the wee brae. A sign here on a beech tree says Spylaw. 'Law' is Scottish for 'a gently rounded hill', often separate or prominent.

Walk past Spylaw Cottage on your left and the road deteriorates into a rough track. A further half a mile or so on this reverts back to tarmac. Follow this road as it kinks right and left through the hamlet of Easter Deans, ignoring a road going off left and uphill. Continue along this road flanked by beech hedges. About a quarter of a mile past Easter Deans a track comes in from the right just past a line of trees. Stay with the tarmac road until about halfway between this line of trees and the woodland ahead, where a track goes off left uphill. This is signposted Mitchell Hill. There appears to be a free-range chicken farm on the right here. At the top of Mitchell Hill is another free-range chicken farm. At this point bear right to pass through the field gate on your right. Then take the left-hand of the two tracks that bears left behind the chicken sheds in a half-moon shape. Once behind the chicken sheds look for a track going off to the right and heading for the line of the old railway embankment and bridge visible on your right.

Once at the embankment climb up it and turn right along the track of the old railway line and across the bridge. Follow this well-worn path into and through the trees, ignoring a footpath to the right and a forest track to the left. After some half a mile of what is almost a track sometimes, you meet a path coming in from the right, bear left here. Some 200 metres further on this path takes you onto the A703. Cross the road and turn left down a rough pavement to reach the Leadburn Inn about 100 metres along on the far side of the A6094.

# 25. Southern Upland Way Sampler: Innerleithen

**Route:** Innerleithen – St Ronan's Wells – Traquair – Cheese Well – Glenmead

**Distance:** 9 miles

**Map:** OS Landranger 73, Peebles and Galashiels

**Start:** Traquair Arms, Innnerleithen

**Access:** By bus, buses run directly from Edinburgh to Innerleithen. The service is adequate on weekdays but a bit sparse on Sundays, but even then you may have to wait but you should get a bus. Get off at the centre of Innerleithen and walk back along the High St. and turn left at the church at the junction of the A72 and B709. The Traquair Arms is about 100 metres down this road on its left-hand side. Ring First Lowland on 0131 663 9233 or call the 'Traveline' on 0800 232323 if in the Edinburgh area. Outwith the Edinburgh area phone 0131 225 3858.

By car, take the A701 out of Edinburgh towards Penicuik. Keep on this road, following the frequent signs for Peebles. It becomes the A703 at Leadburn. At the edge of Peebles take the A72 going left signposted for Galashiels and Innerleithen. As you arrive in Innerleithen take the first road on your right, the B709 signposted for St Mary's Loch and Yarrow. There is a large church and steeple on the right-hand side of the road here. The Traquair Arms is about 100 metres up here on the left. The car park entrance is immediately beyond it, also on the left. If the car park is full you can do a U-turn and return to and cross the A72. Once over the A72 and into Hall St., there is a free car park about 100 metres up here on the right.

---

## Traquair Arms. Tel: 01896 830 229; http://www.trad/inns.co.uk/traquair

This pub was established in 1835 as a coaching inn called Riddles. There is still a stable at the back of the house from where the lady of the house regularly rides. Talking of ladies, this inn has a female ghost. This spirit only manifests herself in the oldest part of the building. She is never spotted save from the rear. This grey lady wears a bustled floor length grey frock. Her hair is always done up in a bun. The pub was extended in 1896 so you are unlikely to see her.

There is, however, nothing ghostly or insubstantial about the food. Beef, some of it local, is a speciality. All the steaks come from Aberdeenshire and are all from Aberdeen Angus grass-fed cattle. This is certified by the Aberdeen Angus Society. Other local food includes haggis and lamb as well as seafood from Eyemouth, whose crystal clear waters make it a Mecca for divers. Landlord Hugh Anderson is a former Merchant Navy catering officer who became a publican and arrived at the Traquair Arms in 1984. Food serving hours are 1200-2100 seven days a week. All food is home cooked. Specialities of the house include steak pie with locally brewed real ale, and finnan savoury which is Scottish smoked haddock, onions, Ayrshire cheddar cheese and double cream. Vegetarians have choices of starters and main courses.

There are also salads and omelettes and sometimes one of the daily specials on the blackboard is vegetarian. The menu changes every three to four months. The standard of cooking is best described by the awards it has won. The Scottish Tourist Board rated it as 'Best Eating Place' in 1997 and it also won the best bar meal section in 1996. The Canadian Automobile Association (I couldn't make this up!) recommends this place as having some of the best pub grub in Britain.

Happily the awards are not only confined to the food. It is featured in CAMRA's 1998 *Good Beer Guide*. It is also in Egon Ronay's *Old Speckled Hen's Guide to Pubs and Inns* for 1997. It is recommended by the *Which Guide to Country Pubs*. It is mentioned favourably in the 1999 *Good Pub Guide*. It is recommended by the Scottish Tourist Board. The real ales mainly come from the local Traquair Brewery. This is an intact brewery from the 1700s discovered by the local laird in the 1960s. It was renovated and produces real ales which are famed worldwide. On draught here are Traquair Bear and Ghillie. There are also bottles of other Traquair brews on sale such as Jacobite, so you could take some home with you. Another real ale on draught is Broughtons Greenmantle and there is Addlestones cask-conditioned cider. Keg products on sale are Guinness, Calders 70/-, Calders Cream, Carlsberg Lager and Broughtons Best. The bar is open 1100-2400 seven days a week.

The pub is nicely furbished in a modern manner with all the facilities you would expect. It is friendly and comfortable. The beer garden is a pleasantly sheltered sun trap with tables and parasols. In winter there are real fires. Children are welcome and a sign at the door assures walkers of a friendly reception. There are walking maps on the wall of the entrance. And entranced is what you will be when you enter. There is sometimes live music in the evenings. Credit cards are accepted.

The Traquair Arms

# Innerleithen

The first record of habitation here is by St Ronan, an early Christian saint. He is supposed to have 'cleked' the devil (caught him with his crook) and cast him into what are now called St Ronan's Wells. These became famous in 1824 when Sir Walter Scott published his novel *St Ronan's Well*, set here. The water of the wells here was reputed to have medicinal qualities. Scott's mother and sister took the waters and this is possibly the source of his inspiration for the book. With fame came visitors and the local laird, Lord Traquair, built a covered pavilion on the site. As it developed into a spa town and tourist resort, other attractions were laid on for visitors, notably the Border Games of the 18th century. These included archery and attracted famous sponsors such as Sir Walter Scott, Henry Glassford Bell and James Hogg, the Ettrick Shepherd. As spa towns declined in popularity, so did Innerleithen. The St Ronan's Wells site was renovated as a tourist attraction by the local council in the 1960s.

But Innerleithen had started to join the modern world before Scott wrote *St Ronan's Well*. In 1788 Alexander Brodie, a wealthy London ironmaster with local connections, established Caerlee Mill in Innerleithen. Like many other local industries this was powered by the waters of the Leithen and the Tweed. This laid down the foundations of a high-quality lambswool and cashmere knitwear industry that flourishes to this day.

Also powered by water was Robert Smail's printing works, and the lade still runs under the floor of it. This remarkable property belongs to the National Trust for Scotland (NTS) and can be visited. For opening hours call the NTS on 0131 226 5922, fax 0131 243 9501. As Innerleithen declined into a sleepy village, the lack of pressure for change preserved this as a microcosm of a turn of the century printers. This family business was established in 1866, and in 1986 the business was being closed when enterprising local people contacted the NTS and had this gem conserved.

The printers did all the local printing, notices etc., as well as a local newspaper. There is a composing room where the type was set. Letters and words were taken and placed in a rack rather like a child's printing set. The compositors were expert in reading upside-down and mirror-image words. There is a machine room where the printing was done and the youngest machine dates from 1925. There is also a paper store where each day the waterwheel was dropped into the lade under the floor to provide power. Later gas and then electricity were used as power. There is a complete set of records for this printing works for over a century. Today this still does some printing as it is a working museum. However, as a museum it does not do commercial printing. It now provides us with a glimpse into the past and makes us grateful for modern inventions such as personal computers and word processors. It is a far cry from the desktop publishing system used to produce this book. For information on the Southern Upland Way there are the following websites:

* http://www.aboutscotland.com/bothy/suw2.html

* www.visitbritain.com

* www.holiday.scotland.net

# The Walk

This is a figure-of-eight walk with the pub at the centre of the figure of eight. One circle of the walk is small and one is large. So perhaps you could do the small walk in the morning, have lunch and do the large one in the afternoon. Alternatively, you could have lunch, do the large walk in the afternoon and on your return have dinner in the Traquair Arms and do the small walk in the evening. There are a number of ways you could combine the two walks, the choice is yours.

## Short Route

Come out of the Traquair Arms and go right along the B709 to the main road. Cross this, the A72, and go directly ahead up Hall Street. Follow this up and around to the right where it becomes St Ronan's Terrace with a sign to St Ronan's Well. This is now an unsurfaced road. Keep on this road uphill until you arrive at St Ronan's Well in front of you, a large, white building. St Ronan's Well was made famous by Sir Walter Scott's eponymous book. There is free water for you to taste with a tap and glass in a pavilion. There is also a museum with various displays, the well itself, information boards and gardens.

Exit St Ronan's Well and turn left down Wells Brae. This leads you to a T-junction where you go right down Chapel St, although it is not signposted here. Follow this down until it forks and take the right-hand fork. Confusingly, the gable end on your left-hand side has a Chapel Street sign on it but you go right here. Then at the main road, A72, bear left across this to Robert Smail's printing works, which you can visit. Details of its opening hours from the NTS on 0131 226 5922. On leaving Robert Smail's, with your back to it turn left and walk down the A72 to the church and steeple and signpost pointing left to St Mary's Loch and Yarrow, B709. Be guided by this sign and the Traquair Arms is 100 metres down here on your left.

## Longer Route

Come out of the Traquair Arms and turn left down the B709. Walk down Traquair Road, past the cemetery on your right and over the Tweed by a bridge with traffic lights. At this point move to the right of the road as the pavement ends and you will then be facing the oncoming traffic. Keep with this road as it bears right and a road to Elibank and Tweed Cycleway goes off on the left. Go past a signpost to 'Traquair $\frac{1}{4}$', past cart tracks left and right and past the pedestrian entrance to Traquair House. Pass other cart tracks on the left and right of this road to arrive at the hamlet of Traquair.

The vehicular entrance to Traquair House is on your right with a notice board giving details of its attractions. Immediately past this is the war memorial on your right and a telephone box on your left. Here, a road goes left marked 'No Through Road' and 'School', there are also two signs indicating that this is the route of the Southern Uplands Way. Go up here. You are now on the Southern Uplands Way. As this tarmac road bears right, go straight ahead on the dirt road signposted for Minch Moor.

Go through a kissing gate to the right of a field gate and keep on this track as it goes through high pastures between dykes and fences. After a flattish bit bear left uphill with pines on your right. Go past a field gate by a stile on its left or a gate on its

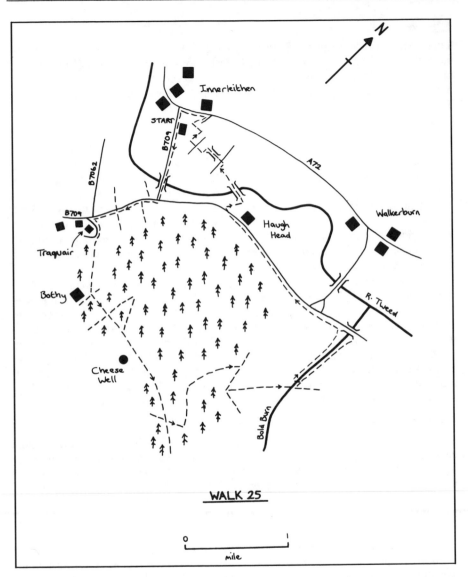

**WALK 25**

0                                    1
└─────────────────────┘
mile

righ; shut the gate if you use it. Keep up the not too steep a hill through a gap in the dyke across the path and past Minch Moor Forest Bothy on your right. You arrive at a forest road across your path. Here a Southern Upland Way waymarker (a thistle) points straight ahead uphill to the forest track into the trees. This is your route.

This takes you to a second forest road across your path. At this point go slightly right over the track, up steps and through a gate as indicated by the thistle waymarker. Follow this well-trodden path to another gate, through it and directly on-wards as guided by the thistle waymarker. Just after this a forest track joins from the left. Keep going straight ahead as guided by the thistle waymarker. As the village of Walkerburn appears through a gap in the trees and hills to your left, keep an eye open on the right for the Cheese Well. This is two small stone slabs rather like gravestones and a trickle of water across the path. The Cheese Well has been here since at least 1654 when it was recorded in Johan Bleau's *Atlas of Scotland*. You are supposed to dip your provisions in the well or leave offerings of cheese to placate the fairies. The Marquis of Montrose and his army retreated along this route in 1645 after the Battle of Philiphaugh. He was leading an army of Highlanders in support of Charles I in the English Civil War. He is rumoured to have lost his treasure chest along here so keep your eyes open for the glint of gold.

Bypass a sign on the right to Minch Moor viewpoint and go straight ahead as indi-cated for Southern Upland Way. You next come to a St Andrew's Cross-shaped junction with a thistle waymarker pointing ahead. Here we depart the Southern Up-land Way, going left on to the semi-tarmac forest road. Follow this road for about a mile and a half as it bends left through the forest and right down the side of a valley. This bit of the walk brings home to you the immensity of the hills. Eventually you come to a sort of T-junction, here dog-leg right downhill. Stay with this road around a hairpin left bend where another road goes straight ahead/leftish. At the fork in the road at the bottom of the valley take the left-hand one.

About 150 metres along here, as the trees end, take the cart track diagonally back-wards on your left. This leads you down to a footbridge across a burn with handrails. Once over this, bear to your left through a gap in the fence then go straight ahead to find a hidden sleeper footbridge over a concealed burn. After this bear right through a field gate, closing it behind you, and follow the faint path beside the fence on your right along the contour line. This path grows into a rudimentary cart track. Keep with this as it becomes more and more a proper cart track with the river and the other cart track on the river's far bank on your right. Go through two field gates and through the farmyard and continue left with the track to skirt the farm buildings on your right. Keep down this now semi-tarmac road towards Walkerburn, now visible in front of you in the Tweed alley. At the T-junction with the minor tarmac road go left.

Walk past the road to Walkerburn on your right and continue up this tarmac road for about a mile until just past Haugh Head Farm on your right. About 100 metres past the farm is a stile on your right. Climb over this and follow the path back and to the right towards the old railway viaduct over the Tweed. Scramble up the embank-ment and turn left across the viaduct to cross the river. Once over, continue along the path in front of you until it ends. Here bear right into Princes St. Then go left between the garages and over the burn by a footbridge.

Go briefly left and right through the passage. Cross the road and pass through the passage again and turn right between wall and fence. Follow the passage around to the left and then to the right and bear right up the small street to the main road through Innerleithen. Turn left up the main road for about 200 metres then turn left at the kirk and sign for the B709 and the Traquair Arms is roughly 100 metres up on your left.

# 26. Southern Upland Way Sampler: Lauder

**Route:** Lauder — Lauder Common — Chester Hill — Burn Mill

**Distance:** 4 miles

**Map:** OS Landranger 73, Peebles and Galashiels

**Start:** The Eagle, Lauder

**Access:** By bus, there is a semi-reasonable bus service from Edinburgh to Lauder, about seven or eight buses a day. On Sundays, however, there are only four buses a day. For details contact First Lowland on 0131 663 9233. Or ring 'Traveline' on 0800 232323 (toll free) if in the Edinburgh area or on 0131 225 3858 if outside the Edinburgh area.

By car, take the A68 out of Edinburgh, signposted for Jedburgh. Keep on this road until it brings you into Lauder. There is a free car park on your left immediately before The Eagle, also on your left. Otherwise there is plenty of on-street unrestricted parking in Lauder, especially in the tollbooth area. Should you miss the car park at The Eagle, the tollbooth area offers you the opportunity to U-turn and return.

---

## The Eagle. Tel: 01578 722426

This building was erected as a manse in the middle of the 17th century. In 1765 it was let as a baker's. Near the beginning of the 19th century it was changed into a coaching inn. It used to have stables at the back and the old bakery ovens were found a few years ago when the kitchen was being renovated.

The name refers to the eagles that haunted the Lammermuir Hills. And speaking of haunting, this pub has a ghost but the supernatural spirit is seldom seen. Today the pub is a haunt of rugby supporters. The Welsh and Irish supporters stay here when their teams are playing at Murrayfield. The pub is split in friendly rivalry over local rugby, the public bar support Melrose and the lounge bar support Jedburgh. Famous customers here have included Jack Charlton and Fraser Hines.

If you prop yourself up at the bar in the lounge you will notice that it is exquisitely carved. Landlady Mrs. Dick tells me that it is a replica of the end of a four-poster bed made by Cumbrian craftsman C. Trippear around 30 years ago. This is a classic country pub in dark wood, stonework, light plaster, colonial-style chairs, exposed beams, old fireplace and early iron lamps. I am sure you get the picture. The public bar has a lovely, old, carved wooden corkscrew coat stand and pictures of old Lauder. It has the usual amenities: cigarette machine, jukebox and fruit machine.

Another usual amenity here is food. This is all good, home-cooked pub grub. The fruit and vegetables are from local suppliers. There is vegetarian choice in starters and main courses. The pub has a good selection including snacks and sandwiches and it is reasonably priced. Food is served from 1200-1400 Monday to Saturday and from 1230-1400 on Sundays. Evening food is served from 1800-2100 seven nights a week.

Between two and four guest real ales are always on tap. On keg are Guinness Extra Cold, Kronenberg 1664, McEwans 70/-, McEwans 80/-, Miller Pilsner and John Smiths Extra Smooth. Opening hours are 1100 – 2300 Monday to Wednesday, Thursday to Saturday 1100 – 2400 and Sunday 1230 – 2300. During these hours a sign at the door welcomes walkers. Lauder is on the route of the Southern Upland Way. There is no children's licence but children can sit with their parents while having a meal. The pub has information about local attractions.

# Lauder

People have lived here for thousands of years. Indeed, a glance at an OS map reveals many traces of ancient Britons. Stone coffins, cists (stone-lined lairs), castles, forts, settlements, chapels, stone circles and cairns are mute testament to the presence of our ancestors here. The Roman road Dere Street passed close by. It was built to connect settlements in northern England with the Antonine Wall.

Lauder was here as long ago as 1120, when David I gave the burgh its charter. At this time Lauder was a medi-eval walled town. Anyone entering had to pay a toll. It had a tollbooth where tolls were paid and markets held. The tollbooth dates back to 1318 and up to 1840 it also, like many other Scottish tollbooths, functioned as a jail. It had three cells; one for men, one for women and a windowless hole under the stairs for major league criminals. The town council met in the upper chamber and the community council meets here to this day. Criminals were tried in the council chamber by JPs, the Provost or Baillies (Scottish Municipal Magistrates).

Medieval times were turbulent and in 1598 the tollbooth was burned and Baillie Lauder killed by a raiding party under the Earl of Home. In 1482 a number of favourites of James III were hung on Lauder Bridge

The tollbooth

(of which no trace remains) by Archibald, Earl of Douglas. The nobles surrounding the king were jealous of the favours received by the king's new friends who were supplanting them. The English took the town in 1547 and held it for three years.

On more peaceful matters, in 1502 James IV renewed the burgh's charter. In 1504 he held court in the town. There were five fairs a year in the town for buying seed corn, hiring farmworkers and selling sheep and cattle. As things grew more settled, part of the wall at the West Port (gate) was knocked down in 1761 to allow access of wheeled vehicles. Later, stagecoaches used Lauder as a stopping place as they travelled between Edinburgh and England. In 1763 Lauder Church was built in the shape of a Greek cross with an octagonal bell-tower. This is on the route of the walk. However, war still occasionally touched Lauder. In 1745 General John Cope rested here in what is known as Cope's House (now a draper's shop) after his defeat at Prestonpans by the Jacobites.

After this Lauder lived peacefully as a market town for the surrounding countryside. In 1995 it was European Architectural Heritage Year. As Lauder is an area of outstanding beauty all the electricity supply was put underground.

The name Lauder is thought to derive from the Leader Water on which it stands. 'Leader' comes from 'laudur', a Celtic word for 'smaller river'. Dere Street gets its name from the Anglo-Saxon word 'deor'. It means 'road into the country of the wild animals'. In addition it is the route from the old province of Deira in England.

## The Walk

Leave The Eagle and carefully cross the main road through the village, A68. Go right along the A68 for about 50 metres until you reach Manse Road. Go left up here and then cross another road lying across your path, bearing slightly left, to continue up Manse Road. Around 50 metres further on this Manse Road forks, take the left-hand fork. Just before the gates of the house named Glebe take the cart track on your right. Glebe lands were those given to a minister to farm to eke out his stipend, so that marries in nicely with Manse Road.

When this cart track forks once out of the trees, take the right-hand, rather overgrown, arm of the split. Walk past an enclosed field fenced in on your left. At the end of this field pass through a field gate in front of you and head forwards to another field gate at some 50 metres distance. At the end of the field after the second gate, turn right uphill heading for the trees keeping the ruined dyke on your left. In the early summer this field can be a blue haze of wild forget-me-nots. At the top of the hill as you reach the trees is a field gate on your left. Once through this gate bear half left, following a faint path towards a field gate visible in the dyke ahead of you. Having negotiated this gate, then walk to your right on the obvious path on the left-hand side of the dyke. This path fades out sometimes but never for very long. You will not get lost as you as keep close company with the dyke on your right. At a gap in the dyke the path bears left towards the obvious small plantation of trees on your left front. Walk through the trees to the far side of the plantation to pick up a clear path on its other side. This path comes to a grassy cart track, turn right along this. You pro-

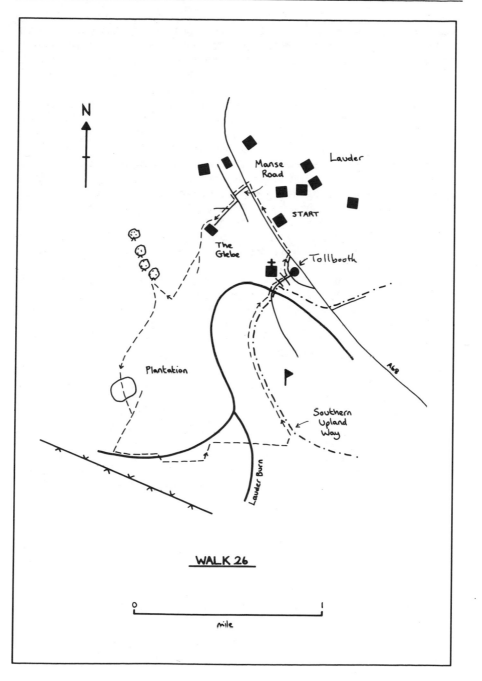

N

Manse
Road

Lauder

START

The
Glebe

Tollbooth

A68

Plantation

Southern
Upland
Way

Lauder Burn

**WALK 26**

0                                      1
mile

ceed on the cart track paralleling the Lauder Burn on your left. The cart track comes to an end as the Lauder Burn appears to turn to cut transversely across your route of travel. A path ahead of you leads you in the direction of the pylons and down into the valley of the burn. The line of the pylons marks the route of an ancient path 'Girthgate' used by pilgrims and monks en route to Border Abbeys.

This well-marked path leads you across what is actually a tributary of the Lauder Burn on stepping stones. Continue on a faint green path and then on a more obvious beaten earth path down the valley of this burn. Stay between the burn on your left and the dyke on your right. This path then takes you half left and deeper into the valley of the burn, away from the dyke. Then turn half right at the burn and walk along with it on your near left for about 40 metres. As the burn turns sharply left, go straight ahead over the valley floor, aiming for the base of the red earth footpath cutting across the shoulder of the hill on the far side of the valley. Climb left up this path through the gorse bushes. This area is hoaching with rabbits.

At the top of the hill you come to a T-junction with a smooth, grassy path which comes from a ladder stile over a dyke on your right. This is the Southern Upland Way. Go diagonally left uphill on it to a small hummock. At the top of the hummock a waymarker ahead (thistle sign) confirms that you are indeed on the Southern Upland Way. Continue along this grassy path with the golf course fence on your close right. Here you may think that you are seeing flying penguins. In reality the black and white chequerboard colours and high-pitched piping cry reveal the presence of oyster-catchers. These seaside wading birds come into the hills in summer to breed.

Continue on this waymarked path as you drop downhill slightly from the golf course and then ascend to parallel it again. At the end of the golf course go through a dyke across your path by a stile in a wooden fence in the dyke. Strangely, a waymarker for the Southern Upland Way only faces in the opposite direction. Proceed downhill through flowering meadows like the water meads of old. At the bottom of the hill on your right is an information board about the Southern Upland Way, turn left here. At the junction of Factors Park and Crofts Road the Southern Upland Way goes right, but we leave it at this point and go directly ahead into the centre of Lauder. Bypass Lauder Church on the left. At the end of Mill Wynd go left heading for the tollbooth and The Eagle is about 100 metres up on your right.